C000296345

Introduction to Bookkeeping

Tutorial

David Cox
Michael Fardon

© David Cox, Michael Fardon, 2021

All rights reserved. No part of this publication may be reproduced, stored in a retrieval system, or transmitted in any form or by any means, electronic, mechanical, photo-copying, recording or otherwise, without the prior consent of the copyright owners, or in accordance with the provisions of the Copyright, Designs and Patents Act 1988, or under the terms of any licence permitting limited copying issued by the Copyright Licensing Agency, Saffron House, 6-10 Kirby Street, London EC1N 8TS.

Published by Osborne Books Limited
Tel 01905 748071
Email books@osbornebooks.co.uk
Website www.osbornebooks.co.uk

Design by Laura Ingham

Printed by CPI Group (UK) Limited, Croydon, CR0 4YY, on environmentally friendly, acid-free paper from managed forests.

British Library Cataloguing in Publication Data
A catalogue record for this book is available from the British Library

ISBN 978 -1-911198-50-5

Contents

Introduction

Qualifications covered

This book has been written specifically to cover the Unit 'Introduction to Bookkeeping' which is mandatory for the following qualifications:

AAT Level 2 Certificate in Accounting

AAT Level 2 Certificate in Bookkeeping

AAT Certificate in Accounting – SCQF Level 6

The book contains a clear text with worked examples and case studies, chapter summaries and key terms to help with revision. Each chapter concludes with a wide range of activities, many in the style of AAT computer based assessments.

Osborne Study and Revision Materials

Additional materials, tailored to the needs of students studying this unit and revising for the assessment, include:

- **Workbooks:** paperback books with practice activities and exams
- **Wise Guides:** pocket-sized spiral bound revision cards
- **Student Zone:** access to Osborne Books online resources
- **Osborne Books App:** Osborne Books ebooks for mobiles and tablets

Visit www.osbornebooks.co.uk for details of study and revision resources and access to online material.

1 The accounting system

this chapter covers...

This chapter is a basic introduction to the accounting system of a business and gives an overview of all the topics that will be explained throughout this book.

It is the aim of the course you are studying that you will acquire the knowledge and skills to enable you to work effectively in an accounting and finance environment.

This chapter describes and explains the basic structure of the accounting system:

- *the range of financial transactions in business, eg buying, selling, making payments*
- *how financial (business) documents, such as invoices, are used to record financial transactions*
- *the way in which financial transactions are first recorded in the books of the business – using 'books of prime entry'*
- *how an accounting system is set up, for example a double-entry system using ledger accounts*
- *how the accounts are brought together in a summary known as the 'trial balance'*
- *the ways in which an accounting system can be used to provide information for the business owners and management, for example how much is owed by customers and how much profit has been made*

FINANCIAL TRANSACTIONS

All businesses carry out a wide range of financial transactions on a daily basis. These transactions will need documenting and then recording in a manual or a digital bookkeeping system. Common transactions include:

selling goods and services

Goods and services can be sold:

- either for immediate payment – known as 'cash' sales, although confusingly this word 'cash' also involves payment by credit or debit card as well as cash itself in the form of notes and coins; or

- for payment at a later date – known as 'credit' sales

making purchases and paying expenses

Examples of purchases and expenses include a wide range of large and small transactions, some more important than others:

- settling purchase invoices, eg paying by cheque or electronically for goods or services received during the previous month

- buying an item for use in the business, eg a new delivery van, paid for by bank transfer

- buying fuel for the delivery van, using the company credit card

- buying postage stamps for the office using cash

payments in and out of the bank account

The money received by the business and the money paid out by the business will pass through the bank account, for example:

- cash, cheque and electronic receipts from selling goods and services

- paying for purchases by cash, cheque or electronic payment

- settling the company credit card by direct debit payment from the bank account

- paying employee wages by bank transfer through the bank account

- drawing cash from the bank for use in the business

the importance of keeping track

As you will see from the above examples, recording financial transactions is a complex process. A business needs to keep track of:

- expenses and purchases
- wages paid
- what each customer owes, and when the money is due
- amounts owed to suppliers, and when the payment is due
- amounts paid into the bank and out of the bank

If these transactions are not recorded accurately, the owner of the business and other interested organisations – such as the bank and the tax authorities – will not know how much money the business is making (or losing!).

DIGITAL BOOKKEEPING SYSTEMS

Most businesses are able to make use of digital bookkeeping systems to record their financial transactions electronically. The form these systems take include:

- spreadsheets, such as Microsoft Excel
- app and cloud-based software, such as Xerox, QuickBooks, Sage
- desktop software, such as Sage
- custom software tailor-made to the specific needs of the business

As to which system is used will depend on the size of the business. We will look more fully at the benefits and drawbacks of using digital bookkeeping systems in Chapter 3.

THE FIVE STAGE ACCOUNTING SYSTEM

The accounting system, which will be set in motion by all the transactions listed on the previous page, can be broken down into five stages. These will be covered in greater detail later in this chapter. These stages (illustrated on the next page) are as follows:

1 A **financial transaction** takes place – a sale, a purchase, a payment.

2 The transaction involves a **financial (business) document**, for example an invoice (a sale), a credit note (returned goods), a petty cash voucher (small cash payments).

3 The document is first recorded by the business, for example a day book (for credit transactions) recording sales of goods or goods returned, a cash book recording payments in and out of the bank, or a petty cash book

which records small cash payments (eg buying postage stamps for use by the business)

These books are known as the **books of prime entry**; this simply means 'the first place a transaction is recorded in the accounting records'.

4   The entries in the books of prime entry, eg the day books, are then transferred to the **ledger accounts** of the business. These are a formal record of the financial transactions and normally involve **double-entry accounts.**

The double-entry system, which involves two entries for each transaction, a debit entry and a credit entry, is explained in more detail on pages 8-11.

5   The final stage in the accounting system covered in your current studies is the **trial balance**. This is a list of the balances of the double-entry accounts. It is used as a check on the accuracy of the account entries and is also a source of information for the business owners and managers: it enables them to monitor items such as expenses and what their customers owe, and also to calculate how much profit the business has made. The trial balance is explained in more detail on pages 12-13.

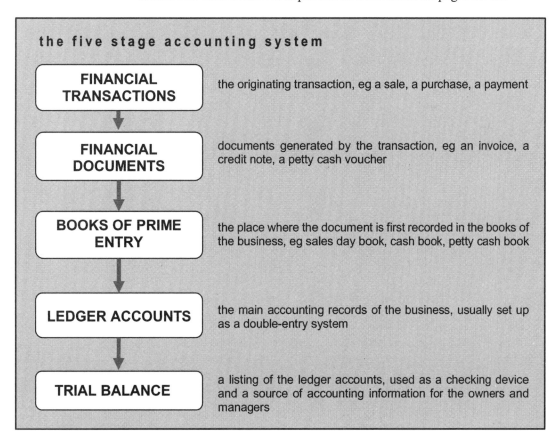

the five stage accounting system

FINANCIAL TRANSACTIONS	the originating transaction, eg a sale, a purchase, a payment
FINANCIAL DOCUMENTS	documents generated by the transaction, eg an invoice, a credit note, a petty cash voucher
BOOKS OF PRIME ENTRY	the place where the document is first recorded in the books of the business, eg sales day book, cash book, petty cash book
LEDGER ACCOUNTS	the main accounting records of the business, usually set up as a double-entry system
TRIAL BALANCE	a listing of the ledger accounts, used as a checking device and a source of accounting information for the owners and managers

We will now explain the last four of these five stages in more detail. The first stage, financial transactions, has already been covered on page 3.

FROM DOCUMENTS TO BOOKS OF PRIME ENTRY

You will need to study a wide variety of financial documents as part of your course. On the next page a Case Study shows how a sales invoice – a **financial document** – is recorded in the sales day book, which is a list of sales invoices issued and a **book of prime entry**. You do not at this stage need to learn all the details of how this record is entered. This will be covered in Chapter 4.

Case Study

FROM DOCUMENT TO BOOK OF PRIME ENTRY

situation

Your business, Computrade, has sold a laptop computer to R S George Limited, for £576.00 (which is list price of £480 plus £96.00 VAT at 20%). The financial document issued is a sales invoice (see below) which requires payment in 30 days' time. The details from this invoice are recorded in a sales day book (see bottom of the page), a book of prime entry.

INVOICE

COMPUTRADE
Ardent House, Mercia Way
Newtown, NT1 6TF
Tel 01722 295875 Fax 01722 295611 Email sales@computrade.com
VAT Reg GB 02756 6865 06

invoice to

R S George Limited
Unit 32 Bruges Trading Estate
Winter Road Maidstone
ME7 2PH

invoice no	**2984**
account	**8934**
your reference	**CT524**
date/tax point	**02 04 20-3**

description	quantity	price	unit	total
Extreme 2120 Laptop	1	480.00	each	480.00

terms
30 days
E & OE

Goods total	480.00
VAT	96.00
TOTAL	576.00

Sales Day Book					
Date	Customer	Invoice No.	Total	VAT	Net
20-3			£	£	£
2 April	R S George Limited	2984	576.00	96.00	480.00

FROM BOOKS OF PRIME ENTRY TO LEDGER ACCOUNTS

The next stage in the accounting system is the transfer of entries in the books of prime entry to the ledger accounts. Books of prime entry, such as that seen on the previous page, are listing devices for financial transactions. They include:

- **day books** for

    - credit sales and sales returns, ie transactions with customers

    - credit purchases and purchases returns, ie transactions with suppliers

    Day books can also be used for recording prompt payment discounts offered to customers or allowed by suppliers. These will be explained later in this book (Chapters 4 and 7).

- **cash book** for recording all payments into and out of the bank account

- **petty cash book** for recording all payments into and out of a cash float used for making small purchases and other small payments

The ledger accounts are the formal bookkeeping records of the business and are kept either manually or by use of a digital bookkeeping system. They form the 'core' of the accounting system and use the double-entry system, ie a debit entry matched by a credit entry.

The flow of accounting information – transaction, book of prime entry, double-entry ledger accounts – is shown on the next page. This gives you an overview of the accounting system. All the stages in this process are fully explained in the chapters that follow.

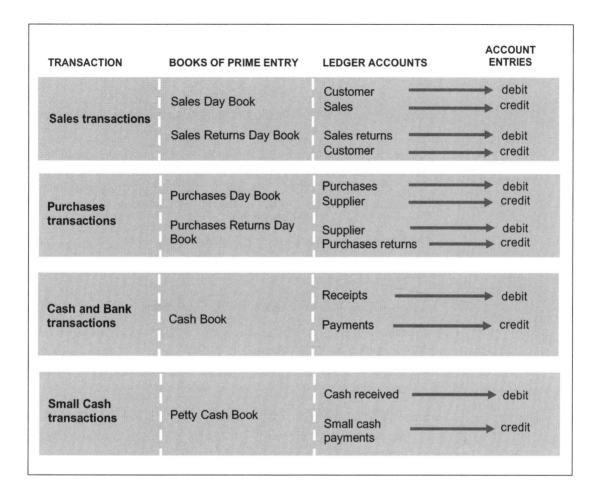

TRANSACTION	BOOKS OF PRIME ENTRY	LEDGER ACCOUNTS	ACCOUNT ENTRIES
Sales transactions	Sales Day Book	Customer	debit
		Sales	credit
	Sales Returns Day Book	Sales returns	debit
		Customer	credit
Purchases transactions	Purchases Day Book	Purchases	debit
		Supplier	credit
	Purchases Returns Day Book	Supplier	debit
		Purchases returns	credit
Cash and Bank transactions	Cash Book	Receipts	debit
		Payments	credit
Small Cash transactions	Petty Cash Book	Cash received	debit
		Small cash payments	credit

LEDGER ACCOUNTS

So far in this chapter we have seen that the accounting system of a business records information from financial transactions and documents (such as invoices and credit notes) into books of prime entry and then into ledger accounts. It is useful at this point to explain what is meant by 'ledgers' and the way in which they are organised.

Most businesses use an accounting system based on the **double-entry bookkeeping system**, in which financial transactions are recorded in the accounts as **debits** and **credits**. There are two equal entries – debit and credit – for the same amount.

Bookkeeping records are kept in one of two forms: handwritten (manual) records or a digital (computer) bookkeeping system.

the ledgers

A **ledger** is traditionally a large book within which each business transaction is entered into individual accounts.

Because of the large number of accounts involved, there are a number of different individual ledgers, both in manual systems and in digital systems:

- **Receivables ledger** (also known as sales ledger) – a personal account is opened for each customer which contains records of sales made on credit (ie buy now, pay later), any returned goods and payments received. This account shows the amount owed by that particular customer. A customer buying on credit is known in accounting language as a 'receivable' or as a 'trade receivable'.

- **Payables ledger** (also known as purchases ledger) – a personal account is opened for each supplier which contains records of purchases made on credit (ie buy now, pay later), any returned goods and payments made to the supplier. This account shows the amount owed to that particular supplier (known as a 'payable' or a 'trade payable').

- **General ledger** – contains a collection of accounts which record all other transactions of the business, such as:

  - assets – these are items owned by a business, eg premises, cars, computers

  - liabilities – items owed by a business, eg overdrafts and bank loans

  - the owner's capital (equity) – this includes the amount invested in the business by the owner and also the profits made by the business

  - expense items – money going out, eg to wages and rent paid

  - income items – money coming in, eg from sales and rent received

  The **general ledger** is sometimes also known as the 'main' ledger or 'nominal' ledger (in digital bookkeeping systems).

Also note that the term 'the ledger' is sometimes used to describe all the individual ledgers grouped together. The ledger structure is shown in the diagram on the next page.

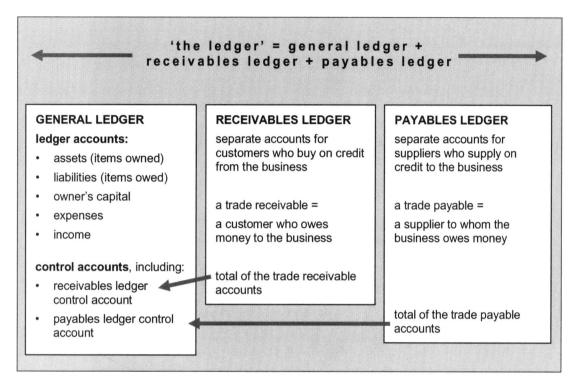

control accounts ('totals' accounts)

Many businesses use **control accounts** to provide them with information about the financial state of the organisation.

Control accounts are 'totals' accounts which summarise a number of other accounts. They are set out in the same way as all other ledger accounts. Examples include:

- **receivables ledger control account** which contains the totals of all the trade receivable accounts in the receivables ledger – this tells the business how much is owing from all its customers, a figure that is important for business owners and managers

- **payables ledger control account** which contains the totals of all the trade payable accounts in the payables ledger – this tells the business how much is owing to all its suppliers at any one time; again this is a figure that is important for anyone running a business

These control accounts are always contained in the general ledger. It is the total of these accounts that is transferred to the trial balance (see next page).

THE TRIAL BALANCE

purpose and format of the trial balance

A trial balance is an important stage in the accounting system. Its purpose is to bring together the balances of all the ledger accounts in the general ledger, setting them out in two columns – a debit column and a credit column – which when added up should show two equal totals.

A simplified trial balance is shown on the next page. You do not need at this stage to know how all this 'works' but just that it is an important accuracy check in the accounting system.

Note that the trial balance is headed up with:

■ the **name** of the business, 'Computrade'

■ the **date** on which it was prepared – this should be done regularly, eg the end of each month, and always the end of the financial year

what the trial balance shows

The trial balance shows the business owner and managers important and useful information. For example, the trial balance on the next page sets out the account balances of Computrade. It shows that:

■ to date, purchases are £35,000 and sales are £58,050

■ £12,500 is owed by customers (trade receivables)

■ £9,350 is owed to suppliers (trade payables)

■ wages paid out to date is £44,100

■ delivery vans have cost £36,000

■ the business has £2,000 in the bank

■ the owner of the business has an investment (capital) worth £105,000

Note that the trade receivables and trade payables figures are 'total' figures and are taken from the receivables ledger and payables ledger control accounts. This makes the trial balance more manageable – it would be difficult to list all the customer and supplier accounts separately.

the trial balance – what next?

A further stage in the accounting system (which you will deal with in your later studies) is the production of **financial statements**, the **statement of profit or loss** and the **statement of financial position**. Although you will not be assessed on these statements at this level, awareness of them will help you in your current areas of study. They are briefly explained on page 14.

the trial balance

Name of business: Computrade
Trial Balance as at 30 June 20-3

	Debit	Credit
	£	£
Purchases	35,000	
Sales		58,050
Trade receivables	12,500	
Trade payables		9,350
Insurance	1,400	
Rent	6,400	
Wages	44,100	
Bank	2,000	
Office equipment	35,000	
Delivery vans	36,000	
Capital		105,000
	172,400	172,400

names of all the individual ledger accounts

totals of the two money amount columns – note that they add up to the same figure, providing an accuracy check of the bookkeeping system

Chapter 11 provides more detail on the workings of the trial balance.

FINANCIAL STATEMENTS

The financial statements of a business are the **statement of profit or loss** and the **statement of financial position**. They are prepared from the accounting records of the business, mainly from the balances of the ledger accounts which form the basis of the trial balance.

what the statement of profit or loss shows

INCOME	minus	EXPENSES	equals	PROFIT

The purpose of the **statement of profit or loss** of a business is to show the day-to-day income that the business has received over a given period for goods sold or services provided. It also sets out the **expenses** incurred, including the cost of producing the products and running expenses.

If income of the business is greater than expenses, the business has made a profit. If income of the business is less than expenses, the business has made a loss.

what the statement of financial position shows

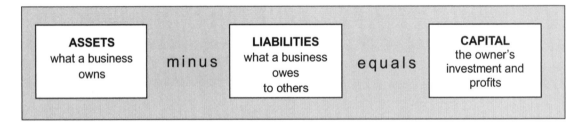

ASSETS what a business owns	minus	LIABILITIES what a business owes to others	equals	CAPITAL the owner's investment and profits

The purpose of the **statement of financial position** of a business is to give a 'snapshot' of the business at a particular date, eg the end of the financial year, and shows the value of the owner's investment in the business. The statement presents a simple equation, known as the **accounting equation**:

assets (owned) minus liabilities (owed) = capital (owner's investment)

If a business owner invests £2,000 in the business and buys a computer, the owner is investing **capital** of £2,000 and also adding an **asset** in the form of a computer costing £2,000. The equation will balance because £2,000 has been added to both sides (to assets and to capital). The accounting equation is explained and expanded in Chapter 3, pages 67-72.

INTERNATIONAL TERMINOLOGY USED IN ACCOUNTING

old and new terms

In your studies of bookkeeping and accounting you will encounter some different ways of expressing common accounting terms. For example, the traditional way of referring to goods held for resale by a shop or by a manufacturer is the word 'stock'; however, you will find that the term 'inventory' is commonly used to mean 'stock'.

This modern terminology is known as **'international accounting terminology'**. There are situations where the international terminology is used instead of the traditional terminology. Examples of this are the financial statements produced by large limited companies.

The table below shows both the international and traditional versions of terms which you are likely to come across in your accounting studies. The table also explains what the terms mean.

international terminology	traditional terminology	what it means
inventory	stock	goods held by a business
trade payable	creditor	a supplier you owe money to
trade receivable	debtor	a customer who owes you money
statement of profit or loss	profit and loss account	financial statement calculating profit (or loss) made by a business
statement of financial position	balance sheet	financial statement showing the assets, liabilities and capital of a business

This book, and AAT Assessments, use the international terminology with which you will become familiar very quickly.

- Digital bookkeeping systems include:
  - spreadsheets
  - app and cloud-based software
  - desktop software
  - custom software

- The accounting system is normally made up of five stages:
  1 financial transactions
  2 financial documents
  3 books of prime entry
  4 ledger accounts
  5 trial balance

- **Financial transactions** are the starting point of the accounting system. They include sales, purchases, expenses, payments in and out of the bank account and small cash (petty cash) transactions.

- Financial transactions normally result in **financial documents**, for example an invoice (for a sale), a credit note (for returned goods), a cheque (for a payment), a petty cash voucher (for a small cash payment).

- Financial documents are recorded in **books of prime entry**, for example separate day books for sales and sales returns, purchases and purchases returns, cash book and petty cash book.

- Next the **ledger accounts** are written up from the books of prime entry. The ledger accounts are normally double-entry accounts, ie two entries are made in the accounts for each transaction – a debit entry and a credit entry.

- As there are so many ledger accounts, **the ledger** is often split into separate ledgers: receivables ledger (for customer accounts), payables ledger (for supplier accounts) and general ledger (all the other accounts, including assets, expenses, income, liabilities, and capital/equity).

- **Control accounts** are 'totals' accounts used to summarise important groups of ledger accounts – receivables ledger control account, payables ledger control account.

- Finally, the balances of the ledger accounts are transferred to the **trial balance**, which is both a checking device and also a source of accounting information for the business owners and managers.

- The **financial statements** of a business – the statement of profit or loss and the statement of financial position – are prepared from the accounts of a business on a regular basis.

Key Terms		
	digital bookkeeping systems	electronic methods of recording financial transactions
	financial document	a term given to a document – such as an invoice – which results from a financial transaction
	'cash' and 'credit' sales/purchases	a 'cash' sale/purchase is where payment is made straightaway; a 'credit' sale/purchase is where payment is made at a later date
	books of prime entry	the place in the books of a business where a financial transaction is recorded for the first time, eg day books, cash book, petty cash book
	day books	book of prime entry listing the details of various financial transactions, eg sales, sales returns, purchases, purchases returns, discounts allowed and discounts received
	cash book	book of prime entry which lists payments in and out of the bank account
	petty cash book	book of prime entry which lists small cash (notes and coins) business expense payments from an office cash fund
	ledger account	the formal accounting record (often in double-entry format) for financial transactions involving individuals (customers and suppliers) and business assets, expenses, income, liabilities and capital
	double-entry accounts	ledger accounts set up on the double-entry system (ie two entries – a debit and a credit – are made for each transaction)
	the ledger	'book' which contains the individual accounts; it is often subdivided into different ledgers, eg receivables ledger, payables ledger, general ledger
	control accounts	'totals' accounts contained in the general ledger
	trade receivable	customer who owes a business money
	trade payable	supplier owed money by a business
	assets	items owned by a business, eg a delivery van

liabilities	items owed by a business, eg a bank loan
capital (equity)	the investment made in a business by the owner(s)
trial balance	a list of the balances of the ledger accounts drawn up in two columns (debit and credit), the totals of which should be the same

Activities

1.1 A 'cash sale' in accounting terms is:

(a)	A sale involving notes and coins	
(b)	A sale with immediate payment	✓
(c)	A sale with payment in the future	

Which **one** of these options is correct?

1.2 A financial document is first recorded in a book of prime entry.

True or false?

1.3 The following groups are **all** books of prime entry:

(a)	Cash book, petty cash book, payables ledger	
(b)	Sales day book, sales returns day book, receivables ledger	
(c)	Cash book, petty cash book, sales day book	✓

Which **one** of these options is correct?

1.4   Transactions recorded in the books of prime entry are transferred to:

(a)	Ledger accounts	✓
(b)	A trial balance	
(c)	A petty cash book	

Which **one** of these options is correct?

1.5   A trade receivable is:

(a)	A supplier owed money by the business	
(b)	A customer who owes money to a business	✓
(c)	A customer who settles straightaway using cash	

Which **one** of these options is correct?

1.6   In double-entry bookkeeping, transactions are recorded using:

(a)	Two debits	
(b)	Two credits	
(c)	One debit and one credit	✓

Which **one** of these options is correct?

1.7   The payables ledger contains the ledger accounts for:

(a)	Customers	
(b)	Suppliers	✓
(c)	Expenses	

Which **one** of these options is correct?

1.8   A liability of a business is:

(a)	An amount owed by that business	✓
(b)	An item owned by that business	
(c)	A cash fund for business expenses	

Which **one** of these options is correct?

1.9   An extract from the trial balance of a shop that sells tiles is shown below.

Name of business: Style & Tile Trial Balance as at 30 June 20-3 (extract)	Debit £	Credit £
Trade receivables	10,500	
Trade payables		6,720
Advertising	1,400	
Insurance	780	
Wages	52,800	
Bank	3,000	
Shop equipment	22,000	
Delivery vans	28,000	
Capital		155,000

On the basis of the figures shown, answer the following questions:

(a)   How much do the customers of Style & Tile owe the business?   *10,500*

(b)   How much does Style & Tile owe its suppliers?   *6720*

(c)   How much does Style & Tile have in the bank?   *3,000*

(d)   How much investment does the owner have in the business?   *~~52,800~~ 155,000*

(e)   Where are the figures for trade receivables and trade payables taken from?   *Ledger/control accounts*

1.10 A payables ledger control account contains the total of accounts of:

(a)	Customers who buy goods and services on a cash basis	
(b)	Customers who buy goods and services on a credit basis	
(c)	Suppliers who sell goods and services on a cash basis	
(d)	Suppliers who sell goods and services on a credit basis	✓

Which **one** of these options is correct?

1.11 The statement of profit or loss shows:

(a)	Income + Expenses = Profit	
(b)	Income – Liabilities = Profit	
(c)	Income – Expenses = Profit	✓

Which **one** of these options is correct?

1.12 The statement of financial position shows:

(a)	Assets – Liabilities = Capital	✓
(b)	Assets + Liabilities = Capital	
(c)	Assets – Expenses = Capital	

Which **one** of these options is correct?

2 Financial documents for sales

this chapter covers...

This chapter examines the procedures involved when a business sells goods or services on credit – which means that payment is made at a later date, possibly a month later.

The important point here is that the business wants to be paid on time and it wants to receive the right amount. It can achieve these aims through the efficient use and monitoring of financial documents.

This chapter covers the areas of:

■ *use of business documents – quotation, purchase order, invoice, delivery note, returns note, credit note, statement*

■ *calculation of document totals and discounts*

■ *calculation of Value Added Tax (VAT)*

■ *coding of documents*

■ *checking and authorisation of documents*

Note that the documents explained in this chapter are often prepared and submitted electronically, eg online orders, invoices, statements and payments. These follow the same principles as paper-based documents.

FINANCIAL DOCUMENTS

When a business sells goods or services, it uses a number of different business documents (listed in the diagram below). A single sales transaction of course involves both seller and buyer. In this chapter we look at the situation from the point of view of the **seller** of the goods or services. The transaction from the point of view of the buyer is explained in Chapter 6. Documents which are used in the **selling** process include:

- price **quotation** which the seller may be asked to provide
- **purchase order** which the seller receives from the buyer
- **delivery note** which goes with the goods from the seller to the buyer
- **invoice** which lists the goods and tells the buyer what is owed
- **returns note** which is sent with any goods that are being returned
- **credit note** which is sent to the buyer if any refund is due
- **statement of account** sent by the seller to remind the buyer what is owed

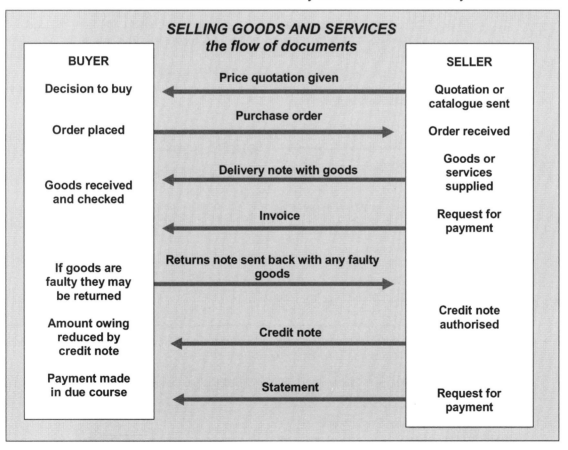

the flow of documents

Before you read the Case Study, make sure you have studied the diagram on the previous page. You will see in the columns representing the buyer and the seller that there are various activities requiring financial documents.

Case Study

COOL SOCKS – A SALES TRANSACTION

situation

Cool Socks Limited manufactures socks in a variety of colours. It supplies a number of different customers, including Trends, a fashion store in Broadfield. In this Case Study, Trends places an order for 100 pairs of socks with Cool Socks. The socks are delivered, but some are found to be faulty, so some of the socks have to be returned. The Case Study looks in detail at the documents involved.

THE PRICE QUOTATION

Before placing the order, the buyer at Trends will need to find out the price of the socks. This can be done by consulting Cool Socks' catalogue or website, or by means of an email or telephone enquiry.

Cool Socks *may* provide a written quotation for the socks if it is requested to do so, although this procedure is more common with higher value orders. A written quotation will look like this:

————— QUOTATION —————

COOL SOCKS LIMITED

Unit 45 Elgar Estate, Broadland, BR7 4ER
Tel 01908 765314   Fax 01908 765951   Email toni@cool.u-net.com
VAT REG GB 0745 4672 76

Trends 4 Friar Street Broadfield BR1 3RF	date **19 09 20-3**

Thank you for your enquiry of 17 September 20-3. We are pleased to quote as follows:

100 pairs Toebar socks (blue) @ £2.36 a pair, excluding VAT.

M. Arnold

Sales Department

PURCHASE ORDER – THE SOCKS ARE ORDERED

The buyer at Trends, once the quoted price has been accepted, will send the authorised purchase order shown below, or submit an online order. The order will have been processed manually, or produced by a digital bookkeeping system.

Note the following details:

- each purchase order has a specific reference number (here it is 47609) – this is useful for filing and quoting on later documents such as invoices and statements; this reference number is an example of **coding** in accounting (see page 40)

- the catalogue number of the goods required is stated in the product code column – this number is a further example of coding

- the quantity of the goods required is stated in the quantity column – socks are normally supplied in pairs!

- the description of the goods is set out in full

- the price is not essential, although some purchase orders will include a price

- the purchase order is signed and dated by the person in charge of purchasing – without this authorisation, the supplier is unlikely to supply the goods (the order will probably be returned)

Trends
4 Friar Street
Broadfield
BR1 3RF
Tel 01908 761234 Fax 01908 761987
VAT REG GB 0745 8383 56

PURCHASE ORDER

Cool Socks Limited,	purchase order no	**47609**
Unit 45 Elgar Estate,	date	**25 09 20-3**
Broadfiled,		
BR7 4ER		

Product code	Quantity	Description
45B	**100 pairs**	**Blue Toebar socks @ £2.36 per pair**

AUTHORISED signature....*D Signer*........................date....*25/09/20-3*....

DELIVERY NOTE – THE SOCKS ARE DELIVERED

A delivery note is despatched with the goods when the order is ready. It is either processed manually in the office or printed out from a digital bookkeeping system, often at the same time as the invoice (see next page). In this case, the delivery note travels with the socks, and a copy will be signed by Trends on receipt. Note the following details:

- the delivery note has a numerical reference (here it is 68873), useful for filing and later reference if there is a query – this is another example of coding

- the method of delivery is stated – here the delivery is by parcel carrier

- the delivery note quotes the purchase order number (47609); this enables the buyer to link the delivery with the original purchase order and is another example of the use of coding

- the delivery note quotes:
  - Cool Socks' catalogue reference 45B as the product code
  - the quantity supplied
  - the description of the goods, but no price – it is not needed at this stage

  These details will be checked by Trends against the goods themselves straightaway so that any discrepancies can be reported without delay.

- the delivery note will be signed and dated by the person receiving the goods as proof of delivery; this process is often carried out electronically – the person receiving the goods is asked to sign a portable electronic device

---

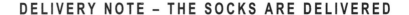

DELIVERY NOTE

COOL SOCKS LIMITED
Unit 45 Elgar Estate, Broadland, BR7 4ER
Tel 01908 765314   Fax 01908 765951   Email toni@cool.u-net.com
VAT REG GB 0745 4672 76

Trends 4 Friar Street Broadfield BR1 3RF	delivery note no	**68873**
	delivery method	**Lynx Parcels**
	your order	**47609**
	date	**02 10 20-3**

Product code	Quantity	Description
45B	**100 pairs**	**Blue Toebar socks**

Received
signature.. *V Williams* ..name (capitals).. *V WILLIAMS* ..date.. *6/10/20-3* ..

INVOICE – THE SELLER REQUESTS PAYMENT

The invoice is the financial document sent by the seller to the buyer stating how much is owed by the buyer of goods or services.

The invoice, like the delivery note, is prepared in the supplier's (seller's) office, and is either processed manually or produced electronically using a digital bookkeeping system.

Invoices produced by different organisations will vary to some extent in terms of detail, but their basic layout will always be the same. The invoice prepared by Cool Socks Limited – illustrated on page 29 – is typical of a typed or electronic document.

An invoice will often be printed as part of a multiple set of documents, which is likely to include a delivery note and a copy invoice for the seller's own records. The copy invoice will normally be filed in numerical order (see 'coding' below). If a digital system is used, the invoice can be called up on screen, referenced by its invoice number.

Note the following details, and refer to the invoice on page 29.

addresses

The invoice shows the address:

- of the seller of the goods – Cool Socks Limited

- where the invoice is to be sent – to Trends

- where the goods are to be sent – if it is different from the invoice address

coding and references

There are a number of important coding references on the invoice:

- the numerical reference of the invoice itself – 787923

- the account number allocated to Trends by the seller – 3993 – for use in the seller's bookkeeping system; note that account references can include letters as well – for example another supplier might give Trends the code TR126

- the original reference number on the purchase order sent by Trends – 47609 – which will enable the shop to link the invoice with the original order

- the product code from the seller's catalogue or product list – here it is 45B

Note that coding on a financial document can be:

- alphabetical – just letters

- numerical – just numbers

- alpha-numerical – a mixture of letters and numbers

date

The date on the invoice is important because the payment date (here one month) is calculated from it. It is also the transaction date used for Value Added Tax (VAT) purposes (see the next page).

the goods

The invoice must specify accurately the goods supplied. The details – set out in columns in the body of the invoice – include:

- **product code** – this is the catalogue number which appeared on the original purchase order and on the delivery note

- **description** – the goods must be specified precisely

- **quantity** – this should agree with the quantity ordered

- **price** – this is the price of each unit shown in the next column

- **unit** is the way in which the unit is counted and charged for, eg pairs of socks; or single items, such as designer dresses, in which case the unit is quoted as 'each'

- **total** is the unit price multiplied by the number of units

- **discount %** is the percentage allowance (often known as 'trade' discount) given to customers who regularly deal with the supplier, ie they receive a certain percentage (eg 10%) deducted from their bill (see page 33 for further explanation of discounts)

- discounts are also given for **bulk purchases** – 'bulk discount' will also be shown in the discount column

- **net** is the amount due to the seller after deduction of trade or bulk discount, and before VAT is added on

totals and VAT

Further calculations are made in the box at the bottom of the invoice:

- **Goods Total** is the amount due to the seller (it is the total of the net column)

- **Value Added Tax (VAT)**, here calculated as 20% of the goods total. VAT is added to produce the invoice final total

- **Total** is the Goods Total plus VAT; it is the amount to be paid to the seller

Note: VAT is a 'sales tax' on the supply of goods and services. The rate of VAT is changed from time-to-time by the Government. In this book a standard VAT rate of 20% is used.

terms

The terms of payment are stated on the invoice. In this case these include:

- **Net monthly** – this means that full payment of the invoice should be made within a month of the invoice date

- **Carriage paid** means that the price of the goods includes delivery charges

- **E & OE** stands for 'errors and omissions excepted' which means that if there is an error or something left off the invoice by mistake, resulting in an incorrect final price, the supplier has the right to rectify the mistake and demand the correct amount

Another term used (not shown here) is **Prompt Payment Discount** (also known as '**Settlement Discount**' or '**Cash Discount**') – a percentage discount given when payment is made early. See pages 35-36 for further details.

INVOICE

COOL SOCKS LIMITED
Unit 45 Elgar Estate, Broadland, BR7 4ER
Tel 01908 765314   Fax 01908 765951   Email toni@cool.u-net.com
VAT REG GB 0745 4672 76

Invoice to

| **Trends** |
| 4 Friar Street |
| Broadfield |
| BR1 3RF |

deliver to

as above

invoice no	**787923**
account	**3993**
your reference	**47609**
date/tax point	**02 10 20-3**

Product code	Description	Quantity	Price	Unit	Total	Discount %	Net
45B	**Blue toebar socks**	100	2.36	pair	236.00	0.00	236.00

terms
Net monthly
Carriage paid
E & OE

GOODS TOTAL	236.00
VAT	47.20
TOTAL	**283.20**

CREDIT NOTE – A REFUND IS DUE TO THE BUYER

A **credit note** is a 'refund' document. It reduces the amount owed by the buyer. The goods, remember, have not yet been paid for. The credit note is prepared by the seller and sent to the buyer. Examples of reasons for a refund by credit note include:

- the goods may have been damaged, lost in transit or they may be faulty
- not all the goods have been sent – this is referred to as 'shortages'
- the unit price on the invoice may be incorrect and the buyer overcharged

In this Case Study, when the staff of Trends unpack the socks in the store room they find that ten pairs are damaged. They contact Cool Socks to report the problem and Cool Socks authorises the return of the socks for credit. These socks will then be sent back to Cool Socks with a request for credit – ie a reduction in the bill for the 10 damaged pairs – with a document known as a returns note (see page 167). Cool Socks will then issue the credit note for £28.32 shown below. Note the following details:

- the invoice number of the original consignment is quoted
- the reason for the issue of the credit note is stated at the bottom of the credit note – here 'damaged' goods
- the details are otherwise exactly the same as on an invoice

---

CREDIT NOTE

COOL SOCKS LIMITED
Unit 45 Elgar Estate, Broadland, BR7 4ER
Tel 01908 765314   Fax 01908 765951   Email toni@cool.u-net.com
VAT REG GB 0745 4672 76

to

Trends		
4 Friar Street		
Broadfield		
BR1 3RF		

credit note no	**12157**
account	**3993**
your reference	**47609**
our invoice	**787923**
date/tax point	**10 10 20-3**

Product code	Description	Quantity	Price	Unit	Total	Discount %	Net
45B	**Blue toebar socks**	**10**	**2.36**	**pair**	**23.60**	**0.00**	**23.60**

Reason for credit		
10 pairs of socks received – damaged		

Goods	**23.60**
VAT	**4.72**
TOTAL	**28.32**

STATEMENT – THE SELLER REQUESTS PAYMENT

A seller will not normally expect a buyer to pay each individual invoice as soon as it is received: this could result in the buyer having to make a number of payments during the month. Instead, a **statement of account** is issued by the supplier to the buyer at the end of the month. This statement shows what is owed by the buyer to the seller. It contains details of:

- any balances (amounts owing) at the beginning of the month – these appear in the debit column with the wording 'balance b/f' in the details column ('b/f' stands for 'brought forward')

- any payments received from the buyer (credit column)

- invoices issued for goods supplied – the full amount due, including VAT (debit column)

- refunds made on credit notes – including VAT (credit column)

- the running balance and, in the box at the bottom, the final net total of all the items

- the bank details required for making payment by a bank BACS or Faster Payments Transfer

The statement issued by Cool Socks to Trends for the period covering the sale and refund is shown on the next page. Note that the balance of £150 owing at the beginning of the month has been paid off in full by a BACS payment on 2 October.

STATEMENT OF ACCOUNT

COOL SOCKS LIMITED

Unit 45 Elgar Estate, Broadland, BR7 4ER
Tel 01908 765314   Fax 01908 765951 Email toni@cool.u-net.com
VAT REG GB 0745 4672 76

to

Trends	account	3993
4 Friar Street		
Broadfield	date	31 10 20-3
BR1 3RF		

Date	Details	Debit £	Credit £	Balance £
01 10 20-3	Balance b/f	150.00		150.00
02 10 20-3	BACS payment 170961		150.00	00.00
02 10 20-3	Invoice 787923	283.20		283.20
10 10 20-3	Credit note 12157		28.32	254.88

Electronic payments: pay Cool Socks Ltd at Albion Bank, Account 11451226, Sort code 904717	TOTAL	254.88

DISCOUNTS

The invoice in the Case Study (shown again on the next page) has a column (second from the right) for a **discount** percentage. The two most common discounts are bulk discount and trade discount, which are simply percentage deductions from the price charged for goods and services.

bulk discount

Discount may be given by sellers to buyers who purchase in large quantities, or over certain money amounts; this is known as **bulk discount**.

trade discount

It is common practice for suppliers to give businesses that order from them on a regular basis an agreed discount – a percentage reduction in the invoiced amount. This is **trade discount** because it applies to businesses 'in the trade' rather than to the general public. In the example on the next page, 10% trade discount has been given by Cool Socks Limited to Trends. Note how the discount percentage is shown in the discount column and the net amount is the amount after deduction of the discount.

The calculations on the Cool Socks invoice are as follows:

Step 1   Calculate the total price before discount
100 x £2.36 = £236.00

Step 2   Calculate the trade discount
£236.00 x 10% (ie 10/100) = £23.60

Step 3   Calculate the net price before VAT
£236.00 – £23.60 = £212.40

Step 4   Calculate the VAT
£212.40 x 20% (ie 20/100) = £42.48

Step 5   Calculate the total invoice price
£212.40 + £42.48 = £254.88

INVOICE

COOL SOCKS LIMITED

Unit 45 Elgar Estate, Broadland, BR7 4ER
Tel 01908 765314   Fax 01908 765951 Email toni@cool.u-net.com
VAT REG GB 0745 4672 76

Invoice to

Trends 4 Friar Street Broadfield BR1 3RF	invoice no	**787923**
	account	**3993**
	your reference	**47609**
deliver to	date/tax point	**02 10 20-3**
as above		

Product code	Description	Quantity	Price	Unit	Total	Discount %	Net
45B	**Blue toebar socks**	**100**	**2.36**	**pair**	**236.00**	**10.00**	**212.40**

terms
Net monthly
Carriage paid
E & OE

Goods total	212.40
VAT	42.48
TOTAL	**254.88**

an invoice with 10% trade discount deducted

prompt payment discount (PPD)

Prompt payment discount (also known as **settlement discount** or **cash discount**) is a discount offered by the seller to the buyer to encourage the buyer to settle up straightaway or in a short space of time rather than waiting the thirty or more days specified on the invoice. For example, the seller might offer an extra 5% discount on an invoice if it is paid within 15 days.

ways of adjusting for VAT when a PPD is deducted

It is important to remember that the VAT on an invoice will **always** be calculated on the invoice total **after** the deduction of trade or bulk discount but will **not** be adjusted for any prompt payment discount (PPD) deducted by the buyer. If PPD is taken, the goods amount and VAT due on the sale will therefore be **less** than that shown on the invoice. These figures will need to be adjusted in the bookkeeping records.

There are two ways in which the seller can reduce the VAT amount and goods total when a PPD (prompt payment discount) is offered. **Important note:** the first alternative listed here is the method that AAT uses in its Assessments and the second is explained here for information only.

▓ **Alternative 1 – the seller issues a credit note (AAT method)**

If the customer pays early, taking advantage of the lower charge, a lower amount of VAT will be due to HM Revenue & Customs (HMRC). The seller will have to issue to the customer a credit note for the amount of the prompt payment discount given. This will include the goods amount and the VAT.

▓ **Alternative 2 – the seller includes a PPD declaration on the invoice**

If the seller does not want to issue a credit note, the seller's invoice must include a written declaration giving the terms of the PPD (eg discount of 5% for an invoice settled within 15 days of the invoice date) and a statement that the buyer should account to HMRC for a lower VAT amount (ie not the amount on the invoice). HMRC recommends that if this method is adopted, this declaration is included on the invoice:

'A discount of X% of the full price applies if payment is made within Y days of the invoice date. No credit note will be issued. Following payment you must ensure you have only recovered the VAT actually paid.'

In the Case Study on the next page, a buyer is offered a prompt payment discount of 5% for payment within 15 days of the invoice date and decides to take the discount **using Alternative 1** (see above) where the seller issues a credit note for the reduction in price and VAT paid.

Case Study

SELAR LTD AND BIYAR LTD – DEALING WITH PPD

situation and how the process works...

- Selar Ltd regularly supplies goods to Biyar Ltd and has offered Biyar Ltd a prompt payment discount of 5% for settlement within 15 days

- Selar Ltd sends an invoice for goods costing £1,000 to Biyar Ltd. An extract of this is shown below. The terms printed at the bottom of the invoice include the 5% PPD that will be offered to Biyar Ltd for payment. The invoice is sent with the goods

- Biyar Ltd decides to pay the invoice within the 15 days and calculates the 5% discount as follows:

  Goods total £1,000 x 5% = £50

  VAT payable = £200 x 5% = £10

  The total discount plus the VAT is therefore £50 + £10 = £60

- Biyar Ltd then calculates the amount due to Selar Ltd and pays the invoice:

Total payable without discount (as on invoice)	£1,200
Less discount	£60
Amount payable	£1,140

- Selar Ltd sends Biyar Ltd a credit note for the total discount including VAT as shown below. The amounts on the £60 credit note are a goods total of £50 and VAT of £10

INVOICE *(extract)*

Selar Ltd to Biyar Ltd

- -

terms

5% prompt payment discount for payment within 15 days of the invoice date

Carriage paid

E & OE

GOODS TOTAL	1,000.00
VAT	200.00
TOTAL	1,200.00

CREDIT NOTE *(extract)*
Selar Ltd to Biyar Ltd

GOODS TOTAL	50.00
VAT	10.00
TOTAL	60.00

VALUE ADDED TAX (VAT) – A 'SALES TAX'

what is Value Added Tax (VAT)?

VAT is a UK sales tax on the selling price charged to buyers.

As we have seen on some of the business documents illustrated in this chapter, VAT is added to the price of items sold after discount has been deducted. VAT is a sales tax paid by the buyer and administered and collected by **HM Revenue & Customs (HMRC)**, a Government Department.

Businesses who are registered for VAT must keep accurate records of VAT paid and collected. This means keeping financial documents such as invoices and credit notes for a minimum period of six years. HM Revenue & Customs tax inspectors visit VAT-registered businesses from time to time to ensure that VAT is being charged correctly.

Note that businesses are generally required to register for VAT once their turnover (sales) exceeds the level set by HMRC. Smaller businesses may have turnover that is below the VAT threshold for registration.

some useful VAT calculations

In your studies you are likely to be asked to carry out a variety of calculations involving VAT. Here are some of the more common ones.

what is the VAT to be charged?

If you need to work out the VAT on a given amount you apply the formula:

$$amount \times \frac{20}{100} \text{ (ie the VAT rate)} = VAT\ payable$$

VAT chargeable on £100 is therefore £100 x $\dfrac{20}{100}$ = £20.00

Note that when calculating VAT, the VAT total is usually rounded down to the nearest penny; eg VAT of £2.5678 becomes £2.56 and not £2.57.

calculating the VAT when the VAT is included but not shown separately

If you are given a total amount – for example, a shop till receipt which does not show the VAT amount – you may need to work out both the VAT content and also the amount before VAT is added (the 'VAT exclusive' amount). The VAT content is worked out by using the formula:

$$\frac{VAT\ percentage\ x\ amount\ which\ includes\ VAT}{100 + VAT\ percentage} = VAT\ content$$

The VAT content can also be found by using the VAT fraction provided by HM Revenue & Customs. For a VAT rate of 20%, the VAT fraction is 1/6. All you have to do to find out the VAT is to divide the amount including VAT by 6. For example, the VAT included in £12 is £12 ÷ 6 = £2.

AUTHORISING AND CHECKING INVOICES

credit limits

The credit limit of a customer is the maximum amount that the seller will allow the customer to owe at any one time.

Part of the accounting control system of a business is to set credit limits for its established customers and to establish limits for new customers. Each time that an invoice is issued, a check should be made against the credit limit of that customer.

authorisation of invoices

Most invoices issued will be within the credit limit and processed with the authority of the person in charge of invoicing.

But what if the credit limit will be exceeded? No business will refuse to supply a good customer. It may be that payment will soon come in from the buyer, or the amount involved is relatively small. In these cases the invoice will need authorisation from the accounts supervisor.

It is quite possible that a credit limit may have to be raised if a customer is buying more goods or services and, of course, is paying invoices on time.

the need to check invoices

Few things are more annoying to a buyer than an incorrect invoice – the wrong goods, the wrong price, the wrong discount, and so on. It wastes the buyer's time and may require an adjusting credit note to be issued. It is essential that a number of important details are checked by the accounts staff of the seller before invoices are authorised and sent out.

The following will need to be checked:

- the purchase order relating to the invoice (this is very important)

- the seller's own record of any price quoted (eg a printed or online catalogue, or a product database)

- the seller's file record of the buyer (either paper or digital) which should give the credit limit and the discount allowed

the checks to be made

- is the **correct customer** being invoiced? There are often customers with similar names; the customer coding must be checked carefully

- are the goods being sent to the **correct place**? Sometimes the delivery address will be different from the address normally held on file

- are the **correct goods** being sent? The product coding on the purchase order must be checked carefully against the description; it is possible that the buyer has quoted an incorrect code

- is the **quantity** correct?

- is the **unit** correct? Is it a box of products or an individual item being requested?

- is the **price** correct?

- is the **correct discount** percentage being allowed to the customer? Do any special terms apply? The list of discounts on customer file will need to be looked at

- are the **calculations** on the invoice correct? This is very important if the invoice has not been produced electronically. The normal checks for a straightforward invoice with trade discount deducted are:

    quantity x unit price = total before discount

    total before discount x discount % = discount

    total before discount – discount = goods total

    goods total x VAT % = VAT

    goods total + VAT = invoice total

If the invoice is for more than one product, all the invoice 'lines' must be checked individually and the addition also checked.

DEALING WITH DISCREPANCIES

Discrepancies on financial documents can occur in the following situations:

■ **The discrepancy is found in the internal checking process,** before the document is issued. In this case the document will have to be passed back to the person or section which made the mistake and a new corrected document will have to be issued and authorised; normally the original document reference number can be retained.

■ **The buyer finds the discrepancy after the document has been issued.** In this case an apology will have to be made by the seller to the buyer and a correcting document issued; under no circumstances should the buyer alter or correct the document.

METHODS OF CODING IN DOCUMENTS

We have already seen in this chapter that **coding** is widely used in the documentation process. Coding is important for two main reasons:

■ it provides an instant and accurate way of referencing customers, suppliers, individual products, purchase orders

■ it enables documents to be traced so that they can be easily accessed; it is important in any business that documents can be found and referred to easily, either in paper format, or electronically on a digital system

Filing systems use either an **alphabetical** or a **numerical** coding system:

■ customer files are normally filed alphabetically by name

■ invoices are normally filed numerically by invoice number

Sometimes coding may be **alpha-numerical**, using a mixture of letters and numbers. For example, customers who have 'JON' as the first three letters of their name – such as 'Jones' – may be coded JON01, JON02, JON03, and so on. If you think about it, alpha-numerical coding is used widely in everyday life: examples include vehicle registration plates, postcodes, tax codes and National Insurance 'numbers'.

Study the invoice extract shown on the next page and see how many accounting-related codes you can identify and what types they are. The answers are shown below the extract.

invoice (extract)

Simway Ltd
4 High Street
Broadfield
BR1 2GF

invoice no	82346
account reference	SIM003
purchase order	47609
date/tax point	07 12 20-3

Product code	Description	Quantity	Price	Unit	Total	Discount %	Net
STPGR	**Stapler (green)**	**10**	**10.70**	**each**	**107.00**	**10.00**	**96.30**

Alphabetical code: product code STPGR

Numerical codes: invoice number 82346

purchase order number 47609

Alpha-numerical code: account reference SIM003

Case
Study

CODING AT WORK

supplier account codes

Legno Ltd, a timber retailer, allocates codes to each of its suppliers. Each code is alpha-numerical, made up of the first three letters of the supplier's name, followed by a two digit number to distinguish between the suppliers when two or more share the same first three letters. It has three suppliers whose account codes start with the letters 'JON':

Supplier	Supplier account code
Jones Supplies	JON01
Jonathan UK Ltd	JON02
Jonas Ltd	JON03

You are to allocate account codes to two new suppliers: Jonsson Ltd and Jonty Supplies.

What codes will you use?

Answer:

Supplier	Supplier account code
Jonsson Ltd	JON04
Jonty Supplies	JON05

sales product codes

Legno Ltd operates a system which allocates general ledger account codes to different types of timber sales. These are entered on the sales invoices and credit notes so that the amount can be entered in the correct account. The ledger codes are as follows:

Product type	General Ledger Code
Pine sales	GL4000
Oak sales	GL4001
Beech sales	GL4002
Ash sales	GL4004

A new trainee asks you to check that he has the right code for an invoice for the sale of oak. He asks if it is GL4002 because that is a code used frequently on invoices. Is the trainee correct?

Answer: No. The code is incorrect. The code for the sale of oak is GL4001.

Chapter Summary

- When a business sells goods or services on credit, it deals with a number of financial documents. The most important of these are the:

  – purchase order

  – delivery note

  – invoice

  – credit note

  – statement of account

- The seller of the goods or services requests payment by means of an invoice and then reminds the buyer by means of a regular statement of account (normally issued monthly).

- Discounts – reductions in the selling price – are often given by the seller to the buyer. These include trade discount, bulk discount and prompt payment discount for early payment. Trade and bulk discounts are deducted by the seller from the invoice total. Prompt payment discount is deducted by the buyer when paying the invoice and is adjusted by means of a credit note issued by the seller.

- Any refund due to the buyer (eg for wrong, damaged or missing goods) is acknowledged and documented by means of a credit note.

- All documents are normally coded (given an alphabetical, numerical or alpha-numerical code) for reference purposes.

- Value Added Tax (VAT), a sales tax payable on most goods and services, is included on invoices and credit notes issued by VAT-registered businesses.

- All documents should be checked carefully by the seller to make sure that the right goods or services have been supplied, and at the right price. It is important that items such as discounts, VAT and totals are calculated correctly.

- Financial documents will need to be authorised before they are issued.

- Any discrepancies found on the documents either by the seller or the buyer should be dealt with promptly.

Key Terms	**purchase order**	a document issued by the buyer of goods and services, sent to the seller, indicating the goods or services required
	delivery note	a document sent by the seller to the buyer with the goods, detailing what has been sent
	invoice	a document issued by the seller of goods or services indicating the amount owing and the required payment date
	credit note	a document issued by the seller of the goods or services reducing the amount owed by the buyer
	statement of account	a document issued by the seller to the buyer, summarising invoices, credit notes issued and payments received, that states the amount owed
	trade discount	a percentage reduction in the selling price given by the seller to the buyer because of the trading relationship
	bulk discount	a discount given by the seller to the buyer for bulk purchases, ie purchases over certain quantities or over certain money amounts
	prompt payment discount	a percentage reduction in the selling price given to the buyer if the buyer pays within a specified short space of time
	Value Added Tax (VAT)	a sales tax calculated on invoices and credit notes issued by VAT-registered businesses
	credit limit	the maximum amount the seller will allow the customer to owe at any one time
	coding	document references using numerical, alphabetical or alpha-numerical identification systems

Activities

2.1 Complete the sentences below by selecting the correct words from the following list:

invoice   **statement of account**   **purchase order**   **delivery note**   **credit note**

(a) A ☐ is used to order goods from the seller.

(b) A ☐ is sent by the seller with the goods to the buyer, giving details of the goods sent.

(c) The document sent by the seller giving details of the terms of the transaction and stating the amount owed is an ☐

(d) A ☐ is sent by the seller to remind the buyer of the amount owed to the seller.

(e) The document sent to a buyer as a formal notification of a refund made is known as a ☐

2.2 Link with lines the three types of discount given by sellers listed on the right with the descriptions in the boxes on the left.

(a)

| a reduction in an amount owed on an invoice where the buyer pays earlier than is normal | **bulk discount** |

(b)

| a discount given by the seller to the buyer which forms part of the terms for regular purchases | **prompt payment discount** |

(c)

| a discount given by the seller for purchases over certain quantities or over certain money amounts | **trade discount** |

2.3   Tippett Brothers supplies goods priced at £159.50 to a customer at a trade discount of 30%. What would the total invoice amount be, assuming a VAT rate of 20% and no further discounts?

2.4   Zeta Stationery sells gel pens and has a special sales offer. A box of ten gel pens normally sells at £8.00 (excluding VAT). Zeta Stationery is offering to give a 20% bulk discount for orders of ten boxes or more. One morning it receives the following orders:

(a)   20 boxes ordered by Osborne Electronics Limited

(b)   50 boxes ordered by Helfield College

(c)   5 boxes ordered by Jim Masters

(d)   1,000 boxes ordered by Trigger Trading Limited

You are to calculate in each case:

- total cost before discount

- discount

- cost after discount

- VAT at the current rate

- invoice total

2.5   Venables Supplies sells computer accessories. The terms it offers its regular customers are as follows:

- 20% trade discount on all orders

- 5% prompt payment discount for settlement of an invoice within 15 days

You are given four invoices to prepare. The goods totals before applying any discounts and applying VAT are as follows:

1   £100

2   £1,650

3   £2,500

4   £10,900

You are to:

(a)   Calculate all four invoice totals after applying trade discount and VAT @ 20%.

(b)   Calculate the total amounts payable after the deduction of prompt payment discount by the buyer.

(c)   State the document used by the seller in each case to deduct the prompt payment discount from the total amount shown on the invoice.

2.6   Examine the invoice and credit note prepared by the seller in Question 2.8 and identify five examples of coding. These examples should include:

(a)   Numerical coding (2 examples)

(b)   Alphabetical coding invoice and credit note (1 example)

(c)   Alpha-numerical coding (2 examples)

2.7   •   Check the invoice extracts shown below.

•   State what is wrong with them.

•   Calculate the correct final totals.

Note: VAT is rounded down to the nearest penny.

Invoice (a)

Description	Quantity	Price	Total	Discount %	Net
Cotton shirts (red)	10	9.50	95.00	20	85.50
				GOODS TOTAL	85.50
				VAT @ 20%	17.10
				TOTAL	102.60

Invoice (b)

Description	Quantity	Price	Total	Discount %	Net
'Crazy Surfin' T-shirts (yellow)	50	5.00	225.00	10	202.50
				GOODS TOTAL	202.50
				VAT @ 20%	40.50
				TOTAL	243.00

2.8   You work in the accounts department of Pool Cleaning Services Limited, a business which maintains swimming pools, spa baths and jacuzzis.

It is 31 July 20-3 and you are looking through the file for the account of Mr Henry Simpson. Your file shows that you issued an invoice on 8 July (shown below) and a credit note on 14 July for a 10% trade discount which should have been deducted from the invoice.

You also note from last month's statement that Mr Simpson still owed you £58.75 on 1 July for a call out charge not yet paid. You received a bank payment for this amount on 4 July.

You are to prepare a statement for Mr H Simpson as at 31 July 20-3. It should show opening and closing balances and transactions for the month. A blank statement is shown on the next page.

INVOICE

Pool Cleaning Services Limited

Unit 5 Neptune Estate, Mereford, MR7 4EF
Tel 01908 352456 Fax 01908 352466 Email mail@poolcleaning-services.com
VAT Reg GB 0745 4872 21

invoice to

H Simpson 45 Bishops Avenue Marston Hackett MR7 9JH	invoice no	**10982**
	account	**HS234**
	your reference	**verbal**
	date/tax point	**08 07 20-3**

Description	Total	Discount	Net
Annual swimming pool service, 27 June 20-3 (Product: ASPS)	290.00	0.00	290.00

Net Total		**290.00**
VAT		**58.00**
TOTAL		**348.00**

terms
Net monthly

extract from credit note No. 2378 dated 14 July			
Description		**Total**	**Discount**	**Net**
Annual swimming pool service (Product:ASPS)		29.00	0.00	29.00

Reason for credit	NET TOTAL	29.00
10% trade discount allowable on invoice	VAT	5.80
	TOTAL	34.80

STATEMENT OF ACCOUNT

Pool Cleaning Services Limited

Unit 5 Neptune Estate, Mereford, MR7 4EF
Tel 01908 352456 Fax 01908 352466 Email mail@poolcleaning-services.com
VAT Reg GB 0745 4872 21

TO

account

date

Date	Details	Debit £	Credit £	Balance £

Electronic payments: pay Pool Cleaning Services Ltd at
Britannia Bank, Account 12397610, Sort code 83 11 20

TOTAL £

2.9 This task is about calculating prompt payment discount.
You are the bookkeeper at Hillier Supplies Limited. Today, 5 March 20-2, you have issued the two invoices below to customers.

<table>
<tr><td colspan="2" align="center">**Hillier Supplies Ltd**
Invoice no: 6748</td></tr>
<tr><td colspan="2">**To:** Merrow plc
Date: 5 March 20-2</td></tr>
<tr><td></td><td>£</td></tr>
<tr><td>30 x Product 34 at £20 each</td><td>600.00</td></tr>
<tr><td>VAT @ 20%</td><td>120.00</td></tr>
<tr><td>TOTAL</td><td>720.00</td></tr>
</table>

Terms: 2.5% discount if payment received within 10 days of date of invoice

<table>
<tr><td colspan="2" align="center">**Hillier Supplies Ltd**
Invoice no: 6749</td></tr>
<tr><td colspan="2">**To:** Barton Ltd
Date: 5 March 20-2</td></tr>
<tr><td></td><td>£</td></tr>
<tr><td>120 x Product 173 at £15 each</td><td>1,800.00</td></tr>
<tr><td>VAT @ 20%</td><td>360.00</td></tr>
<tr><td>TOTAL</td><td>2,160.00</td></tr>
</table>

Terms: 2% discount if payment received within 14 days of date of invoice

(a) The accounts supervisor asks you to:

- calculate how much will be received from each customer if the prompt payment discount is taken

- calculate the date by which the amounts will be received if the prompt payment discount is taken (choose from the date options below)

Customer	£	Date
Merrow plc		
Barton Ltd		

Date options
5 March 20-2
15 March 20-2
16 March 20-2
19 March 20-2
20 March 20-2

(b)   If either customer takes up the prompt payment discount, what document will you issue to them?

(a)	Delivery note	
(b)	Credit note	
(c)	Returns note	
(d)	Statement of account	

Which **one** of these options is correct?

3 Double-entry and the accounting equation

this chapter covers...

- *the need for accounts and what they are used for*
- *how double-entry accounts are organised into ledgers*
- *the format of double-entry accounts*
- *the principles of debits and credits and the dual effect of each transaction*
- *how the bank account fits into the double-entry system*
- *making entries in double-entry accounts*
- *deciding whether an entry made in a double-entry account is debit or credit*
- *how double-entry accounts relate to the accounting equation*
- *the operation of the accounting equation*
- *balancing double-entry accounts*
- *the use of digital bookkeeping systems*

important note

This book uses the term 'bank account' to mean both an account held at a bank and also a ledger account set up by a business to record bank transactions. To avoid confusion, all ledger accounts in this book use capital letters for the start of the account name, but the account held at the bank is referred to using small letters. The rule is:

Bank **A**ccount = a ledger account in the books of the business

bank account = an account held at a bank

INTRODUCTION TO DOUBLE-ENTRY ACCOUNTS

double-entry accounts and the accounting system

As we saw in Chapter 1, double-entry accounts are prepared from the books of prime entry, which include day books and cash books.

Books of prime entry record financial transactions and are prepared from business documents, which include invoices and bank payments. The phrase 'prime entry' means 'the first place where information is entered'. Books of prime entry are covered in detail in later chapters of this book.

The diagram below shows how the double-entry accounts fit into the earlier stages of the accounting system.

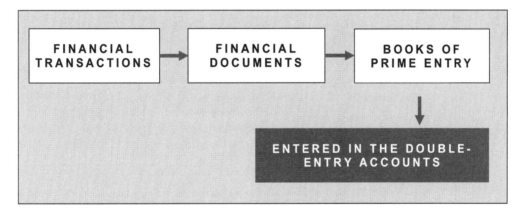

what do double-entry accounts record?

Double-entry accounts form the 'core' of the accounting system. They are a record of financial transactions:

■ what is owed on credit by individual customers as a result of sales

■ what is owed on credit to individual suppliers as a result of purchases

■ income items

■ expense items

Double-entry accounts can be:

■ accounts for types of income (sales, rent received) or expenses (purchases, insurance, wages)

■ accounts for assets (items owned)

■ accounts for liabilities (items owed)

how are double-entry accounts organised?

Double-entry accounts are grouped for convenience in different **ledgers** (for credit sales, credit purchases, general accounts). These are shown in the diagram below and are explained in more detail in later chapters.

All the ledgers grouped together are called '**the ledger**', which we have seen already in Chapter 1. To summarise:

'the ledger' = receivables ledger & payables ledger & general ledger

RECEIVABLES LEDGER

accounts for customers

- who buy on credit from the business

- who owe money to the business

PAYABLES LEDGER

accounts for suppliers

- who supply on credit to the business, and

- to whom the business owes money

GENERAL LEDGER

accounts for

- assets (items owned)

- liabilities (items owed)

- owner's capital

- expenses

- income

DOUBLE-ENTRY 'T' ACCOUNTS

In manual accounting systems, double-entry accounts are customarily set out in the form of a 'T' with the account name at the top; they are known as 'T accounts' – see the example below:

Debit (dr)	Account name	Credit (cr)

Each account has two sides:

- a **debit** side (often written as 'dr') on the left

- a **credit** side (often written as 'cr') on the right

You can remember this using the phrase '**Dr**ive on the left and **Cr**ash on the right'. If you do not normally drive on the left you could use the phrase '**D**ozy **L**ions **C**annot **R**un'.

A double-entry transaction makes entries in **two accounts** – a debit entry in one account and a credit entry in the other account.

In the example below, a business has paid an insurance premium from its bank account. The accounts record two aspects of the transaction: the insurance expense and the deduction from the bank account.

The debit entry goes to the Insurance Account and the credit entry to the Bank Account. If you are wondering why the Insurance Account entry is a debit and the Bank Account entry a credit, we will explain the rules over the next few pages.

This process is known as the **dual effect** of double-entry bookkeeping: every transaction makes a change to two accounts.

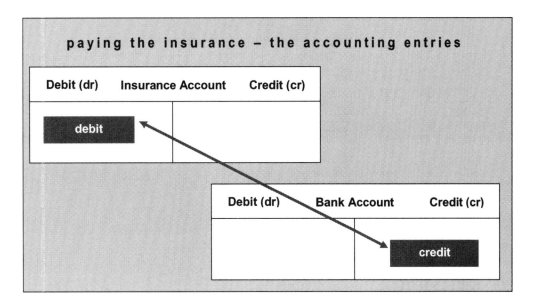

BANK ACCOUNTS – DEBITS AND CREDITS

Virtually all businesses make use of a bank account. Transactions passing through the account held at the bank – for example, money received, payments made – will need recording in the accounts of the business.

Bank Account in the accounting system of a business is a separate record of the money paid into and out of the bank.

The problem for the bookkeeper is that the terms 'debit' and 'credit' are used differently by the bank and a business. In fact they are the opposite way round. This can prove confusing when dealing with a bank statement:

- a bank sees a **debit** as a **payment out** of a customer's account

- a bank sees a **credit** as a **payment into** a customer's account

Businesses, however should always think as follows:

- **money paid into the bank is always a debit** in the accounting system of the business

- **money paid out of the bank is always a credit** in the accounting system of the business

This 'left to right' flow of money in and out of the Bank Account as set up in the ledgers of a business can be seen as follows:

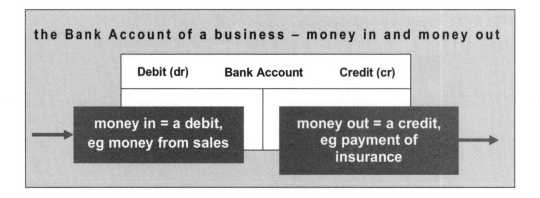

the Bank Account of a business – money in and money out

Debit (dr)	Bank Account	Credit (cr)
money in = a debit, eg money from sales		money out = a credit, eg payment of insurance

debit or credit?

When a financial transaction is recorded as an entry in the Bank Account of a business as part of the double-entry system, it is easy to work out whether it is a credit or a debit by using the 'money in = debit; money out = credit' rule. It is then straightforward to work out whether the entry in the other account involved in the transaction is a debit or credit. The rules are:

■ **payment into the bank . . . money in = a debit . . .**

so the other entry must be a credit

Example:

£1,000 received from sales paid into the bank. The entries are:

Debit: Bank Account £1,000   Credit: Sales Account £1,000

■ **payment out of the bank . . . money out = a credit . . .**

so the other entry must be a debit

Example:

£500 insurance premium paid out of the bank account by electronic transfer. The entries are:

Debit: Insurance Account £500   Credit: Bank Account £500

Note from each of these two entries:

■ the debit and credit entries are for the same amount

■ the debit entry is listed first and the credit entry is listed second

Not every double-entry transaction involves the Bank Account, but many do, and it is a very useful starting point for getting to grips with debits and credits. The two transactions just explained are illustrated on the next page.

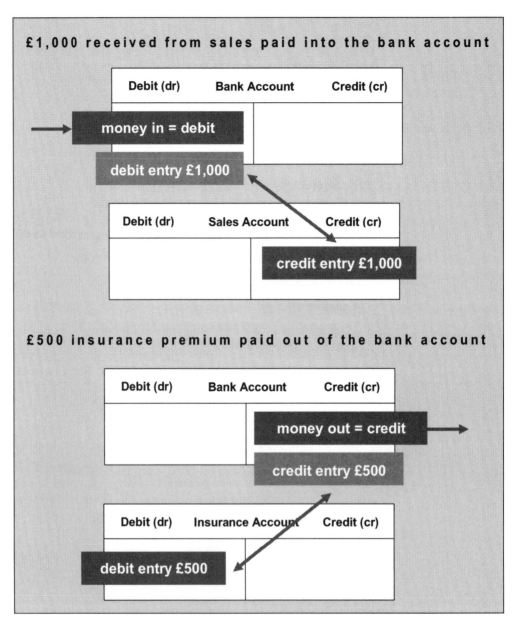

We will now go a step further and illustrate the full format of double-entry accounts and the information that needs to be recorded in the account.

ENTRIES IN A DOUBLE-ENTRY ACCOUNT

In this chapter the double-entry accounts have so far been displayed as a simple 'T'. This 'T' format is a useful way of displaying the account, but a full double-entry account is more detailed and will have a number of columns.

You will need to know how to enter the transaction details in these columns.

As you will see in the example below, there are two lines of detail on the account:

- the account name and the 'debit' and 'credit' headings at the top; remember that the account name has a capital letter at the beginning (see the 'important note' on page 52)

- on the next line down are the transaction column headings (date, details, £); these are the same on the debit and on the credit sides

Study the account format and read the notes about the transaction details that follow.

The transaction here shows how the Bank Account is entered up for insurance of £500 paid out from the bank on 30 March 20-3 (remember: payment out of bank = credit entry).

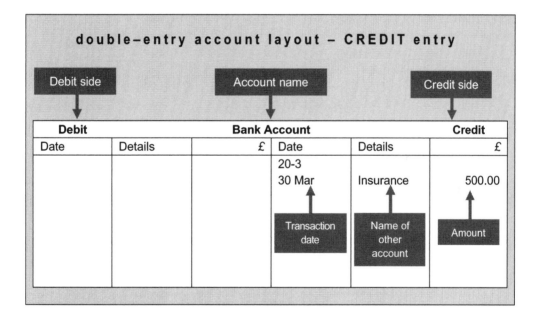

- **date** – the year date is normally entered on the next line down of the date column and the actual date and transaction details on the following line; note that the month is often abbreviated – here it is '30 Mar' (30 March)

- **details** – this is the other account that has been used in the double-entry transaction; here the other account is Insurance Account and the entry will be a debit because the Bank Account entry is a credit ('money out = a credit')

- **£** – this is the amount column; obviously the '£' refers to the UK pound but you might also see a $ or a € sign if that is appropriate; occasionally you may also find that £ and pence (or dollars and cents) are separated into two columns

The entry to the Insurance Account for the above transaction is shown below.

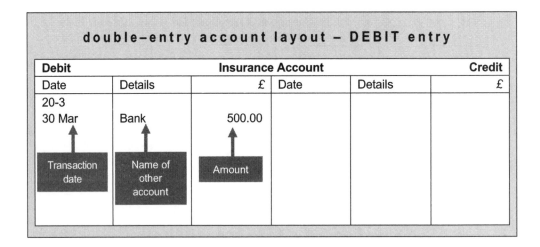

RULES FOR DEBITS AND CREDITS

So far in this chapter we have seen that:

- money paid into the bank results in a **debit** entry to Bank Account in the accounting system of the business

- money paid out of the bank results in a **credit** entry to Bank Account in the accounting system of the business

Bank Account

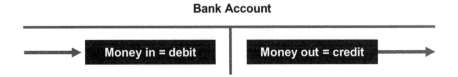

We will now look in more detail at the 'other' accounts involved in the transactions, identifying which are normally debit or credit entries to the accounts.

entries that are always debits

Some entries in the double-entry accounts are always debits because the other account entry is the **credit side of Bank Account** and the transaction involved is a payment of money going out of the business. They include:

- **purchases** – goods bought for resale or materials used for manufacturing

- **expenses** – expenses of running the business, eg rent, advertising, insurance

- **assets bought** – items bought for use in the business, eg computers, vehicles

entries that are always credits

Some entries in the double-entry accounts are **always credits** because the other account entry is the **debit side of Bank Account** and the transaction involved is a receipt of money coming into the business. They include:

- **sales** – money received for goods sold or services provided

- **capital** – money paid in by the owner

- **loans** – money borrowed from the bank or other sources

Examples of debits and credits are illustrated in the diagram below which uses the simple 'T' account and shows the account names in order to makes things clearer. Note that:

- money received entries: **debit** Bank Account and **credit** the account recording the receipt

- money paid out entries: **credit** Bank Account and **debit** the account recording the expense

- the description entered in each account is the name of the other account in the transaction

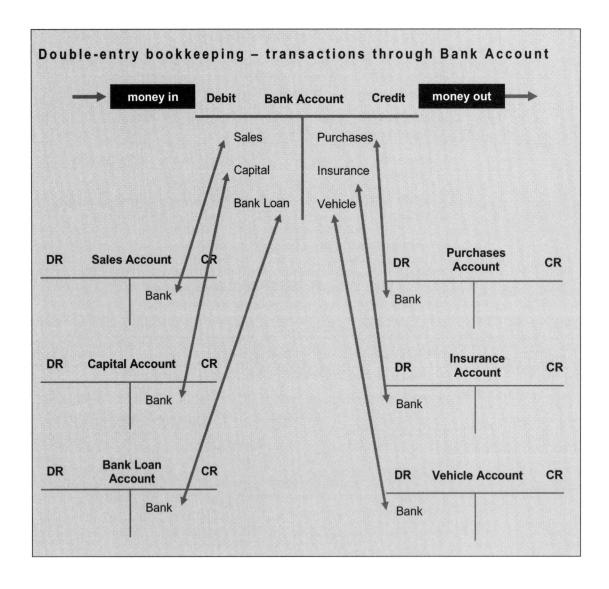

The Case Study which follows puts into practice the double-entry theory covered so far in this chapter, and uses the full layout of the double-entry accounts.

Case Study

PRONTA PIZZA – DOUBLE-ENTRY IN PRACTICE

Riccardo has just started a new pizza home delivery business. He has put in capital of £30,000 himself and raised loans of £10,000 from the bank and £10,000 from his brother Carlo. He has paid all this money into a business account at Albion Bank so that he can pay for all that he needs to start and run the business.

He asks his bookkeeper to enter the transactions shown in the table below into his cash book (which contains the Bank Account). He then asks the bookkeeper to set up and to record the entries in the bookkeeping system.

amounts received and paid into the bank		date of payment
Capital introduced by Riccardo	£30,000	15 January 20-3
Bank loan	£10,000	16 January 20-3
Loan from brother Carlo	£10,000	18 January 20-3
amounts paid out of the bank		
Equipment for cooking	£10,000	22 January 20-3
Van for pizza deliveries	£15,000	25 January 20-3
Materials purchased	£3,000	28 January 20-3
Insurance	£2,000	31 January 20-3

Riccardo's Bank Account in the books of Pronta Pizza after these entries have been made is shown below. The 'other' double-entry accounts follow on the next two pages.

Debit			Bank Account			Credit
Date	**Details**	**£**	**Date**	**Details**		**£**
20-3			20-3			
15 Jan	Capital	30,000	22 Jan	Equipment		10,000
16 Jan	Bank loan	10,000	25 Jan	Van		15,000
18 Jan	Carlo Loan	10,000	28 Jan	Purchases		3,000
			31 Jan	Insurance		2,000
	money in = debit			money out = credit		

The 'other entries' for payments into the Bank Account – ie credits

Debit				Capital Account	Credit
Date	**Details**	**£**	**Date**	**Details**	**£**
			20-3		
			15 Jan	Bank	30,000

Debit				Bank Loan Account	Credit
Date	**Details**	**£**	**Date**	**Details**	**£**
			20-3		
			16 Jan	Bank	10,000

Debit				Carlo Loan Account	Credit
Date	**Details**	**£**	**Date**	**Details**	**£**
			20-3		
			18 Jan	Bank	10,000

The 'other entries' for payments out of the Bank Account – ie debits

Debit				Equipment Account	Credit
Date	**Details**	**£**	**Date**	**Details**	**£**
20-3					
22 Jan	Bank	10,000			

Debit				Van Account	Credit
Date	**Details**	**£**	**Date**	**Details**	**£**
20-3					
25 Jan	Bank	15,000			

Debit	Purchases Account				Credit
Date	**Details**	**£**	**Date**	**Details**	**£**
20-3 28 Jan	Bank	3,000			

Debit	Insurance Account				Credit
Date	**Details**	**£**	**Date**	**Details**	**£**
20-3 31 Jan	Bank	2,000			

A NOTE ON CASH AND CREDIT TRANSACTIONS

The difference between cash and credit transactions is straightforward:

Cash sale = cash received straightaway

Credit sale = cash received at a later date

Cash purchase = cash paid straightaway

Credit purchase = cash paid at a later date

The double-entry bookkeeping described so far in this chapter relates also to **cash transactions**, ie money received and paid straightaway.

Where goods are sold or purchased now and settled later, the **credit transactions** will involve two double-entry transactions:

- the **first** on the date when the sale or purchase is made but no entry is made in Bank Account – the amount is entered in the customer or supplier account in the ledgers to record the transaction

- the **second** at a later date when the amount is paid and recorded in Bank Account and the customer or supplier account in the ledgers

These account entries will be covered in detail in Chapter 4 'Accounting for sales, returns and discounts' and in Chapter 7 'Accounting for purchases, returns and discounts'. In conclusion, all you need to note at this stage is:

- a **cash** sale or purchase requires just **one** double-entry transaction

- a **credit** sale or purchase requires **two** double-entry transactions on different dates:

  – the first when the credit sale or credit purchase takes place

  – the second when the transaction is paid

DEBITS AND CREDITS – CONCLUSION

'cash' transactions involving the bank account

Study the table below which gives examples of 'cash' double-entry transactions involving payments in and out of the bank. The column 'money in/out' indicates whether the payments are into or out of the bank.

	money in/out	debit	credit
buying an asset	out	asset account	bank account
receiving a bank loan (liability)	in	bank account	loan account
owner contributing capital	in	bank account	capital account
business paying wages (expense)	out	wages account	bank account
business receiving rent (income)	in	bank account	rent received account
business purchasing materials	out	purchases account	bank account

balances of accounts

So far in this chapter we have concentrated on the rules for debit and credit **entries** made in the double-entry accounts. These rules also extend to the double-entry account **balances**. As we will see at the end of this chapter, double-entry accounts are balanced regularly – in other words the amount that is 'held' in each account is calculated, just as your bank calculates how much money is held in your bank account, and is your bank 'balance'.

debits and credits – the rules

The table set out below shows which accounts normally have **debit** entries and balances and which accounts normally have **credit** entries and balances.

DEBITS	CREDITS
Assets (items bought and owned by the business)	**Liabilities** (amounts owed by the business, eg loans)
Customer accounts (money due to be paid by customers to the business)	**Supplier accounts** (money due to be paid to suppliers by the business)
Expenses of the business	**Sales and other types of income** received by the business
Purchases of goods for resale or manufacturing	**Capital**

accurate recording of transactions

By now you should have a good idea of the principles of debits and credits. However, it is important to ensure that bookkeeping transactions are entered accurately into the accounts. In a manual system, common errors include:

■ omitting to record entries for a transaction

■ duplication of transactions by recording the same transaction twice

■ making one entry only, eg a debit entry without making the credit entry

■ entering transactions the wrong way round, eg a debit entry recorded as a credit, and the credit entry recorded as a debit

■ entering the wrong amount in one or both accounts

■ making the entry in the wrong account, eg the customer account of J Smith, instead of T Smith's account

Always be aware of the need for accuracy in bookkeeping. The consequences of inaccurate entry in manual systems will have an effect on the results and may lead to the owner of the business receiving wrong information.

DOUBLE-ENTRY AND THE ACCOUNTING EQUATION

the accounting equation

In Chapter 1 we outlined the financial statements of a business – the **statement of profit or loss** and the **statement of financial position** – which are the end result of the accounting process. The statement of profit or loss shows how much profit (or loss) has been made and the statement of financial position shows how the assets of a business are financed. The statement of financial position illustrates what is known as the accounting equation:

assets (what a business owns and is owed)

minus   *liabilities (what is owed by the business)*

equals   *capital/equity (the owner's investment and profits)*

ASSETS what a business owns and is owed	minus	LIABILITIES what a business owes to others	equals	CAPITAL the owner's investment and profits

To help explain this equation we will now look at the concept of 'financial position' on a personal basis. If someone asked you what your financial position is, you might say:

'I have a total of £2,000 in the bank and in cash and I am owed £500 by a friend. I owe £100 to my brother.

My financial position is as follows: I have £2,000 plus the £500 owed to me by my brother, but I have to pay £100 to my friend, so I have £2,400.'

If you then express this in accounting terms (ie assets, liabilities and capital) you can see how the accounting equation works. Study the table below and then the accounting equation on the next page.

amount	personal situation	accounting term
£2,000	what you own	an asset
+ £500	what you are owed	an asset
− £100	what you owe	a liability
= £2,400	your financial position	capital

ASSETS £2,000 owned + £500 owed to you = £2,500	minus	LIABILITIES what you owe = £100	equals	CAPITAL your financial position = £2,400

the accounting equation and double-entry

The accounting equation is a useful way of looking at how the double-entry accounting works. As we have seen, each financial transaction is recorded in the bookkeeping system and results in two entries being made in the ledgers – a debit and a credit.

Where the accounting equation becomes relevant is that each equal debit and credit entry will always ensure that the equation balances.

We can illustrate this by seeing how example financial transactions:

- are entered in the double-entry accounts as debits and credits
- alter the accounting equation so that the equation still balances

1   starting a business by paying money into the bank

You pay £30,000 into the bank as capital to start your business. The account entries are:

Debit: Bank Account £30,000 Credit: Capital Account £30,000

Here, you are increasing assets by a debit entry of £30,000 and increasing capital by a credit entry of £30,000.

The accounting equation (£30,000 – £0 = £30,000) balances:

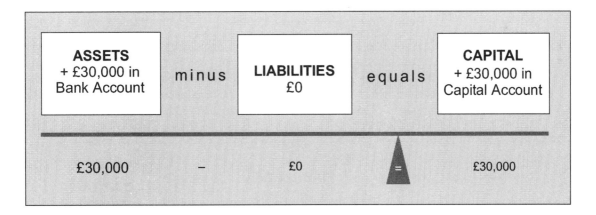

ASSETS + £30,000 in Bank Account	minus	**LIABILITIES** £0	equals	**CAPITAL** + £30,000 in Capital Account
£30,000	–	£0	=	£30,000

2   a bank loan which is paid into the bank account

You receive a bank loan (a liability) of £10,000 which goes straight into the business account at the bank (an asset). The account entries will be:

Debit: Bank Account £10,000   Credit: Bank Loan Account £10,000

Here you are **increasing assets** by a debit entry of £10,000 and **increasing liabilities** by a credit entry of £10,000. The accounting equation is now £40,000 (Assets) *minus* £10,000 (Liabilities) = £30,000 (Capital). The equation still balances because the increase in assets (a 'plus') is compensated for by the increase in liabilities (a 'minus') on the same side of the equation.

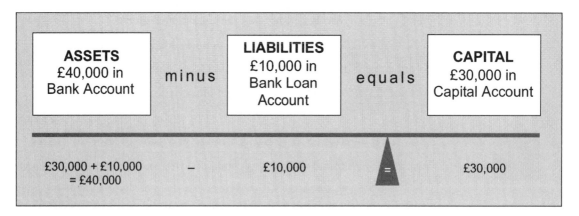

buying a computer (an asset)

You buy a computer (an asset) for £5,000 using money from the business bank account (also an asset). The account entries will be:

Debit: Computer Account £5,000   **Credit: Bank Account £5,000**

Here you are **increasing assets** by a debit entry of £5,000 to Computer Account and **decreasing assets** by a credit entry of £5,000 to Bank Account. The accounting equation is unchanged and still balances because you have just switched money from one asset (the bank account) to another asset (the computer). The equation now looks like this:

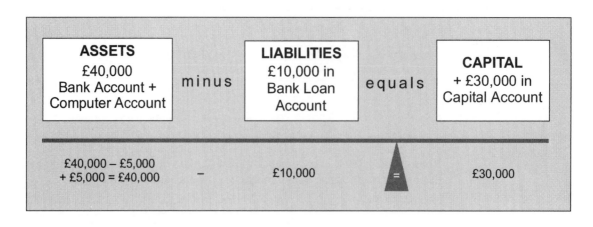

repaying part of the bank loan (a liability)

You repay £1,000 of the bank loan (a liability) using money from the business bank account (an asset). The account entries will be:

Debit: Bank Loan Account £1,000   Credit: Bank Account £1,000

Here, you are **decreasing a liability** with a debit entry of £1,000 to the Bank Loan Account and **decreasing an asset** by a credit entry of £1,000 to the Bank Account.

The equation still balances because the decrease in assets is compensated for by the decrease in liabilities on the same side of the equation. The equation now looks like this:

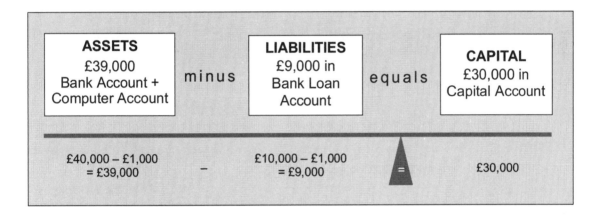

double-entry rules for changes in assets, liabilities and capital

You will see from the four examples on the last few pages that increases and decreases in assets, liabilities and capital follow a strict pattern which ensures that the accounting equation always balances:

- an **increase in an asset** is always a **debit entry**

- a **decrease in an asset** is always a **credit entry**

- an **increase in a liability** is always a **credit entry**

- a **decrease in a liability** is always a **debit entry**

- an **increase in capital** is always a **credit entry** (capital – which includes profit – is effectively a liability of the business which is owed to the owner)

These rules are set out in the summaries shown below.

<table>
<tr><td>

asset accounts

examples of assets:

  property

  vehicles

  computers

  inventory

  money due from customers

  money in the bank and cash

entries to the asset account:

DEBIT	CREDIT
asset increase	asset decrease

</td><td>

liability and capital accounts

examples of liabilities:

  bank loans

  bank overdrafts

  loans from other sources

  money due to suppliers

entries to the liability account:

DEBIT	CREDIT*
liability decrease	liability increase

*an increase in capital is also a credit entry

</td></tr>
</table>

BALANCING ACCOUNTS

In a manual bookkeeping system it is good practice to balance double-entry accounts at regular intervals in order to calculate the 'total' of the account. This process provides the owner of the business with valuable information, such as:

- the amount owing to each supplier (trade payable)

- the amount owed by each customer (trade receivable)

- the amount of sales and purchases and expenses

- the amount of VAT due to, or from, HM Revenue & Customs

These accounts are set out in the payables, receivables and general ledgers.

PAYABLES LEDGER	RECEIVABLES LEDGER	GENERAL LEDGER
suppliers who have supplied on credit – 'trade payables'	customers who have bought on credit – 'trade receivables'	other accounts such as sales, purchases, VAT, assets, loans and expenses

We will now see how to balance accounts from all three ledgers. Note that, with digital bookkeeping systems there is no need to balance accounts – the balance is available at any time.

BALANCING PAYABLES LEDGER ACCOUNTS

Set out below is an example of a supplier's account (Donato Wholesale) which has been written up in the payables ledger of Pronta Pizza (a pizza take-away business) during the month, but has not yet been balanced. Purchases made from the supplier are entered on the credit (right-hand) side of the account and faulty goods returned (purchases returns) to the supplier are entered on the debit (left-hand) side of the account.

Dr			Donato Wholesale Account			Cr
20-3	**Details**	**£**	**20-3**	**Details**		**£**
14 Jul	Purchases returns	25.00	13 Jul	Purchases		320.00
22 Jul	Purchases returns	75.00	20 Jul	Purchases		80.00
			24 Jul	Purchases		200.00

Now study the way in which this account is balanced at the end of July:

Dr			Donato Wholesale Account		Cr
20-3	**Details**	**£**	**20-3**	**Details**	**£**
14 Jul	Purchases returns	25.00	13 Jul	Purchases	320.00
22 Jul	Purchases returns	75.00	20 Jul	Purchases	80.00
31 Jul	Balance c/d **1**	500.00	24 Jul	Purchases	200.00
	2	600.00		**2**	600.00
			1 Aug	Balance b/d **3**	500.00

The debit and the credit columns are added up separately and the totals noted down (eg on a piece of paper). The totals are £600 on the credit side (three purchases items) and £100 (two purchases returns items) on the debit side.

Nothing is entered in the account at this stage. You should then follow the following procedure:

1 The difference between the totals of the two sides (ie £600 – £100 = £500) is the **balance** of the account; this is entered in the account:

- in the money column on the side of the smaller total (here, the debit side)

- on the next available line down on that side

- with the date of the balancing (here, it is 31 July)

- with the words 'Balance c/d', which is an abbreviation of 'Balance carried down' in the details column

2 Both sides of the account are now added up and the totals (which should be identical, and the higher of the two totals calculated earlier) are entered in the money columns on both sides of the account on the same line; here, the figure is £600.

A single line is drawn above the totals and a line (or a double line) underneath the totals.

3 As we have entered an extra £500 on the debit side in Step 1, we need to compensate for this by entering £500 on the credit side of the account, below the totals entered in Step 2. This ensures that the account shows the £500 account balance on the correct side. Note that the date here is not the month-end date (31 July) but the first day of the following month (1 August). The abbreviation 'Balance b/d' used here stands for 'Balance brought down'.

BALANCING RECEIVABLES LEDGER ACCOUNTS

On the previous page we balanced a payables ledger account. This showed how much a supplier, Donato Wholesale, is owed by Pronta Pizza at the end of the month. The balance of this account (£500) is on the **credit** side of the account, representing an amount **owed by** a business, a liability.

It therefore follows that if you turn to the receivables ledger which shows the opposite situation, ie amounts **owed to** Pronta Pizza by a customer, you will then find the balance of a customer account on the **debit** side of the ledger account, because an amount **owed to** a business is always a **debit**.

Study the example below of a balanced customer account – Albion Hotel – and read the notes that follow. You will see that sales are recorded on the debit (left-hand) side of the account and goods returns (sales returns) are on the credit (right-hand) side.

Dr			Albion Hotel Account		Cr
20-3	**Details**	**£**	**20-3**	**Details**	**£**
6 Jul	Sales	200.00	Jul 9	Sales returns	20.00
8 Jul	Sales	50.00	Jul 16	Sales returns	30.00
22 Jul	Sales	150.00	Jul 31	Balance c/d **1**	350.00
	2	400.00		**2**	400.00
1 Aug	Balance b/d **3**	350.00			

1 The balance of **£350** is the difference between the total of the debit entries (**£400**, ie £200 + £50 + £150) and the total of the credit entries (**£50**, ie £20 + £30). It is entered on the credit side, ie the side with the lower total.

2 Both sides are added up to produce a total of £400. A single line is drawn above the totals and a thicker single line (or a double line) underneath them.

3 As we have entered an extra £350 on the credit side in Step 1, we need to compensate for this by entering £350 on the debit side of the account, below the totals entered in Step 2. This ensures that the account shows the £350 account balance on the correct side. Note that the date here is not the month-end date (31 July) but the first day of the following month (1 August). The abbreviation 'Balance b/d' used here stands for 'Balance brought down'.

BALANCING GENERAL LEDGER ACCOUNTS

general ledger balances

You can normally rely on the rule that a payables ledger account has a balance brought down on the credit side and a receivables ledger account has a balance brought down on the debit side.

For General Ledger accounts, some usually have debit balances and some usually have credit balances:

- **debit account balances** = where **money is spent by the business**, ie spent on purchases, money refunded because of returns, expenses paid

- **credit account balances** = where **money is received by the business**, ie from sales, refunds received and other items of income

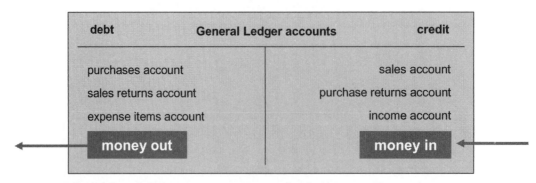

The balancing process is exactly the same as with the payables ledger and receivables ledger accounts, although it is common for the transaction entries to be on one side only.

The account below shows weekly payments for £250 recorded in the Rent Paid Account of a business. As you can see, these entries are all debits. If there was a refund of rent paid, it would be entered on the credit side and would reduce the final debit balance by that amount.

Dr			Rent Paid Account			Cr
20-3	**Details**	**£**	**20-3**	**Details**		**£**
1 Feb	Bank	250.00	28 Feb	Balance c/d		1,000,00
8 Feb	Bank	250.00				
15 Feb	Bank	250.00				
22 Feb	Bank	250.00				
		————				————
		1,000.00				1,000,00
		————				————
1 Mar	Balance b/d	1,000.00				

THE USE OF DIGITAL BOOKKEEPING SYSTEMS

As we have seen in this chapter, double-entry bookkeeping can be kept using a manual system, based on handwritten records. However, many businesses – even the smallest ones – keep their records electronically using digital bookkeeping systems in the form of:

- spreadsheets, such as Microsoft Excel
- app and cloud-based software, such as Xero, QuickBooks, Sage
- desktop software, such as Sage
- custom software, tailor-made to the specific needs of the business

Features of digital bookkeeping systems include:

- on-screen preparation of sales invoices, which can be sent electronically to the customer, with automatic updating of accounts in the receivables ledger

- electronic recording of purchases invoices, with automatic updating of accounts in the payables ledger

- electronic importing of transactions from bank records

- electronic payments to suppliers and for expenses

- automatic updating of general (nominal) ledger

- importing transactions from sources such as third-party software, csv (comma-separated values) files, and spreadsheets

Benefits of digital bookkeeping systems include automatic:

- balancing of the cash book

- completion of the transfer of data from books of prime entry to the ledgers

- completion of the transfer of data into the control (totals) accounts

- reconciliation of the receivables and payables ledgers to their respective control accounts

- creation of a trial balance from the general ledger accounts

- processing of recurring entries, such as regular payments for rent

- reports available on demand, such as trial balance, supplier and customer lists, customer statements

As well as the above, digital bookkeeping systems save time with faster data entry from its formatted screens and built-in databases of customer and supplier details. Digital systems reduce errors and omissions because both the debit and credit entries of each double-entry transaction are completed at the same time.

Drawbacks of digital bookkeeping systems include:

- transactions could be duplicated by recording the same transaction twice

- creation of errors when a recurring entry changes, eg the amount or frequency of the transaction

- other errors such as omitting a transaction, entering the wrong amount, and recording the entry to the wrong account

Because of the way it works, a digital bookkeeping system balances automatically but this does not mean that the entries are correct. The consequences of inaccurate entry will have an effect on the results from the system.

Chapter Summary

■ Double-entry accounts are an integral part of the accounting system of a business and are written up from books of prime entry.

■ Double-entry accounts form the core of the accounting system and record items such as income, expenses, amounts owed by customers, amounts owed to suppliers, assets, liabilities and capital.

■ Double-entry bookkeeping requires that two entries are made in the accounts for each transaction – a debit and a credit in separate accounts.

■ Double-entry accounts are normally set up in the form of a 'T' with debit entries on the left and credit entries on the right.

■ Double-entry accounts are organised in different ledgers (books): receivables ledger (credit customer accounts), payables ledger (credit supplier accounts) and general ledger (the rest of the accounts, including Bank Account).

■ Money amounts received are recorded on the left-hand side of the Bank Account (debits) and payments made are recorded on the right-hand side (credits). This rule helps to work out debits and credits: if the transaction is a bank payment (credit) the other entry must be a debit; if the transaction is a bank receipt (debit) the other entry is a credit.

■ The table below is a guide as to which entries are debits and which entries are credits in their accounts:

Debits	Credits
Purchases	Sales
Expenses	Income
Assets	Liabilities
Money owed by credit customers	Money owed to credit suppliers
	Capital

- The Accounting Equation relates directly to double-entry bookkeeping:

Assets – Liabilities = Capital

Double-entry transactions change the figures in the Accounting Equation, but ensure that it always balances. The changes in the assets, liabilities and capital in the Accounting Equation follow these rules:

Debits	**Credits**
Increases in assets	Decreases in assets
Decreases in liabilities	Increases in liabilities
	Increases in capital

- Ledger accounts are balanced regularly to provide information about the financial activity of a business. Payables Ledger account balances are normally credit, Receivables Ledger balances are normally debit and General Ledger balances can be either debit or credit.

- Digital bookkeeping systems include
    - spreadsheets
    - app and cloud-based software
    - desktop software
    - custom software

- It is important that bookkeeping transactions – for both manual and digital systems – are entered accurately. The consequences of inaccurate entry will have an effect on the results.

Key Terms	**books of prime entry**	the first place in the accounting records of a business where financial transactions are recorded, using details from business documents
	day book	a book of prime entry which lists the details of various financial transactions, eg Sales Day Book (a list of sales invoices) and Cash Book (compiled from bank transactions)
	cash book	the book of prime entry which lists payments in and out of an account at the bank; it can also act as the 'Bank Account' ledger account in the double-entry system
	double-entry bookkeeping	an accounting system which normally involves two entries for each transaction – a debit and a credit; this is known as the 'dual effect' of double-entry bookkeeping
	ledger accounts	double-entry accounts for financial transactions involving individuals (credit customers and credit suppliers), assets, purchases, expenses, income, liabilities and capital
	the ledger	contains the individual ledger accounts; it is normally subdivided into different categories: – receivables ledger (customer accounts) – payables ledger (supplier accounts) – general ledger (all other accounts)
	statement of financial position	one of the financial statements of a business; it shows the owner's capital in the business (investment and profits) calculated as assets (items owned and amounts owed to the business) minus liabilities (amounts owed by the business)
	accounting equation	assets – liabilities = capital This calculates the capital of the business (ie the owner's investment and profits made) in terms of assets and liabilities – in other words, the financial position of the business owner; it always balances if the double-entry bookkeeping is carried out correctly

account balancing

the process of calculating the difference between the totals of the debit and credit columns of a ledger account in order to provide information to management about the financial activity of the business

digital bookkeeping systems

electronic methods of keeping bookkeeping records – main advantages are speed and reduction in errors; will automatically balance but errors may still occur

Activities

3.1   Which is the main source for the writing up of the double-entry accounts? Select **one** option.

(a)	The ledgers	
(b)	Financial documents	
(c)	Books of prime entry	
(d)	The trial balance	

3.2   The ledger that contains the accounts of customers who buy on credit is the:

(a)	General ledger	
(b)	Receivables ledger	
(c)	Payables ledger	

Which **one** of these options is correct?

3.3   The rule for entries in the Bank Account in the cash book is:

(a)	Money in is a debit, money out is a credit	
(b)	Money out is a debit, money in is a credit	
(c)	The debit entries and credit entries always add up to the same amount	

Which **one** of these options is correct?

3.4   The table below lists transactions recorded in a Bank Account in the cash book of a business. Tick the appropriate column to indicate whether the entry will be a debit or a credit in the Bank Account.

	Debit	Credit
Payment of wages		
Cash received from sales		
Payment of an invoice by a credit customer		
Payment of an insurance premium		
Loan received from a finance company		
Loan repayment made		
Bank charges		

3.5   The table below lists transactions recorded in the Bank Account of a business. Write the name of the two accounts involved in the double-entry in the correct column. The first example is completed to show what is required. The name of the account (other than Bank Account) is shown in bold type.

	Debit	Credit
Payment of **wages**	Wages	Bank
Payment of **insurance**		
Money received from **sales**		
Purchases made		
Loan received from the bank		
Loan repayment		
Telephone bill paid		
Repairs bill paid		
Rent received from office space rented out		

3.6 The Bank Account shown below has been written up by the bookkeeper, but the double-entry in the appropriate other accounts needs to be completed. You have been asked to do this, using the blank accounts set out below. You should complete the account name, date, details and amount for each entry. Enter the transactions in the accounts in date order.

You may photocopy the blank accounts on the next page if you wish or you can download a copy from www.osbornebooks.co.uk.

Debit			Bank Account			Credit
Date	**Details**	**£**	**Date**	**Details**		**£**
20-3			20-3			
1 May	Sales	975.00	6 May	Telephone		265.00
11 May	Sales	456.70	12 May	Insurance		678.00
14 May	Bank loan	5,000.00	15 May	Purchases		2760.90

Debit			....Account			Credit
Date	**Details**	**£**	**Date**	**Details**		**£**

Debit			....Account			Credit
Date	**Details**	**£**	**Date**	**Details**		**£**

Debit			....Account			Credit
Date	**Details**	**£**	**Date**	**Details**		**£**

Debit			....Account		Credit
Date	**Details**	**£**	**Date**	**Details**	**£**

Debit			....Account		Credit
Date	**Details**	**£**	**Date**	**Details**	**£**

3.7 Some account **balances** are debit balances and some account balances are credit balances. Complete the table below by entering the following account names in the correct column:

Purchases   Capital   Expenses   Liabilities   Supplier Accounts (money owed to suppliers)

Customer Accounts (money owed by customers)   **Assets Sales Income**

Debit balances	Credit balances

3.8   Some account **entries** are normally debits and some are normally credits.

Tick the appropriate column in the table below, indicating whether the type of account listed in the left-hand column normally requires a debit entry or a credit entry.

Type of account	Debit ✓	Credit ✓
Asset bought by the business		
Liability (eg bank loan taken out)		
Capital introduced by the owner		
Sales made by the business		
Purchases made by the business		
Expenses of the business		
Customer who owes the business money		
Supplier who is owed money by the business		

3.9   Which is the correct formula for the accounting equation? Select **one** option.

(a)	Liabilities – Assets = Capital	
(b)	Assets – Liabilities = Capital	
(c)	Assets + Liabilities = Capital	
(d)	Assets + Capital = Liabilities	

3.10   Insert the correct figures in the blank boxes of the accounting equation table below.

Assets £	Liabilities £	Capital £
120,000	45,000	
	61,000	95,000
265,500	86,500	
88,000		50,000
	37,500	90,000
345,700		209,000

3.11   An increase or a decrease in an asset, liability, or capital will result in either a debit or a credit to the asset, liability, or capital accounts.

Indicate with a tick in the table what type of entry – debit or credit – will be brought about by the increase or decrease described in the column on the left.

Transaction	Debit ✓	Credit ✓
Increase in capital account		
Increase in liability account		
Decrease in asset account		
Decrease in liability account		
Increase in asset account		

3.12   Enter the business transactions set out below into the double-entry bookkeeping system.

All the transactions pass through the Bank Account, so you will have to write the entries in the Bank Account and also work out what the 'other' accounts will be. No credit sales or purchases are involved.

You can draw up your own accounts, photocopy the accounts on page 85, or download blank accounts from www.osbornebooks.co.uk.

Date 20-4	Transaction
3 Feb	Paid in capital of £10,000
4 Feb	Received bank loan of £25,000
6 Feb	Sales of £1,340
10 Feb	Purchases of £750
14 Feb	Paid business rates of £450
15 Feb	Purchases of £2,760
18 Feb	Sales of £860
21 Feb	Paid for advertising costing £138
25 Feb	Sales of £2,640
28 Feb	Paid wages of £3,560

3.13 You are working as a bookkeeper for Sphere Sports which is a distributor for footballs and tennis balls. You have been handed the ledgers and asked to balance the four accounts shown on the next two pages. The date is 31 March 20-3.

(a)

Dr				Cr		
20-3	**Details**	**£**	**20-3**	**Details**		**£**
			23 Mar	Purchases		248.00
			25 Mar	Purchases		78.75
			30 Mar	Purchases		180.00

Solo Suppliers Account (Payables Ledger)

(b)

Dr				Cr		
20-3	**Details**	**£**	**20-3**	**Details**		**£**
23 Mar	Purchases returns	80.00	24 Mar	Purchases		120.00
26 Mar	Purchases returns	70.00	27 Mar	Purchases		360.00
			30 Mar	Purchases		170.00

Atletico Supplies Account (Payables Ledger)

(c)

Dr				Cr		
20-3	**Details**	**£**	**20-3**	**Details**		**£**
23 Mar	Sales	450.00	24 Mar	Sales returns		80.00
26 Mar	Sales	70.00	30 Mar	Sales returns		70.00
27 Mar	Sales	180.00				

Trajan Sports Account (Receivables Ledger)

(d)

Dr	Office Expenses Account (General Ledger)				Cr
20-3	Details	£	20-3	Details	£
4 Mar	Bank	75.20			
6 Mar	Bank	191.00			
8 Mar	Bank	34.65			
15 Mar	Bank	63.46			

3.14 Identify whether the following statements regarding bookkeeping systems are true or false.

Statement	True	False
A digital bookkeeping system is always completely accurate		
An inaccurate entry in a manual bookkeeping system may lead to the owner of the business receiving wrong information		
A digital bookkeeping system can import data from sources such as third-party software		

3.15 Identify whether the following statements regarding digital bookkeeping systems are advantages or disadvantages.

Statement	Advantages	Disadvantages
The system is able to reconcile the receivables ledger to receivables ledger control account		
The system automatically creates a trial balance		
The system saves time with faster data entry		
A change in the amount and/or frequency of recurring entries may not be identified		

3.16 Identify **four** features of a digital bookkeeping system.

1.
2.
3.
4.

4 Accounting for sales, returns, and discounts

this chapter covers...

This chapter focuses on using the accounting system to record the details of sales, sales returns, and discounts allowed (using the credit note system – see pages 35-36).

Having looked in previous chapters at the documents and procedures involved in selling on credit, we will now take the financial documents of sales invoices, credit notes for sales returns and discounts allowed and record them in books of prime entry (day books) and in the bookkeeping system of general ledger and receivables ledger.

We will be using three books of prime entry:

- *sales day book*
- *sales returns day book*
- *discounts allowed day book*

Information from these day books is then transferred into the bookkeeping system using accounts in general ledger and receivables ledger.

The chapter also covers the methods of coding, which are used to trace transactions through the accounting system.

Note:

In this chapter we focus on the accounting for credit sales, sales returns, and discounts allowed. Cash sales will be seen when we study the cash book in Chapter 9.

THE ACCOUNTING SYSTEM

We have seen earlier in Chapter 1 (page 4) that the accounting system comprises a number of stages of recording and presenting financial transactions:

- financial documents

- books of prime entry (eg day books)

- double-entry bookkeeping

- trial balance

In this chapter we look at how financial documents for credit sales, sales returns, and discounts allowed transactions are recorded in the books of prime entry, together with the entries to be made in the double-entry bookkeeping accounts. Books of prime entry are used in manual bookkeeping systems, or they can be set up in a computer spreadsheet. They are not used in digital bookkeeping because these systems automatically update as financial documents are entered.

ACCOUNTING FOR CREDIT SALES, SALES RETURNS, AND DISCOUNTS ALLOWED

In accounting, the term 'sales' means: **the sale of goods in which the business trades**.

This means that an office stationery shop will record as sales things such as photocopier paper, ring binders, etc. The income from the goods in which the business trades is described as **revenue income**. By contrast, if the shop sells off its old cash till when it is replaced with a new one, this is not recorded as sales but, instead, is accounted for as the sale of an asset – such income is described as **capital income**.

'Sales returns' are when goods previously sold on credit are returned to the business by its customers.

'Discounts allowed' (or **prompt payment discount**) is a discount offered by a supplier to customers in order to encourage customers to settle up straightaway or in a short time from the invoice date; it is discounts allowed in the accounting system of the seller.

The diagram on the next page shows the order in which the accounting records are prepared for credit sales, sales returns, and discounts allowed transactions.

You will see that the steps are:

- start with a **financial document** – either a sales invoice (for sales) or a credit note issued (for sales returns and discounts allowed)

- enter it in the appropriate **book of prime entry** (the first accounting book in which the financial document is recorded and summarised), sales day book, sales returns day book, or discounts allowed day book

- transfer the information from the book of prime entry into the double-entry accounts in the **general ledger**

- transfer the information from the book of prime entry into the accounts of trade receivables – ie the customers – in the **receivables ledger** (also known as **sales ledger**)

accounting for credit sales and sales returns

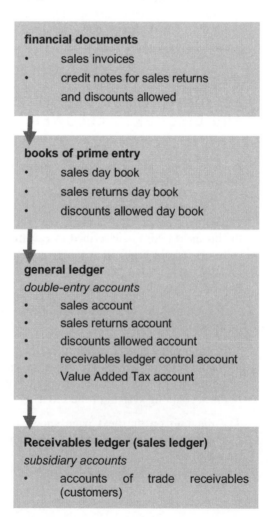

We will now look in more detail at the mechanics of the books of prime entry and the double-entry bookkeeping system. We shall then apply the accounting system to the recording of credit sales, sales returns, and discounts allowed.

BOOKS OF PRIME ENTRY

The books of prime entry include a number of **day books** which list money amounts and other details taken from financial documents.

The day books used for credit sales, sales returns and discounts allowed are:

- sales day book
- sales returns day book
- discounts allowed day book

These are called books of prime entry because they are the first place in the accounting system where financial documents are recorded. Note that books of prime entry are not part of double-entry bookkeeping, but are used to give totals which are then entered into the accounts.

The reasons for using books of prime entry are:

- the totals from the books of prime entry can be checked before they are entered into the ledger accounts
- the use of books of prime entry for a large number of regular transactions, such as sales, means that there are fewer transactions to enter into the double-entry accounts
- the work of the accounts department can be divided up – one person can enter transactions in the books of prime entry, while another can concentrate on the double-entry accounts

A sales day book is written up as shown on the next page, with sample entries which will have been taken from individual sales invoices:

Sales Day Book						SDB21
Date	Details	Invoice number	Account code	Total	VAT*	Net
20-4				£	£	£
5 Jan	Doyle & Co Ltd	901	RL058	144	24	120
8 Jan	Sparkes & Sons Ltd	902	RL127	192	32	160
13 Jan	T Young	903	RL179	96	16	80
15 Jan	A-Z Supplies Ltd	904	RL003	240	40	200
21 Jan	Sparkes & Sons Ltd	905	RL127	144	24	120
31 Jan	Totals for month			816	136	680
				GL1200	GL2200	GL41003

*VAT = 20%

Notes:

- sales day book is prepared from financial documents – sales invoices issued to customers

- the code 'SDB21' at the top of the day book is used for cross-referencing to the bookkeeping system: here it indicates that this is page 21 of the sales day book (SDB)

- the **account code** column cross-references here to 'RL' – the Receivables Ledger – followed by the account number of the trade receivable (customer)

- the **total** or **gross** column records the amount of each financial document, ie after VAT has been included

- the code 'GL' beneath the totals amounts refers to the account numbers in the General Ledger

- sales day book is totalled at appropriate intervals – daily, weekly, or monthly (as here) – and the total of the **net** column tells the business the amount of credit sales for the period

- the amounts from sales day book are recorded in the ledger accounts

a note on day books and Value Added Tax

When a business is VAT-registered, VAT is charged on invoices and credit notes issued to customers. When writing up day books from VAT invoices and credit notes:

- enter the total amount of the invoice or credit note into the 'total' column

- enter the VAT amount in the VAT column

- enter the net amount of the invoice or credit note, before VAT is added, in the 'net' column

Later in this chapter we shall see how the VAT columns from the sales, sales returns, and discounts allowed day books are entered into the double-entry accounts.

PREPARING THE SALES DAY BOOK

The sales day book lists the credit sales made by a business. Following the issue of an invoice for each transaction, the sales day book is prepared from sales invoices, as seen on page 96. In the sales day book, we take the sales invoices that have been checked and authorised, and enter the following details:

- date of invoice

- customer name

- sales invoice number

- cross reference to the customer's account number in the receivables ledger, eg 'RL058'

- total amount of the invoice into the total or gross column

- VAT amount shown on the invoice

- net amount of the invoice (often described as 'goods total'), before VAT is added

The next step in the accounting process is to make entries in the ledger accounts contained in the general ledger and in the receivables ledger.

GENERAL LEDGER AND RECEIVABLES LEDGER

Within an accounting system there are often a number of ledger sections – for example general ledger, receivables ledger and payables ledger. In accounting for sales transactions, we will make use of the following ledgers:

- **general ledger** (also often referred to as the nominal ledger) containing sales account, sales returns account, receivables ledger control account, Value Added Tax account, together with other accounts kept by the business

- **receivables ledger (sales ledger)**, which is a subsidiary ledger to general ledger, and contains the accounts of the trade receivables

The diagram on the next page illustrates the way in which ledgers and accounts are used in connection with sales:

GENERAL LEDGER

- **sales account** – to record sales invoices issued

- **sales returns account** – to record credit notes issued for sales returns

- **discounts allowed account** – to record credit notes issued for prompt payment discount allowed

- **receivables ledger control account** – to record the total amount of trade receivables

- **Value Added Tax account** – to record the VAT amounts of credit sales and sales returns

RECEIVABLES LEDGER

ledger containing the separate subsidiary accounts for each **trade receivable**, ie customers who owe money to the business

Notes:

■ **General ledger** also contains a number of other accounts – for example accounts for items such as purchases, expenses, receipts and payments, and also the assets and liabilities of the business.

■ **Receivables ledger** is a subsidiary ledger to general ledger because it gives a detailed breakdown of the amount of the receivables ledger control account in the general ledger. It does this by showing the separate accounts for each trade receivable of the business: these accounts are called **subsidiary accounts** because they provide a record of individual amounts owed by each trade receivable. The total of these accounts should always equal the balance (total amount) of the receivables ledger control account.

ACCOUNTING SYSTEM FOR CREDIT SALES

The accounting system for credit sales fits together in the following way:

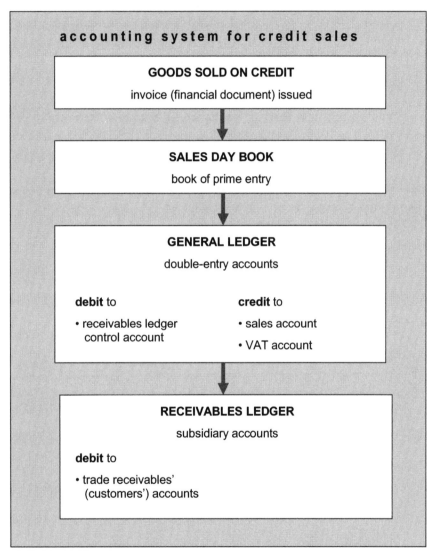

We will now look in more detail at the sales day book and the accounting system for credit sales.

In the examples which follow, we will assume that the business is registered for Value Added Tax, and therefore VAT is charged on invoices issued to customers.

The VAT rate used in the examples is 20%.

BOOKKEEPING FOR CREDIT SALES

After the sales day book has been prepared and totalled, the information from it is transferred to the double-entry system in the general ledger.

The completed sales day book is shown below, followed by the accounts in the general ledger which record the credit sales transactions listed in the sales day book.

Sales Day Book						SDB21
Date	**Customer name**	**Invoice number**	**Account code**	**Total**	**VAT**	**Net**
20-4				£	£	£
5 Jan	Doyle & Co Ltd	901	RL058	144	24	120
8 Jan	Sparkes & Sons Ltd	902	RL127	192	32	160
13 Jan	T Young	903	RL179	96	16	80
15 Jan	A-Z Supplies Ltd	904	RL003	240	40	200
21 Jan	Sparkes & Sons Ltd	905	RL127	144	24	120
31 Jan	Totals for month			816	136	680
				GL1200	GL2200	GL4100

GENERAL LEDGER

Dr		Receivables ledger control account (GL1200)			Cr
20-4			£	20-4	£
31 Jan	Sales Day Book SDB21		816		

Dr		Value added tax account (GL2200)			Cr
20-4			£	20-4	£
				31 Jan Sales Day Book SDB21	136

Dr		Sales account (GL4100)			Cr
20-4			£	20-4	£
				31 Jan Sales Day Book SDB21	680

Note that from the sales day book on the previous page:

■ the total of the total column, £816, has been debited to receivables ledger control account (which records the asset of receivables)

■ the total of the VAT column, £136, has been credited to VAT account

■ the total of the net column, £680, has been credited to sales account (which has given value)

■ each entry in the general ledger is cross-referenced back to the page number of the sales day book; here the reference is 'SDB21'

The last step is to record the amount of sales made to each trade receivable. We do this by recording the sales invoices in receivables ledger as follows:

RECEIVABLES LEDGER

Dr		A-Z Supplies Ltd (RL003)		Cr
20-4		£	20-4	£
15 Jan	Sales SDB21	240		

Dr		Doyle & Co Ltd (RL058)		Cr
20-4		£	20-4	£
5 Jan	Sales SDB21	144		

Dr		Sparkes & Sons Ltd (RL127)		Cr
20-4		£	20-4	£
8 Jan	Sales SDB21	192		
21 Jan	Sales SDB21	144		

Dr		T Young (RL179)		Cr
20-4		£	20-4	£
13 Jan	Sales SDB21	96		

Notes:

■ the sales day book incorporates an account code column, used to cross-reference each transaction to the account of each trade receivable in the receivables ledger (RL); this enables a particular transaction to be traced from financial document (invoice issued), through the book of prime entry (sales day book), to the trade receivable's account

■ each entry in the receivables ledger is cross-referenced back to the page number of the sales day book; here the reference is 'SDB21'

subsidiary accounts/memorandum accounts

The accounts in receivables ledger are prepared following the principles of double-entry bookkeeping. However, they are **subsidiary accounts,** which means they are used to provide a note of how much each trade receivable owes to the business.

As such they are not part of double-entry but are represented in the general ledger by receivables ledger control account. This means that, here, the £816 debit entry is split up in the receivables ledger between the four trade receivables' subsidiary accounts. Note that subsidiary accounts are often referred to as **memorandum accounts**.

ACCOUNTING SYSTEM FOR SALES RETURNS

Sales returns (or returns in) are when goods previously sold on credit are returned to the business by its customers. A credit note (see page 30) is the financial document issued by a business when it makes a refund to a customer who has bought goods on credit. A credit note reduces the amount owed by the trade receivable.

The accounting procedures for sales returns involve:

■ **financial documents** – credit notes issued to customers

■ **book of prime entry** – sales returns day book

■ **double-entry accounts** – general ledger (sales returns account, which records the total net amount of credit notes issued; Value Added Tax account, which records the VAT amount of sales returns; and receivables ledger control account, which records the asset of trade receivables)

■ **receivables ledger** – the subsidiary accounts for each individual trade receivable of the business

The accounting system for sales returns is shown in the diagram on the next page.

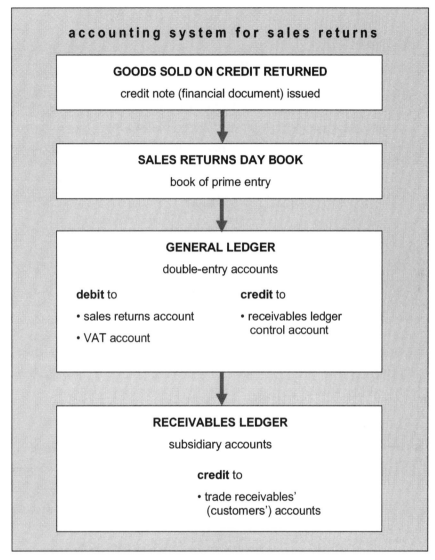

We will now look in more detail at the sales returns day book and the double-entry accounts for sales returns. Note that the business is registered for Value Added Tax.

SALES RETURNS DAY BOOK

The sales returns day book uses virtually the same layout as the sales day book seen on page 96 of this chapter. It operates in a similar way, storing up information about sales returns transactions until such time as a transfer is made into the double-entry accounts system. The financial documents for sales returns day book are credit notes issued to customers.

The sales returns day book is written up as follows, with sample entries:

Sales Returns Day Book						SRDB5
Date	**Customer name**	**Credit note no**	**Account code**	**Total**	**VAT***	**Net**
20-4				£	£	£
15 Jan	T Young	702	RL179	48	8	40
27 Jan	A-Z Supplies Ltd	703	RL003	144	24	120
31 Jan	Totals for month			192	32	160
				GL1200	GL2200	GL4110

* VAT = 20%

Notes:

■ the sales returns day book is prepared from credit notes (or copies of credit notes) issued to customers

■ the day book is totalled at appropriate intervals – weekly or monthly

■ the VAT-inclusive amounts from the total column are credited to the trade receivables' individual subsidiary accounts in receivables ledger

■ the total of the VAT column is transferred to the debit of the VAT account in general ledger

■ the total of the net column tells the business the amount of sales returns for the period. This amount is transferred to the debit of sales returns account in general ledger

■ the total or gross column records the amount of each credit note issued, ie after VAT has been included. This amount is transferred to the credit of receivables ledger control account in general ledger

BOOKKEEPING FOR SALES RETURNS

After the sales returns day book has been written up and totalled, the information from it is transferred into the double-entry system.

The accounts in the general ledger to record the transactions from the above sales returns day book (including any other transactions already recorded on these accounts) are as follows:

GENERAL LEDGER

Dr	Receivables ledger control account (GL1200)		Cr		
20-4		£	20-4		£
31 Jan	Sales Day Book SDB21	816	31 Jan	Sales Returns Day Book SRDB5	192

Dr	Value added tax account (GL2200)		Cr		
20-4		£	20-4		£
31 Jan	Sales Returns Day Book SRDB5	32	31 Jan	Sales Day Book SDB21	136

Dr	Sales returns account (GL4110)		Cr		
20-4		£	20-4		£
31 Jan	Sales Returns Day Book SRDB5	160			

The last step is to record the amount of sales returns from each trade receivable. We do this by recording the sales returns in the subsidiary accounts for each trade receivable in the receivables ledger as follows:

RECEIVABLES LEDGER

Dr	A-Z Supplies Ltd (RL003)		Cr		
20-4		£	20-4		£
15 Jan	Sales SDB21	240	27 Jan	Sales Returns SRDB5	144

Dr	T Young (RL179)		Cr		
20-4		£	20-4		£
12 Jan	Sales SDB21	96	15 Jan	Sales Returns SRDB5	48

ACCOUNTING SYSTEM FOR DISCOUNTS ALLOWED

As noted on page 35, HM Revenue & Customs permits two methods of accounting for Value Added Tax when a prompt payment discount (PPD) is offered by the supplier:

1 The supplier's invoice charges the normal rate of VAT (currently 20%) on the net value of the goods or services, eg net £100, VAT £20, total £120. If a 5% PPD is offered by the supplier and taken up by the customer, then the supplier issues a credit note for the amount of the PPD which, for the example above, will be net £5, VAT £1, total £6.

2 If the supplier does not wish to have a policy of issuing credit notes then the supplier's invoice must include:

– the terms of the PPD

– a statement that the customer can only recover as input tax (see Chapter 7) the VAT paid to the supplier which, for the example above, will be net £95, VAT £19, total £114

HM Revenue & Customs recommends that the following statement is used on the invoice: *'A discount of X% of the full price applies if payment is made within Y days of the invoice date. No credit note will be issued. Following payment you must ensure you have only recovered the VAT actually paid.'*

Important note: in this section we see how the accounting for PPD in the supplier's books, ie discounts allowed, is carried out using the method where a credit note is issued by the supplier. Note that this method is used by AAT to assess PPD transactions. A sample credit note for PPD is shown on page 37.

When accounting for discounts allowed by using credit notes, a Discounts Allowed Day Book (DADB) is used to record credit notes issued by the supplier for PPD and sent to the customer. The accounting system is shown on the next page.

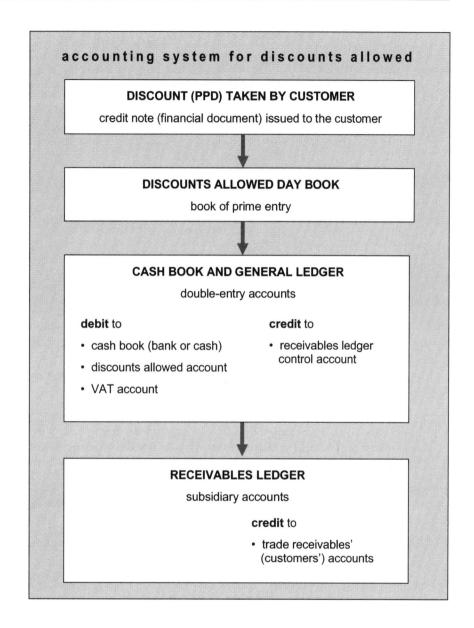

We will now look in detail at the discounts allowed day book and the double-entry accounts to record prompt payment discount in the books of the supplier. Note that the business is registered for Value Added Tax.

DISCOUNTS ALLOWED DAY BOOK

Discounts allowed day book (DADB) uses virtually the same layout as the sales day book seen on page 96.

In order to see how the discounts allowed day book and the bookkeeping entries are recorded, we will use the following sales invoice issued by James Ltd to a customer, XJ Ltd:

INVOICE	
Number 5480	
From James Ltd	10 August 20-2
To XJ Ltd	

	£
Goods total	1,000.00
VAT	200.00
Total	1,200.00

Terms: 5% prompt payment discount for payment within ten days

Note: if the customer pays after ten days, the payment will be for £1,200 and no PPD entries will be required.

If the customer pays within ten days, the payment will be net £950, VAT £190, total £1,140. The supplier will issue a credit note for £60 (ie £50 + VAT £10) which will be recorded by the supplier in the discounts allowed day book as follows:

Discounts Allowed Day Book						DADB1
Date	Customer name	Credit note no	Account code	Total	VAT	Net
20-2				£	£	£
19 Aug	XJ Ltd	DA100	RL243	60	10	50
31 Aug	Totals for month			60	10	50
				GL1200	GL2200	GL3480

Notes:

- the discounts allowed day book is prepared from credit notes (or copies of credit notes) for PPD issued to customers

- the day book is totalled at appropriate intervals – weekly or monthly (only one transaction in the example on the previous page)

- the VAT-inclusive amounts from the total column are credited to the trade receivables' individual subsidiary accounts in receivables ledger

- the total of the VAT column is transferred to the debit of the VAT account in the general ledger

- the total of the net column tells the business the amount of discounts allowed for the period. This amount is transferred to the debit of discounts allowed account in the general ledger

- the total column records the amount of each credit note issued, ie after VAT has been included. This amount is transferred to the credit of receivables ledger control account in the general ledger

BOOKKEEPING FOR DISCOUNTS ALLOWED

After the discounts allowed day book has been written up and totalled, the information from it is transferred into the double-entry system as follows:

| Date | Details | Account code | Cash Book* (debit side) | | | | | CB015 |
			Cash	Bank	VAT	Cash sales	Trade receivables	Other income
20-2			£	£	£	£	£	£
19 Aug	XJ Ltd	RL243		1,140			1,140	

*the layout of the cash book is explained fully in Chapter 9

GENERAL LEDGER

Dr	Discounts allowed account (GL3480)		Cr
20-2		£	20-2	£
19 Aug	Discounts Allowed Day Book DADB1	50		

Dr	Value added tax account (GL2200)		Cr
20-2		£	20-2	£
19 Aug	Discounts Allowed Day Book DADB1	10		

Dr				Receivables ledger control (GL1200)			Cr
20-2			£	20-2			£
				19 Aug	Bank CB015		1,140
				19 Aug	Discounts Allowed Day Book DADB1		60

The last step is to record the amount of discounts allowed in the subsidiary account of the trade receivable in the receivables ledger as follows:

RECEIVABLES LEDGER

Dr				XJ Ltd (RL 243)			Cr
20-2			£	20-2			£
10 Aug	Sales SDB		1,200	19 Aug	Bank CB015		1,140
				19 Aug	Discounts Allowed Day Book DADB1		60

THE USE OF ANALYSED SALES DAY BOOKS

As well as the layout of the day books we have seen so far in this chapter, a business can use analysed day books whenever it needs to analyse its sales and sales returns between:

- different types of goods sold, eg paint, wallpaper, brushes, or services supplied

- different departments, eg a store with departments for furniture, carpets and curtains, hardware

For example, a business with two different types of sales – sales type 1 and sales type 2 – will write up its sales day book as follows:

				Sales Day Book				SDB48
Date	Customer name	Invoice number	Account code	Total	VAT*	Net	Sales type1	Sales type 2
20-4				£	£	£	£	£
9 Aug	DIY Limited	1478	RL059	240	40	200	200	–
12 Aug	T Lane	1479	RL108	144	24	120	100	20
16 Aug	Comet Traders Limited	1480	RL038	336	56	280	100	180
23 Aug	Southern Ltd	1481	RL211	192	32	160	160	–
31 Aug	Totals for month			912	152	760	560	200
				GL1200	GL2200		GL4160	GL4170

VAT = 20%

Analysed sales day books and sales returns day books can be adapted to suit the particular needs of a business. Thus, there is not a standard way in which to present the books of prime entry – the needs of the user of the information are all important. By using analysed day books, the owner of the business can see how much has been sold by types of goods and services, or by departments.

Notes:

■ the account code column is to 'RL' (Receivables Ledger) and the customer's account number

■ the code 'GL' beneath the totals amounts refers to the account numbers in General Ledger

■ the analysis columns – here sales type 1 and sales type 2 – show the amount of sales net of VAT (ie before VAT is added)

■ the analysis columns analyse the net amount – by products sold or services supplied – from sales invoices

METHODS OF CODING IN ACCOUNTING SYSTEMS

As a business grows, methods of coding need to be used to trace transactions through the accounting system, ie through financial documents, books of prime entry, double-entry bookkeeping and the trial balance. As we have seen earlier when studying financial documents, there are a number of different systems of coding in use:

■ **alphabetical**, where letters are used, eg 'ABC'

■ **numerical**, where numbers are used, eg '123'

■ **alpha-numerical**, where both letters and numbers are used, eg 'ABC123'

Uses of coding in the stages of the accounting system are:

financial documents

■ each document, eg invoice, credit note, is numbered

■ goods listed on invoices have reference number or letters, eg catalogue reference, which, when a digital bookkeeping system is used, enables the business to analyse sales by product

books of prime entry

■ each page of the day books is numbered

■ the number of the document, eg invoice, credit note, is recorded

■ the code of the trade receivables or trade payables account is recorded (eg 'RL' for receivables ledger), followed by the account number or short name (see below)

ledger accounts

■ the accounting system is divided into sections: general ledger, receivables ledger, and payables ledger

■ general ledger accounts are numbered and are often arranged in a particular order, for example:

0100 – 1399 Assets

2100 – 2399 Liabilities

3100 – 3399 Capital

4100 – 4399 Sales

5100 – 5399 Purchases

6100 – 6399 Expenses

■ each account in the receivables ledger is coded eg 'RL058' (or some accounting systems use an abbreviated name, or short name, eg the account of Peterhead Trading Company might be coded as 'PETER')

■ alternatively, in receivables ledger an alpha-numerical code – such as 'PET001' – is used; this comprises the first three letters of the customer's name followed by three numbers indicating the first (001) second (002) third (003) etc account use of the same first letter (here 'PET001' is coded as the first account to use 'P')

Case Study

WYVERN TRADERS – CREDIT SALES AND RETURNS

This Case Study shows how credit sales and sales returns are recorded in the accounting system of a business. The Case Study makes use of:

- **books of prime entry**
  - sales day book
  - sales returns day book
- **general ledger accounts**
  - sales account
  - sales returns account
  - Value Added Tax account
  - receivables ledger control account
- **receivables ledger accounts**
  - trade receivables' subsidiary accounts

The Chapter Summary (pages 116-119) also includes diagrams which summarise the procedures for recording credit sales and sales returns transactions in the accounting system.

situation

Wyvern Traders is a wholesaler of stationery and office equipment. The business is registered for VAT. The VAT rate is 20%. The following are the credit sales and sales returns transactions for April 20-4:

20-4	
2 Apr	Sold goods to P Woodhouse, £200 + VAT, invoice no 2416
9 Apr	P Woodhouse returns goods, £80 + VAT, we issue credit note no 12
14 Apr	Sold goods to Blackheath Limited, £80 + VAT, invoice no 2417
21 Apr	Blackheath Limited returns goods, £40 + VAT, we issue credit note no 13
26 Apr	Sold goods to P Woodhouse, £160 + VAT, invoice no 2418

solution

The day books, general ledger and receivables ledger accounts are illustrated on the next two pages: arrows indicate the transfers from the day books to the individual accounts. Note that some accounts have been repeated on both pages in order to show, on the same page, the accounts relating to a particular day book: in practice a business would keep all the transactions together in one account.

Sales Day Book						SDB30
Date	Customer name	Invoice number	Account code	Total	VAT	Net
20-4				£	£	£
2 Apr	P Woodhouse	2416	RL248	240	40	200
14 Apr	Blackheath Ltd	2417	RL027	96	16	80
26 Apr	P Woodhouse	2418	RL248	192	32	160
30 Apr	Totals for month			528	88	440
				GL1200	GL2200	GL4100

General Ledger

Dr   **Receivables ledger control account (GL1200)**   Cr

Date	Details	£	Date	Details	£
20-4			20-4		
30 Apr	Sales Day Book SDB30	528			

Dr   **Value added tax account (GL2200)**   Cr

Date	Details	£	Date	Details	£
20-4			20-4		
			30 Apr	Sales Day Book SDB30	88

Dr   **Sales account (GL4100)**   Cr

Date	Details	£	Date	Details	£
20-4			20-4		
			30 Apr	Sales Day Book SDB30	440

Receivables Ledger

Dr   **Blackheath Ltd (RL027)**   Cr

Date	Details	£	Date	Details	£
20-4			20-4		
14 Apr	Sales SDB30	96			

Dr   **P Woodhouse (RL248)**   Cr

Date	Details	£	Date	Details	£
20-4			20-4		
2 Apr	Sales SDB30	240			
26 Apr	Sales SDB30	192			

Sales Returns Day Book						SRDB4
Date	Customer name	Credit note number	Account code	Total	VAT	Net
20-4				£	£	£
9 Apr	P Woodhouse	12	RL248	96	16	80
21 Apr	Blackheath Ltd	13	RL027	48	8	40
30 Apr	Totals for month			144	24	120
				GL1200	GL2200	GL4100

General Ledger

Dr		Receivables ledger control account (GL1200)				Cr
Date	Details	£	Date	Details		£
20-4			20-4			
30 Apr	Sales Day Book SDB30	*528	30 Apr	Sales Returns Day Book SRDB4		144

Dr		Value added tax account (GL2200)				Cr
Date	Details	£	Date	Details		£
20-4			20-4			
30 Apr	Sales Returns Day Book SRDB4	24	30 Apr	Sales Day Book SDB30		*88

Dr		Sales returns account (GL4110)				Cr
Date	Details	£	Date	Details		£
20-4			20-4			
30 Apr	Sales Returns Day Book SRDB4	120				

Receivables Ledger

Dr		Blackheath Ltd (RL027)				Cr
Date	Details	£	Date	Details		£
20-4			20-4			
14 Apr	Sales SDB30	*96	21 Apr	Sales Returns SRDB4		48

Dr		P Woodhouse (RL248)				Cr
Date	Details	£	Date	Details		£
20-4			20-4			
2 Apr	Sales SDB30	*240	9 Apr	Sales Returns SRDB4		96
26 Apr	Sales SDB30	*192				

*transactions entered previously

The diagrams below and on the two next pages summarise the material we have studied so far in this chapter. They show the procedures for recording transactions in the accounting system for credit sales, sales returns and discounts allowed.

Further chapter summary points follow on page 119.

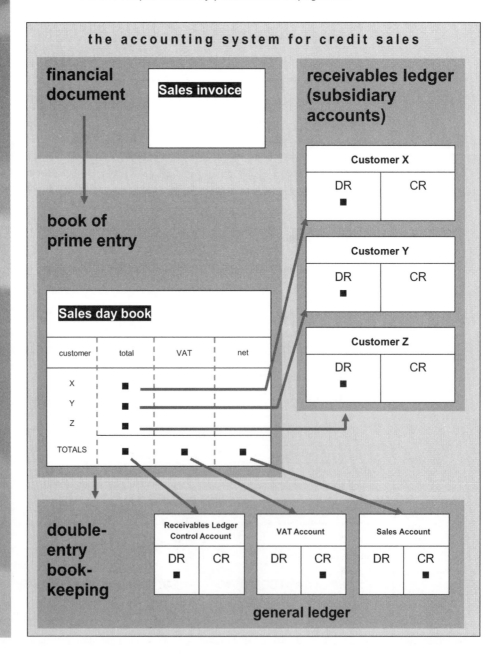

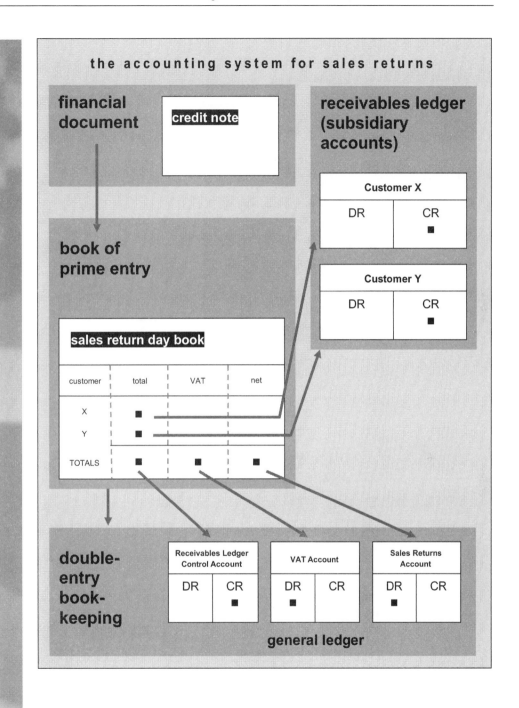

the accounting system for sales returns

financial document

credit note

receivables ledger (subsidiary accounts)

book of prime entry

sales return day book

customer	total	VAT	net
X	■		
Y	■		
TOTALS	■	■	■

Customer X

DR	CR
	■

Customer Y

DR	CR
	■

double-entry book-keeping

Receivables Ledger Control Account		VAT Account		Sales Returns Account	
DR	CR	DR	CR	DR	CR
	■	■		■	

general ledger

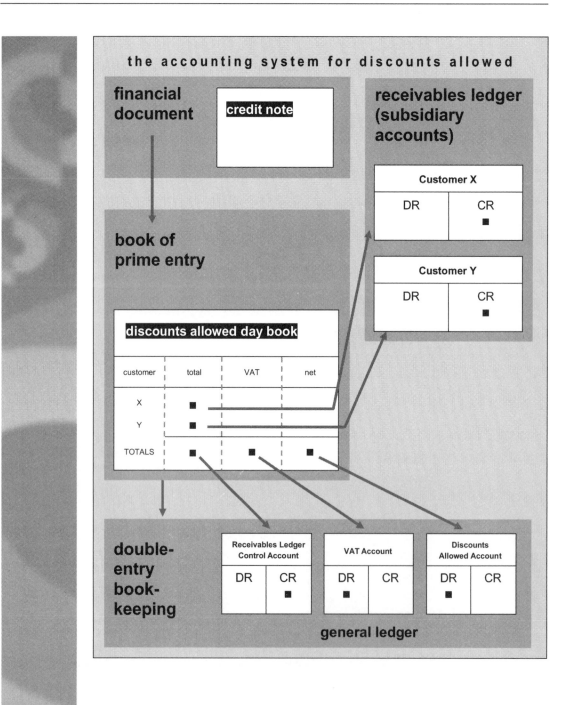

- The accounting system comprises a number of specific stages of recording and presenting financial transactions:
  - financial documents
  - books of prime entry (eg day books)
  - double-entry bookkeeping
  - trial balance

- The financial documents relating to credit sales are:
  - sales invoices
  - credit notes for sales returns and discounts allowed

- Sales day book is the book of prime entry for credit sales. It is prepared from sales invoices sent to customers.

- Sales returns day book is the book of prime entry for sales returns. It is prepared from credit notes issued to customers.

- Discounts allowed day book is the book of prime entry for discounts allowed. It is prepared from credit notes for prompt payment discount issued to customers.

- Analysed sales and sales returns day books are used when a business wishes to analyse its sales between different departments or different types of goods sold or services supplied.

- Recording credit sales in the double-entry system uses:
  - financial documents, sales invoices
  - book of prime entry, sales day book
  - double-entry accounts in the general ledger
  - subsidiary accounts in the receivables ledger

- Recording sales returns in the double-entry system uses:
  - financial documents, credit notes for sales returns issued to customers
  - book of prime entry, sales returns day book
  - double-entry accounts in the general ledger
  - subsidiary accounts in the receivables ledger

- Recording discounts allowed in the double-entry system uses:
  - financial documents, credit notes for prompt payment discount issued to customers
  - book of prime entry, discounts allowed day book
  - double-entry accounts in the general ledger
  - subsidiary accounts in the receivables ledger

<table>
<tr><td rowspan="1" style="background:black;color:white;">Key Terms</td><td></td><td></td></tr>
</table>

Key Terms	**financial documents**	source documents for the accounting records
	books of prime entry	the first accounting books in which transactions are recorded
	coding	cross-referencing methods used to trace transactions through the accounting system
	ledger	section of an accounting system, eg general ledger, receivables ledger, payables ledger
	sales	the sale of goods in which the business trades
	revenue income	income from the goods in which the business trades
	capital income	income from items other than the goods in which the business trades, eg a shop selling its old cash till
	sales returns	goods previously sold on credit which are returned to the business by its customers
	discounts allowed	prompt payment discount offered by a supplier to customers in order to encourage customers to settle up straightaway or in a short time from the invoice date; it is discounts allowed in the accounting system of the seller
	sales day book	book of prime entry prepared from sales invoices
	sales returns day book	book of prime entry prepared from credit notes issued to customers
	discounts allowed day book	book of prime entry prepared from credit notes for prompt payment discount issued to customers
	analysed sales day book	day books which incorporate analysis columns, for example between
		– different departments
		– different types of goods sold, or services supplied
	general ledger	ledger section which includes
		– sales account
		– sales returns account
		– discounts allowed account

	– receivables ledger control account
	– Value Added Tax account
receivables ledger	subsidiary ledger section which contains the subsidiary accounts of the trade receivables (customers)
subsidiary account (memorandum account)	a subsidiary ledger (eg receivables ledger) account which provides a record of individual amounts (eg owing by trade receivables to the business)

Activities

4.1 Which **one** of the following is a book of prime entry?

(a)	Sales day book	
(b)	Sales account	
(c)	Receivables ledger account of T Smith	
(d)	Value Added Tax account	

4.2 Which **one** of the following is in the right order?

(a)	Sales invoice; sales day book; sales account; VAT account; receivables ledger control account; customer's account	
(b)	Sales day book; receivables ledger control account; customer's account; sales account; VAT account; sales invoice	
(c)	Sales day book; sales invoice; customer's account; sales account; VAT account; receivables ledger control account	
(d)	Sales account; VAT account; receivables ledger control account; customer's account; sales invoice; sales daybook	

4.3 Which **one** of the following shows the correct general ledger entries to record discounts allowed?

(a)	Debit receivables ledger control; debit VAT; credit discounts allowed	
(b)	Credit receivables ledger control; credit discounts allowed; credit VAT	
(c)	Debit discounts allowed; debit VAT; credit receivables ledger control	
(d)	Debit discounts allowed; credit receivables ledger control; credit VAT	

4.4 Explain in note format:

(a) The principles of recording a credit sales transaction in the accounting system.

(b) The principles of recording a sales returns transaction in the accounting system.

For Activities 4.5 and 4.6:

- work in pounds and pence, where appropriate

- the rate of Value Added Tax is to be calculated at 20% (when calculating VAT amounts, you should ignore fractions of a penny, ie round down to a whole penny)

- use a coding system incorporating the following:

sales day book	*– SDB50*	*general ledger account numbers*	
sales returns day book	*– SRDB18*	*receivables ledger control account*	*– GL1200*
		sales account	*– GL4100*
receivables ledger account numbers		*sales returns account*	*– GL4110*
A Cox	*– RL032*	*Value Added Tax account*	*– GL2200*
Dines Stores	*– RL048*		
E Grainger	*– RL055*		
M Kershaw	*– RL090*		
D Lloyd	*– RL095*		
Malvern Stores	*– RL110*		
Pershore Retailers	*– RL145*		
P Wilson	*– RL172*		

4.5 Wyvern Wholesalers sells office stationery to other businesses in the area. During April 20-5 the following credit transactions took place:

20-5

2 Apr   Sold goods to Malvern Stores £55 + VAT, invoice no 4578 issued

5 Apr   Sold goods to Pershore Retailers £65 + VAT, invoice no 4579 issued

7 Apr   Sold goods to E Grainger £28 + VAT, invoice no 4580 issued

9 Apr   Sold goods to P Wilson £58 + VAT, invoice no 4581 issued

12 Apr   Sold goods to M Kershaw £76 + VAT, invoice no 4582 issued

14 Apr   Sold goods to D Lloyd £66 + VAT, invoice no 4583 issued

19 Apr   Sold goods to A Cox £33 + VAT, invoice no 4584 issued

22 Apr   Sold goods to Dines Stores £102 + VAT, invoice no 4585 issued

23 Apr   Sold goods to Malvern Stores £47 + VAT, invoice no 4586 issued

26 Apr   Sold goods to P Wilson £35 + VAT, invoice no 4587 issued

29 Apr   Sold goods to A Cox £82 + VAT, invoice no 4588 issued

You are to:

(a) Record the above transactions in Wyvern Wholesalers' sales day book for April 20-5, using the format shown below.

(b) Record the accounting entries in Wyvern Wholesalers' general ledger and receivables ledger. (You will need to retain the ledger accounts for use with Activity 4.6.)

	Sales Day Book					SDB50
Date	**Customer name**	**Invoice number**	**Account code**	**Total** £	**VAT** £	**Net** £

4.6 The following details are the sales returns of Wyvern Wholesalers for April 20-5. They are to be:

(a) Recorded in the sales returns day book for April 20-5, using the format shown on the next page.

(b) Recorded in the general ledger and receivables ledger (use the ledgers already prepared in the answer to Activity 4.5).

20-5

8 Apr   Pershore Retailers returns goods £20 + VAT, credit note no 572 issued

12 Apr   E Grainger returns goods £28 + VAT, credit note no 573 issued

16 Apr   D Lloyd returns goods £33 + VAT, credit note no 574 issued

28 Apr   Malvern Stores returns goods £20 + VAT, credit note no 575 issued

30 Apr   A Cox returns goods £40 + VAT, credit note no 576 issued

Sales Returns Day Book						SRDB18
Date	Customer name	Credit note number	Account code	Total £	VAT £	Net £

4.7 You are employed by Johnson Limited as an accounts assistant. The business has a manual accounting system. Double-entry takes place in the general ledger; individual accounts of trade receivables are kept as subsidiary accounts in the receivables ledger. The VAT rate is 20%.

Notes:

- show your answer with a tick, words or figures, as appropriate

- coding is not required

(a) The following credit transactions all took place on 30 June 20-9 and have been recorded in the sales day book as shown below. No entries have yet been made into the ledger system.

Sales day book

Date 20-9	Customer name	Invoice number	Total £	VAT £	Net £
30 June	Bowne Ltd	610	960	160	800
30 June	Jamieson & Co	611	4,944	824	4,120
30 June	Pottertons	612	3,888	648	3,240
30 June	Wells plc	613	2,928	488	2,440
	Totals		12,720	2,120	10,600

What will be the entries in the general ledger?

General ledger

Account name	Amount £	Debit	Credit

What will be the entries in the receivables ledger?

Receivables ledger

Account name	Amount £	Debit	Credit

(b) The following credit transactions all took place on 30 June 20-9 and have been recorded in the sales returns day book as shown below. No entries have yet been made into the ledger system.

Sales returns day book

Date 20-9	Customer name	Credit note number	Total £	VAT £	Net £
30 June	Lloyd & Co	CN 47	576	96	480
30 June	Wyvern Stores	CN 48	1,248	208	1,040
	Totals		1,824	304	1,520

What will be the entries in the general ledger?

General ledger

Account name	Amount £	Debit	Credit

What will be the entries in the receivables ledger?

Receivables ledger

Account name	Amount £	Debit	Credit

(c) The following discounts allowed transactions all took place on 30 June 20-9 and have been recorded in the discounts allowed day book as shown below. No entries have yet been made into the ledger system.

Discounts allowed day book

Date 20-9	Customer name	Credit note number	Total £	VAT £	Net £
30 June	Sanchos Ltd	DA 122	24	4	20
30 June	Belton Stores	DA 123	36	6	30
		Totals	60	10	50

What will be the entries in the general ledger?

General ledger

Account name	Amount £	Debit	Credit

What will be the entries in the receivables ledger?

Receivables ledger

Account name	Amount £	Debit	Credit

4.8 The following is taken from the coding lists used at a business called Fashion Trading.

Customer	Sales ledger account code
Allens Stores	ALL001
Dart Enterprises	DAR001
Dennis & Co	DEN002
Eden Contracts	EDE001
Ginger Trading	GIN001
Jarvis & Co	JAR001
New Wave Fashions	NEW001
Number 1 Store	NUM002
Riverside Trading	RIV001
Toast Ltd	TOA001
Ye Olde Stores	YEO001

You are to set up the receivables ledger account codes for the new customers shown below.

Customer name	Receivables ledger account code
Dymock Trading Co	
Hedgehog Fashions	
Jones & Co	

4.9 Sales invoices have been prepared and partially recorded in the sales day book, as shown below.

(a) Complete the entries in the sales day book by inserting the appropriate figures for each invoice.

(b) Total the last five columns of the sales day book.

Sales day book

Date 20-9	Customer name	Invoice number	Total £	VAT £	Net £	Sales type 1 £	Sales type 2 £
30 June	Yanez & Co	1621		240			1,200
30 June	Napier Stores	1622	1,920			1,600	
30 June	Beale Ltd	1623	768		640		640
	Totals						

4.10 You are the bookkeeper at Newtown Trading Ltd and have prepared the following invoice today, 15 July 20-4:

	£
Newtown Trading Ltd Invoice no: 24761	
To: Sparks & Co **Date:** 15 July 20-4	
10 Toner cartridges at £20 each	200.00
VAT @ 20%	40.00
TOTAL	240.00
Payment by BACS preferred	

(a) You are to record the invoice in the digital bookkeeping system by:

– selecting the correct daybook

– making the necessary entries

Daybook	
Sales day book	
Sales returns day book	
Purchases day book	
Discounts allowed day book	

Date 20-4	Name	Invoice number	Total £	VAT £	Net £

(b) Identify the general ledger account into which the net amount will be entered.

Purchases: toner cartridges	
Sales: copier paper	
Sales: toner cartridges	
Sales returns: toner cartridges	

(c) Identify how the amount will be recorded in the general ledger account selected in (b).

as a debit entry	
as a credit entry	

4.11 This task is about totalling and balancing ledger accounts.

The following customer's account is in the receivables ledger at the close of the financial year on 30 June 20-2:

20-2	Details	Amount £	20-2	Details	Amount £
1 June	Balance b/f	3,627	10 June	Bank	1,483
4 June		2,184	21 June	Sales Returns	210
				Total	

Complete the account by:

- inserting the balance carried down, together with date and details
- inserting the totals
- inserting the balance brought down together with date and details

Note:

- for details, choose from: Balance b/d, Balance c/d, Difference
- for date, choose from: 1 June, 30 June, 1 July, 31 July

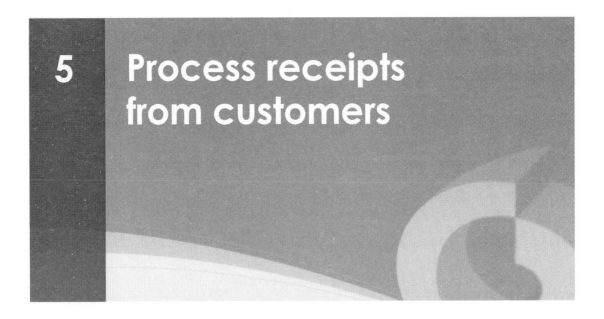

5 Process receipts from customers

this chapter covers...

The earlier chapters of this book have explained how a business sells its goods and services on credit, issues invoices, credit notes and statements which help to ensure that the right money is received at the right time.

This chapter explains the way in which a business processes a receipt from a customer who has bought goods on credit. It continues the Case Study in Chapter 2 in which Cool Socks, a manufacturer, has sold socks to Trends, a fashion store.

A payment by a business such as Trends in settlement of sales transactions will need to be checked and verified against documentation that includes:

- *the remittance advice sent by the buyer and any payment sent by the buyer*
- *sales invoices and credit notes issued by the seller*
- *the statement of account issued by the seller*
- *the record of what is owing on the buyer's account in the receivables ledger of the seller*

In checking this documentation, the seller will have to look out for any discrepancies which may be the result of an error made by the buyer, such as:

- *overpayments*
- *underpayments*
- *incorrect discounts taken*
- *other discrepancies: incorrect amounts, incorrect details, timing differences, missing and/or duplicated transactions*

Receipts from customers have to be allocated to the outstanding item on the customer's account.

FINANCIAL DOCUMENTS – SOME REVISION

When a business makes a sale on credit terms, it uses a number of financial documents which are sent to the buyer. These include the:

- **invoice**, which sets out the details of the sales transaction, including

  - the date

  - the sales price and any trade or bulk discount given, and VAT (sales tax) added

  - the total amount due

  - the date when payment is required (which is often 30 days after the date of the invoice)

- **credit note**, which is used if any refund is due and is deducted from the amount owing to the seller – for example a deduction made for faulty goods

- **customer statement**, which sets out the invoices and credit notes issued and any payments received over a set period (often a month), all resulting in a final total outstanding

FINANCIAL DOCUMENTS – REMITTANCE ADVICE

A further financial document which is important to the payment process is the **remittance advice**. This is an advice which states the amount of money sent by a credit buyer to the seller in full or part settlement of an account. A remittance advice is used:

- to advise the sending of a payment **direct to the seller's bank account** by electronic bank transfer such as **BACS** or **Faster Payments**; or

- **to accompany a cheque** – a practice which is becoming less common as more businesses and individuals make payments electronically and online

These two types of remittance advice are illustrated on the next two pages. The remittance advices both relate to payments made to Cool Socks, the business introduced as a Case Study in Chapter 2. They both contain references to:

- the buyer's purchase order reference

- the seller's invoice or credit note number

Other details include the amount being sent and the means of payment, ie a cheque enclosed or a payment direct to the bank account of the seller through BACS or Faster Payments electronic bank transfer systems.

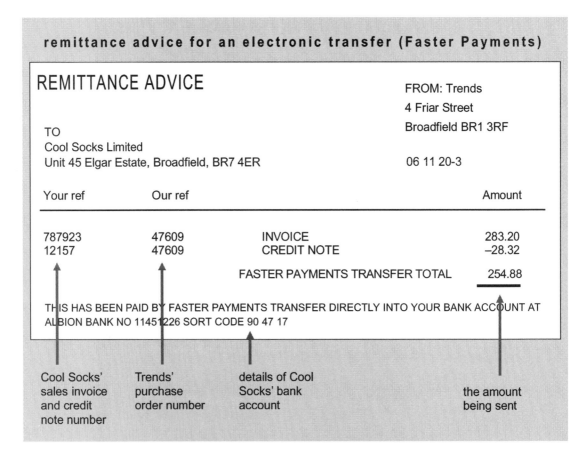

remittance advice for an electronic transfer (Faster Payments)

REMITTANCE ADVICE

FROM: Trends
4 Friar Street
Broadfield BR1 3RF

TO
Cool Socks Limited
Unit 45 Elgar Estate, Broadfield, BR7 4ER

06 11 20-3

Your ref	Our ref		Amount
787923	47609	INVOICE	283.20
12157	47609	CREDIT NOTE	−28.32
		FASTER PAYMENTS TRANSFER TOTAL	254.88

THIS HAS BEEN PAID BY FASTER PAYMENTS TRANSFER DIRECTLY INTO YOUR BANK ACCOUNT AT ALBION BANK NO 11451226 SORT CODE 90 47 17

Cool Socks' sales invoice and credit note number

Trends' purchase order number

details of Cool Socks' bank account

the amount being sent

electronic payment remittance advice

- this remittance advice relates to a Faster Payments bank transfer made by Trends in payment of its account with Cool Socks Limited. The advice has been emailed from Trends' accounts department

- the details include the invoice amount and the credit note amount, together with the payment made – these details help with the checking process.

- the bank account details on the advice set out Cool Socks' bank account number and sort code in full. Some remittance advices may not provide the account number in full for security reasons

- Cool Socks will need to check its bank account in due course to ensure that the amount has been received

checks to be made

Cool Socks needs to check a number of details on this advice against the sales documentation and the receivables ledger account of the customer making payment. This is to make sure that there are no errors or discrepancies and that the right amount has been sent for the right transactions. This process is explained in full in the Case Study on pages 137-141.

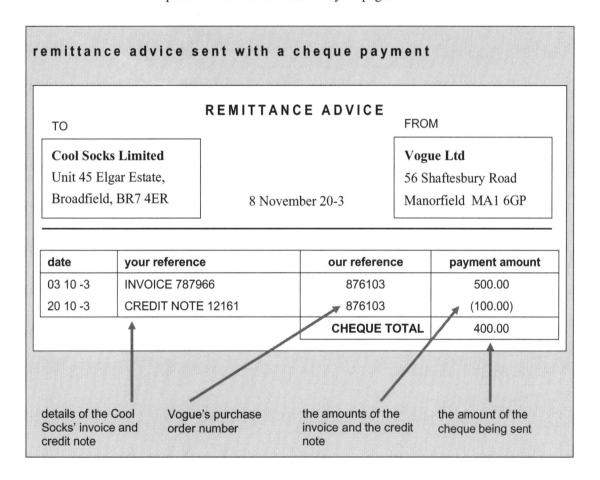

remittance advice sent with a cheque payment

REMITTANCE ADVICE

TO   FROM

Cool Socks Limited   **Vogue Ltd**
Unit 45 Elgar Estate,   56 Shaftesbury Road
Broadfield, BR7 4ER   8 November 20-3   Manorfield MA1 6GP

date	your reference	our reference	payment amount
03 10 -3	INVOICE 787966	876103	500.00
20 10 -3	CREDIT NOTE 12161	876103	(100.00)
		CHEQUE TOTAL	400.00

details of the Cool Socks' invoice and credit note

Vogue's purchase order number

the amounts of the invoice and the credit note

the amount of the cheque being sent

remittance advice sent with a cheque

- this remittance advice is for a payment from Vogue Ltd – a cheque for £400 – sent together through the post to Cool Socks
- the advice shows the amounts of an invoice for £500 and a credit note for £100 taken into account when calculating the £400 payment
- these details will help Cool Socks in its checking process, which will involve the sales documentation and the receivables ledger account for its customer, Vogue Ltd

- cheques are becoming a less common means of settling customer accounts, but they are still used by more traditional businesses
- if a customer's cheque is received in payment, it will need to be checked carefully to make sure it is correctly written out and has all the necessary details on it

checking the cheque

A **cheque** has to be in writing and signed by the person or business paying the money. All the details on a cheque have to be accurate and correct for it to be acceptable as a means of payment.

There are therefore a number of important basic checks that need to be carried out on a cheque before it can be paid in:

- is the cheque signed? – it is invalid if it is not
- is the name written after the word 'pay' correct? – the bank will not accept it if it is not
- is the cheque in date? – a cheque becomes invalid after six months
- the amount in words and figures must be the same

The cheque below shows all these details:

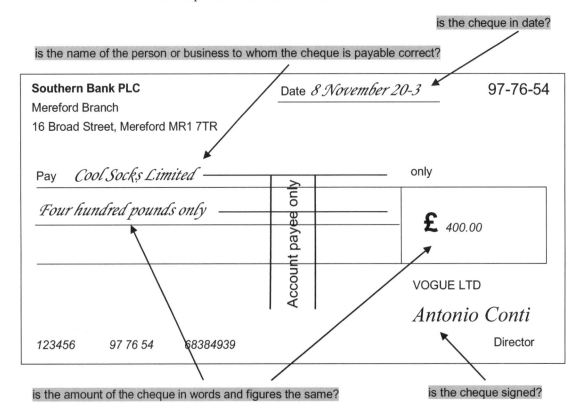

If the business (Cool Socks) accepting payment by cheque does not check these details before paying it in, Vogue Ltd's bank (Southern Bank) may refuse to pay it and will return it to Cool Socks' bank. If everything is in order, the amount will be deducted from Vogue Ltd's bank account.

Now read the Case Study which follows. Note the internal checks that are made by Cool Socks when Trends settles its account.

Case Study

COOL SOCKS – PROCESSING THE RECEIPT

situation

Cool Socks Limited, a manufacturer of socks, supplies Trends, a fashion store in Broadfield. In this Case Study, Trends sends a payment and remittance advice, which is checked by Cool Socks for errors and discrepancies.

The financial documents issued so far by Cool Socks are an invoice for socks supplied (see next page), a credit note for £28.32 (not illustrated) for some faulty socks returned and a statement of account issued to Trends at the end of the month (see page 139).

The amount due is £283.20 (invoice amount) minus £28.32 (credit note amount) equals £254.88.

INVOICE

COOL SOCKS LIMITED
Unit 45 Elgar Estate, Broadfield, BR7 4ER
Tel 01908 765314 Fax 01908 765951 Email toni@cool.u-net.com
VAT Reg GB 0745 4672 76

Invoice to

Trends
4 Friar Street
Broadfield
BR1 3RF

invoice no	**787923**
account	**3993**
your reference	**47609**
date/tax point	**02 10 20-3**

deliver to

as above

Product code	Description	Quantity	Price	Unit	Total	Discount %	Net
45B	Blue toebar socks	100	2.36	pair	236.00	0.00	236.00

terms

Net monthly

Carriage paid

E & OE

GOODS TOTAL	236.00
VAT	47.20
TOTAL	283.20

—————— STATEMENT OF ACCOUNT ——————

COOL SOCKS LIMITED

Unit 45 Elgar Estate, Broadfield, BR7 4ER

Tel 01908 765314 Fax 01908 765951 Email toni@cool.u-net.com

VAT Reg GB 0745 4672 76

TO

Trends		
4 Friar Street	account	**3993**
Broadfield	date	**31 10 20-3**
BR1 3RF		

date	details	debit £	credit £	balance £
01 10 20-3	Balance b/f	150.00		150.00
02 10 20-3	Faster payment 170961		150.00	00.00
02 10 20-3	Invoice 787923	283.20		283.20
10 10 20-3	Credit note 12157		28.32	254.88

Pay Cool Socks Ltd at Albion Bank, Account 11451226, Sort code 904717

TOTAL	254.88

Notes on the statement and the ledger account

The statement of account illustrated above has four entries. The first two relate to full payment of last month's account for £150 and can be ignored. The last two relate to this Case Study and are highlighted by the grey frames:

- the third entry is the invoice for £283.20 issued on 2 October to Trends
- the last entry is the credit note for £28.32 issued on 10 October to Trends

The amount owed by Trends to Cool Socks (the account balance) is £254.88.

These entries have been entered by Cool Socks in the double-entry bookkeeping system, in the **receivables ledger account** for Trends shown below.

Debit	Receivables Ledger: Trends Account						Credit
20-3	**Details**	**£**	**p**	**20-3**	**Details**	**£**	**p**
1 Oct	Balance b/d	150	00	2 Oct	Bank	150	00
2 Oct	Sales	283	20	10 Oct	Sales returns	28	32

receipt of the remittance advice

On 6 November Cool Socks received a remittance advice by email (see below) from Trends stating that £254.88 has been paid into the bank account of Cool Socks Limited by using a Faster Payments transfer.

What checks should Cool Socks make to make sure the payment of £254.88 is correct and valid?

REMITTANCE ADVICE

FROM: Trends
4 Friar Street
Broadfield BR1 3RF

TO
Cool Socks Limited
Unit 45 Elgar Estate,
Broadfield, BR7 4ER

06 11 20-3

Your ref	Our ref		Amount
787923	47609	INVOICE	254.88
12157	47609	CREDIT NOTE	−28.32
		FASTER PAYMENTS TRANSFER TOTAL	254.88

THIS HAS BEEN PAID BY FASTER PAYMENTS TRANSFER DIRECTLY INTO YOUR BANK ACCOUNT AT ALBION BANK NO 11451226 SORT CODE 90 47 17

---

solution

The following checks could be made by the accounts department of Cool Socks.

Question Are the remittance advice details correct?

Answer Check the original documentation. The answer is 'Yes'.

- invoice number 787923 and credit note number 12157 agrees with the 'Your ref 787923 and 12157' of the remittance advice

- the Trends purchase order number 47609 (to be found in the Cool Socks filing system) is quoted on the remittance advice

Question   Is the remittance advice amount of £254.88 correct?

Answer   Answer is 'Yes'. Invoice value £283.20 minus credit note value £28.32 = £254.88

This can be verified from the statement issued by Cool Socks on 31 October and also from the receivables ledger account of Trends in the accounts of Cool Socks. Both (see page 139) show the two figures (£283.20 and £28.32) which result in the total amount owing of £254.88.

Question   Are there any missing or duplicated transactions?

Answer   Check the receivables ledger account for Trends against the remittance advice. The amount paid of £254.88 settles the invoice minus the credit note in full. There are no missing or duplicated transactions.

Question   Are there any timing differences?

Answer   Timing differences often occur at the end of a month when, for example, a seller issues an invoice but it is not recorded in the buyer's bookkeeping system until the first day or so of the new month.

Here there are no timing differences as the account of Trends in Cool Socks' receivables ledger is the same as the statement of account issued, and the receipt from Trends.

Note that Cool Socks would not need to carry out all these checks, but a minimum requirement is likely to be:

- a check of the documentation references (especially the invoice and credit note number), and

- a calculation of the amount paid – from figures obtained from the customer statement issued or from the receivables ledger account

DEALING WITH DISCREPANCIES

The Case Study on the previous five pages has explained the checks that should be made by the seller when a remittance advice is received from a credit customer. In this example, all was correct. Normally this is the case, but there are situations where references do not tie up or, more often, the amount is wrong. These **discrepancies** can occur when:

■ there is an **underpaymen**t – not enough money has been received

■ there is an **overpayment** – too much money has been received

■ the buyer has made a mistake in deducting **prompt payment discount**

■ other differences – incorrect amounts, incorrect details, timing differences, missing and/or duplicated transactions

underpayments

There are number of reasons why a credit customer may not send enough money when settling an account. These are described below, together with the action that should be taken in each case by the seller.

reason   the customer has made a genuine mistake with the figures

solution   the seller should contact the customer and explain the problem; the customer should be asked for an adjusting payment or advised that it will be adjusted in the next statement

reason   the customer has not paid all the invoices which are due because there is a dispute over one of them

solution   the seller should contact the customer and attempt to resolve the problem; if necessary the matter may have to be referred to the accounts supervisor

overpayments

There are a number of reasons why a credit customer may send too much money when settling an account. This is not a common experience! These reasons are described below and appropriate solutions are suggested.

reason   the customer has made a genuine mistake with the figures

solution   the seller should contact the customer and explain the situation; the ideal solution for the seller is to keep the extra money and wait for the next statement to make the necessary adjustment; it is possible that the customer may want the money returned (it may be a large amount), in which case an adjusting refund payment may need to be made

reason   the customer has not taken into account a credit note or has paid an invoice twice in error

solution   the seller should contact the customer and explain the situation; the ideal solution for the seller is to retain the extra money and wait for the next statement to make the necessary adjustment, unless the customer urgently needs the money, in which case an adjusting refund payment will need to be made

other discrepancies

As we have seen in the Case Study, other discrepancies that need to be identified include:

- are the details correct on the records and documents?
- are the amounts correct?
- are there any missing or duplicated transactions?
- are there any timing differences? (For example, look for transactions dated at the end of a month that are not recorded until the beginning of the following month.)

discrepancies with prompt payment discount

Prompt payment discount is an 'early payment discount' where a seller allows a customer to deduct a percentage discount from the invoice total if payment is made within a specified period of time, eg seven days.

Prompt payment discount is explained on pages 35-36. The main problem with prompt payment discount is that the amount is not stated on the invoice itself – just the discount percentage – and the calculation is left to the customer. This is where errors can occur as the customer can get it wrong.

When a business offers prompt payment discount, it is set out in the 'Terms' section at the bottom of the invoice, eg:

Prompt payment discount of 2.5% for payment within 7 days of the invoice date.

If the goods total before VAT is £100, the discount available if the invoice is paid within 7 days of the invoice is (£100 x 2.5)/100 = £2.50.

The correct total amount actually payable is therefore:

£100 minus £2.50	= £97.50
plus VAT @ 20% on £97.50	= £19.50
	= £117.00

As you can see from this, there is plenty of room for customer error:

- the amount of discount calculated by the customer may be incorrect

- the customer may take the discount after the seven days has elapsed

- the customer may take a discount when it is not being offered at all

In each of these three cases, the seller will have to contact the customer and explain the nature of the discrepancy.

Examples of these errors are shown in the Case Study which follows on the next page.

Case Study

PROMPT PAYMENT DISCOUNT DISCREPANCIES

situation

You work in the accounts department of Cool Socks Limited. The company offers to some (but not all) customers a prompt payment discount of 2.5% on invoices which are paid within 7 days of the invoice date.

When prompt payment discount is made available, the 'Terms' section at the bottom of the invoice always states:

"Prompt payment discount of 2.5% for payment within 7 days of the invoice date."

The date is 25 November and you have to check three invoices which have had prompt payment discount deducted by the customer. The accounts supervisor asks you to report and correct any discrepancies you find. The current VAT rate is 20%.

Invoice 1 – payment amount received £1,140

Dated 22 November. Terms state that 2.5% prompt payment discount is available for payment within 7 days. Goods total is £1,000, VAT £200 and discount of £60 (including VAT) deducted.

Invoice 2 – payment amount received £468

Dated 8 November. Terms state that 2.5% prompt payment discount is available for payment within 7 days. Goods total is £400, VAT £80 and discount of £12 (including VAT) is deducted.

Invoice 3 – payment amount received £292.50

Dated 22 November. There is no mention of a 2.5% prompt payment discount in the 'Terms' section of the invoice. Goods total is £250 and VAT is £50. Cash discount of £7.50 has been taken by the customer.

solution

> **Answers**
>
> **Invoice 1:** the discount deducted is calculated at 5% (£60 including VAT) and should be at 2.5% (£30 including VAT). The payment should have been £975 + VAT £195 = £1,170.
>
> **Invoice 2:** the 7 day period for deduction of prompt payment discount has expired and therefore no discount should be deducted. The payment should have been £400 + VAT of £80 = £480.
>
> **Invoice 3:** there is no prompt payment discount available on this invoice but, despite this, the customer has taken 2.5% (£7.50). The payment should have been £300.

ALLOCATING RECEIPTS

When payment is received from a customer, it is important to allocate the amount correctly to the outstanding – or open – items in the customer's account in receivables ledger. By allocating, we mean the process of matching the payment received to the outstanding items. The general rule is that receipts are allocated to older transactions first, in the following order:

- opening balance
- invoices, in full or part payment
- credit notes, utilised in full or part against invoices

If there is an unresolved dispute on an invoice then the customer may not have sent payment for that item, which will remain outstanding. Usually, remittance advices indicate the outstanding items that the customer is settling. Where items remain outstanding after allocating a payment, they will total to the balance carried forward on the account.

Allocation of receipts is especially important when using a digital bookkeeping system. The payment must be allocated to each invoice as either fully or partly paid, with credit notes being used against invoices. If this is not done, the system will show that invoices appear to remain unpaid, or partly unpaid, which gives a false position of the customer's account.

Chapter Summary

- When a customer who has bought goods or services on credit makes payment of the account, the customer will send a **remittance advice** to the seller.

- Payment may be received by cheque or by electronic bank transfer (eg BACS or Faster Payments).

- When a remittance advice is received, it must be checked carefully against the sales documentation held by the seller and the customer's account in the seller's receivables ledger. The amount received must be the correct amount. The documentation checked includes invoices, credit notes and the remittance advice itself.

- If a cheque is received, it must be checked to ensure that it is acceptable.

- If payment is made by electronic bank transfer (eg BACS or Faster Payments), the bank statement must be checked to ensure that the payment has been received.

- Discrepancies relating to payments received can be caused by:

  - **underpayments** – a disputed invoice may not have been included

  - **overpayments** – a credit note may have been ignored or an invoice paid twice

  - problems with **prompt payment discount** – discount rate incorrect, discount period expired, no discount available

  - other discrepancies: incorrect amounts, incorrect details, timing differences, missing and/or duplicated transactions

- In all cases, discrepancies must be communicated to the customer so that an appropriate adjustment can be made.

- Receipts are allocated to the outstanding items on the customer's account in receivables ledger.

Key Terms

remittance advice	an advice received from a customer telling the seller that a payment has been made
BACS	Bankers Automated Clearing Services – an electronic bank transfer system which makes payment direct from one bank account to another; often used for multiple payments made at the same time
Faster Payments	an electronic bank transfer system which makes payment direct from one bank account to another – often used for individual payments
prompt payment discount	a percentage reduction in the selling price given to the buyer if the buyer pays within a specified short space of time
allocation of receipts	process of matching the payment received for the outstanding items on the customer's account in receivables ledger

Activities

5.1 A business which receives a remittance advice from a customer is likely to check it against the following documents or accounts:

(a)	Delivery note, invoice, customer statement	
(b)	Delivery note, invoice, receivables ledger account	
(c)	Invoice, purchase order, customer statement	
(d)	Invoice, receivables ledger account, customer statement	

Which **one** of the above options is correct?

5.2 On an invoice which offers prompt payment discount:

(a)	The prompt payment discount calculation is always shown	
(b)	The prompt payment discount percentage is shown	
(c)	The VAT (sales tax) is worked out on the goods total after the prompt payment discount is deducted	
(d)	The final invoice total takes into account the prompt payment discount deducted	

Which **one** of these options is correct?

5.3 On the next three pages are set out remittance advices and associated documents.

You are to check the remittance advices against the documents and:

1   Identify and describe any discrepancies that you find.

2   Suggest the action that could be taken by the supplier in each case.

(a) **remittance advice sent to the seller**

REMITTANCE ADVICE

FROM: Trends
4 Friar Street
Broadfield BR1 3RF

TO
Cool Socks Limited
Unit 45 Elgar Estate,
Broadfield, BR7 4ER

06 12 20-3

Your ref	Our ref	Amount
788101	47645	490.00
	FASTER PAYMENTS TRANSFER **TOTAL**	490.00

THIS HAS BEEN PAID BY FASTER PAYMENTS TRANSFER DIRECTLY INTO YOUR
BANK ACCOUNT AT ALBION BANK NO 11451226 SORT CODE 90 47 17

statement sent by the seller to the customer

——— STATEMENT OF ACCOUNT ———

COOL SOCKS LIMITED
Unit 45 Elgar Estate, Broadfield, BR7 4ER
Tel 01908 765314 Fax 01908 765951 Email toni@cool.u-net.com
VAT Reg GB 0745 4672 76

TO

Trends
4 Friar Street
Broadfield
BR1 3RF

account **3993**

date **30 11 20-3**

Date	Details	Debit £	Credit £	Balance £
01 11 20-3	Balance b/f	249.57		249.57
02 11 20-3	Payment received		249.57	00.00
02 11 20-3	Invoice 788101	490.00		490.00
10 11 20-3	Credit note 12189		49.00	441.00
	TOTAL			441.00

(b) **remittance advice sent to the seller**

	TO	**REMITTANCE**	FROM	
	Cool Socks Limited Unit 45 Elgar Estate, Broadfield, BR7 4ER	**ADVICE** 8 December 20-3	**Vogue Ltd** 56 Shaftesbury Road Manorfield MA1 6GP	

date	our reference	our reference	payment amount
03 11 -3	INVOICE 788106	876213	500.00
15 11 -3	INVOICE 788256	876287	220.10
20 11 -3	CREDIT NOTE 12218	876287	(22.01)
		TOTAL	698.09

sales ledger account of the customer in the accounting records of the seller

Debit				Vogue Ltd			Credit	
20-3	**Details**	**£**	**p**	**20-3**	**Details**	**£**	**p**
3 Nov	Sales	500	00	20 Nov	Sales returns	22	01
15 Nov	Sales	220	10				
17 Nov	Sales	625	85				

(c) **remittance advice sent to the seller**

REMITTANCE ADVICE

TO
Chico Importers
34 Oldfield Street,
London EC1 6TR

FROM:
RTC Fashions
85 Fish Street
Stourminster ST1 8RT

03 12 20-3

Your ref	Our ref		Amount
10956	1078	less 5% prompt payment discount	638.40
		FASTER PAYMENTS TRANSFER **TOTAL**	638.40

THIS HAS BEEN PAID BY FASTER PAYMENTS TRANSFER DIRECTLY INTO YOUR BANK ACCOUNT AT HRBC BANK ACCOUNT NO xxxx6534 SORT CODE 40 47 17

invoice sent by the seller

INVOICE

CHICO IMPORTERS
34 Oldfield Street, London EC1 6TR
Tel 0208765322 Fax 0208765564 Email sales@chicoimporters.com
VAT Reg GB 0745 4672 76

Invoice to

RTC Fashions
85 Fish Street
Stourminster
ST1 8RT

invoice no	10956
account	834
your reference	1078
date/tax point	5 11 20-3

Product code	Description	Quantity	Price	Unit	Total	Discount %	Net
5674R	T shirts (red)	200	3.50	each	700.00	20.00	560.00

terms

Net monthly

Carriage paid

Goods total	560.00
VAT	112.00
TOTAL	672.00

5.4 You are the bookkeeper at A-Z Trading and are processing customer transactions.

A receipt of £5,270 has been received from a credit customer, Kamat Limited. The following is an extract for Kamat Limited from your digital bookkeeping system, together with the remittance advice.

April sales list: Kamat Ltd		
Date 20-4	Details	Amount £
3 April	Invoice 7624	1,410
12 April	Credit note 105	−340
23 April	Invoice 7711	1,875
26 April	Credit note 115	−65
28 April	Invoice 7769	2,350

Remittance Advice: Kamat Ltd To: A-Z Trading 30 April 20-4		
Date 20-4	Details	Amount £
3 April	Invoice 7624	1,410
21 April	Credit note 105	−340
23 April	Invoice 7711	1,785
26 April	Credit note 115	65
28 April	Invoice 7796	2,350
TOTAL: Paid by BACS 30 April		5,270

(a) You are to identify the discrepancies (if any) between the transactions from the sales list and the transactions in the remittance advice.

20-4	Details	£	Discrepancies
3 April	Invoice 7624	1,410	
10 April	Credit note 105	−340	
19 April	Invoice 7711	1,875	
25 April	Credit note 115	−65	
28 April	Invoice 7769	2,350	

For the discrepancies column, choose from the following options (use each once only):

No discrepancy
Incorrect date
Incorrect invoice number
Incorrectly recorded
Incorrect amount

(b) What will be the balance of Kamat Limited's account after the payment of £5,270 has been allocated to its account?

Balance of Kamat Ltd's trade receivables account	
(a) £40 underpaid	
(b) £40 overpaid	
(c) £65 underpaid	
(d) £65 overpaid	

(c) An invoice to supply goods for £3,860 plus VAT has been sent to Robens Limited, offering prompt payment discount of 2% for payment within seven days.

What will be the amount payable by Robens Limited if it pays within seven days?

£ [   ]

(d) The following remittance advice has been received by A-Z Trading from Hanford & Co:

Hanford & Co
BACS remittance advice
To: A-Z Trading
Date: 30 April 20-4
Amount: £3,170
Detail:
- £2,170 part payment of balance at 1 April 20-4
- £1,000 part payment of invoice 7695
- Full allocation of credit note 121 to invoice 7695

You are to show the outstanding amount for each entry after the remittance has been allocated.

Date 20-4	Detail	£	Outstanding amount £
1 April	Opening balance	3,150	
15 April	Invoice 7695	1,875	
28 April	Credit note 121	-325	

6 Financial documents for purchases

this chapter covers...

*In Chapter 2 we described the financial documents prepared by a **seller** of goods and services on credit. This chapter looks at the situation from the purchaser's point of view and describes the procedures and documents involved when goods and services are **bought** on credit.*

The chapter covers the following areas:

■ *the use of financial documents for the purchase of goods and services – quotation, purchase order, delivery note, goods received note, purchase invoice, goods returns note, credit note*

■ *the checking of the supplier's documents received against the purchaser's documents*

■ *the calculation of document totals, including discounts and VAT*

■ *the coding and filing of documents*

■ *the checking and authorisation of documents*

■ *dealing with discrepancies*

This chapter covers the treatment of financial documents until payment is made. The processes of calculating and making payment are covered in Chapter 8.

FINANCIAL DOCUMENTS – THE PURCHASER'S POINT OF VIEW

When a business **sells** goods and services, its main concern is that it provides what has been ordered and that it gets paid on time. When a business **orders** goods and services, on the other hand, it will want to ensure that:

■ the correct goods and services are provided – on time

■ they are charged at the right price

The traditional procedure is for the purchaser to accumulate on file – often stapled together – a series of documents which will be checked against each other as they are produced or come into the office, eg copy purchase order, delivery note, goods received note, invoice, credit note, statement, and so on. These will often be kept in a 'pending invoices' file until payment is made, when they will go into a 'paid invoices' file – as shown in the diagram below.

This chapter covers the treatment of financial documents until payment is made. Calculating and making payment is covered in Chapter 8.

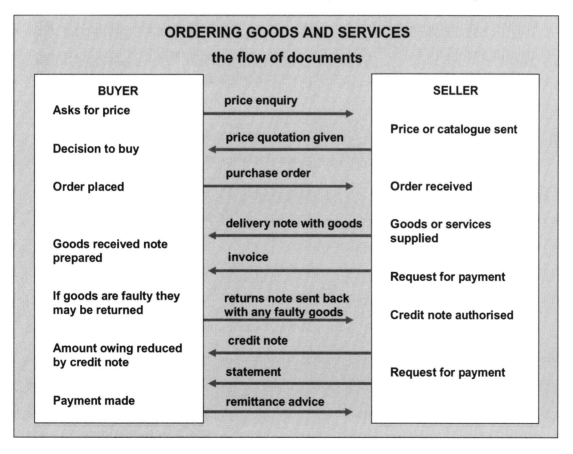

ORDERING PROCEDURES

getting prices and requesting quotations

When ordering goods or services, a business needs to know the price that will be charged. The business is likely to 'shop around' to get the best price available. Enquiries can be made by telephone, looking at catalogues and price lists, and comparing website price lists and product descriptions.

Another way of getting a price is by asking for a written (or emailed) quotation from the seller. The format of a quotation given by Cool Socks to its customer 'Trends' is shown below.

—— QUOTATION ——

COOL SOCKS LIMITED
Unit 45 Elgar Estate, Broadfield, BR7 4ER
Tel 01908 765314 Fax 01908 765951 Email toni@cool.u-net.com
VAT Reg GB 0745 4672 76

Trends 4 Friar Street Broadfield BR1 3RF	date 19 09 20-3

Thank you for your enquiry of 17 September 20-3. We are pleased to quote as follows:

100 pairs Toebar socks (blue) @ £2.36 a pair, excluding VAT

M Arnold

Sales Department

The quotation will note if any discounts – bulk or trade – are offered to the buyer.

the ordering process

As soon as the buyer is happy with the price provided on a quotation, or obtained from a price list, the ordering process can begin. The diagram on page 155 shows the traditional method of ordering goods and services: a purchase order is issued, the goods (or services) are delivered (or provided) and an invoice is sent for payment by the customer.

The purchase order can be in paper format (see next page) or it can be made online.

documents for purchases

This chapter concentrates on the traditional method of purchasing using paper documents. Electronic methods are based on the same principles. The documents are:

- purchase order
- delivery note
- goods received note
- purchase invoice

When a business purchases goods, it is important that the accounting system includes checks and controls to ensure that:

- the correct goods have been received in an acceptable condition
- the correct terms (including discounts) and price have been applied
- the goods are paid for within the terms agreed with the seller

PURCHASE ORDER

A purchaser, when the price of the product has been obtained, normally issues a **purchase order**. It is essential that this purchase order is **authorised** by the appropriate person, who signs and dates the form. A business keeps a copy of every purchase order it issues and often files them in numerical order (each order has a numerical code).

The purchase order for Blue Toebar socks from the Cool Socks Case Study in Chapter 2 is shown below.

Trends   **PURCHASE ORDER**

4 Friar Street

Broadfield

BR1 3RF

Tel 01908 761234 Fax 01908 761987

VAT Reg GB 0745 8383 56

Cool Socks Limited	
Unit 45 Elgar Estate,	purchase order no **47609**
Broadfield,	
BR7 4ER	date **25 09 20-3**

product code	quantity	description
45B	**100 pairs**	**Blue Toebar socks**

D.Signer   *25/09/20-3*

AUTHORISED signature.. date.........................

DELIVERY NOTE

When the goods ordered are despatched by the seller they will normally be accompanied by a **delivery note**.

The delivery note shown below was described in the Cool Socks Case Study in Chapter 2. The main features are as follows:

- the delivery note has a numerical reference (here it is 68873), useful for filing and later reference if there is a query

- the method of delivery is stated – here the delivery is by parcel carrier

- the delivery note quotes the purchase order number – 47609 – this enables the buyer to 'tie up' the delivery with the original purchase order

- the delivery note quotes:

  - Cool Socks' catalogue reference 45B as the product code

  - the quantity supplied

  - the description of the goods, but no price – it is not needed at this stage

These details will be checked against the goods themselves straightaway so that any discrepancies can be reported without delay.

If the business purchasing the goods uses a **goods received note** (see next page) this will also be completed at this stage.

■ the delivery note will be signed and dated by the person receiving the goods as proof of delivery. This signature process can also be carried out electronically – the person receiving the goods is asked to sign a portable electronic device

---

──── DELIVERY NOTE ────

COOL SOCKS LIMITED
Unit 45 Elgar Estate, Broadfield, BR7 4ER
Tel 01908 765314 Fax 01908 765951 Email toni@cool.u-net.com
VAT Reg GB 0745 4672 76

Trends	delivery note no	**68873**
4 Friar Street	delivery method	**Lynx Parcels**
Broadfield	your order	**47609**
BR1 3RF	date	**02 10 20-3**

product code	quantity	description
45B	**100 pairs**	**Blue Toebar socks**

Received

signature...*V Williams*... name (capitals)...*V WILLIAMS*.................... date...*5/10/20-3*...

GOODS RECEIVED NOTE

Some businesses use an internal document known as a goods received note (GRN). The buyer records on this document the receipt of the goods and the details set out on the delivery note or advice note sent by the supplier.

The GRN is essentially a checklist on which is recorded:

■ the name of the supplier

■ the quantity and details of the goods ordered

■ the purchase order number

■ the name of the carrier and any carrier reference number

As the goods are received and checked in, the GRN is ticked and signed to indicate that the right quantity and description of goods has been received.

The GRN forms part of the payment authorisation process: only when a completed and correct GRN is approved by the accounts department can the relevant invoice be paid.

Shown below is the goods received note relating to the Case Study in Chapter 2 in which the shop 'Trends' ordered socks from Cool Socks Limited.

Note that the receipt of the 100 pairs of socks has been recorded, and also the fact that 10 pairs are damaged.

Trends		GOODS RECEIVED NOTE

Suppliers

Cool Socks Limited Unit 45 Elgar Estate, Broadfield, BR7 4ER	GRN no date	**1871** **05 10 20-3**

quantity	description	order number
100 pairs	**Blue Toebar socks**	**47609**

carrier   **Lynx Parcels**   consignment no   **8479347**

received by *V Williams*   checked by   *R Patel*

condition of goods (please tick and comment)	good condition damaged ✓ (10 pairs) shortages	**Copies to** Buyer Accounts Stockroom	✓ ✓ ✓

PURCHASE INVOICE

You will already be familiar with the **purchase invoice** because it is the **sales invoice** sent out by the person selling the goods or services. In the Chapter 2 Case Study, the sales invoice sent by Cool Socks becomes the purchase invoice received by Trends, the buyer:

INVOICE

COOL SOCKS LIMITED
Unit 45 Elgar Estate, Broadfield, BR7 4ER
Tel 01908 765314 Fax 01908 765951 Email toni@cool.u-net.com
VAT Reg GB 0745 4672 76

Invoice to

Trends
4 Friar Street
Broadfield
BR1 3RF

invoice no	**787923**
account	**3993**
your reference	**47609**
date/tax point	**02 10 20-3**

deliver to

as above

Product code	Description	Quantity	Price	Unit	Total	Discount %	Net
45B	Blue toebar socks	100	2.36	pair	236.00	0.00	236.00

terms

Net monthly

Carriage paid

E & OE

GOODS TOTAL	236.00
VAT	47.20
TOTAL	283.20

CHECKING INVOICE, DELIVERY NOTE AND PURCHASE ORDER

The purchase documents must be checked carefully by the purchaser. This involves two separate procedures carried out by the accounts department:

■ checking the documents – the invoice, delivery note (or GRN) and copy purchase order – against each other

■ checking the calculations on the invoice

Checking the documents involves the following:

check 1 – goods received and delivery note

When the goods are received they should be checked against the delivery note – the quantities should be counted and the condition of the goods checked and noted on a GRN, if required. Any discrepancies or damage should be notified immediately to the supplier so that replacements can be sent or the buyer credited with the value of the missing or damaged goods (ie the amount due reduced by the issue of a credit note).

check 2 – delivery note and purchase order

The delivery note should then be checked in the accounts department against a copy of the original purchase order (see illustration on page 25):

■ supplier catalogue number – has the right type of goods been delivered?

■ quantity – has the right number been delivered?

■ specifications – are the goods delivered to the same specifications as those ordered?

■ purchase order reference number – do the goods and the delivery note relate to the purchase order?

If all is in order, the delivery note will be filed with the copy purchase order under the purchase order reference number, ready for checking against the invoice when it arrives.

check 3 – invoice, delivery note and purchase order

When the invoice is received from the supplier, it should be checked against the delivery note and the purchase order (which should be filed together). The points to look at are:

■ **invoice and delivery note**

Are the details of the goods on the invoice and delivery note the same? The product code, description and quantity of the goods should agree.

■ **invoice and purchase order**

Has the correct price been charged? The unit price quoted by the supplier or obtained from the supplier's catalogue will be stated on the purchase order, and should agree with the unit price stated on the invoice. If there is a difference, it should be queried with the supplier.

---

task

Look at the invoice, the purchase order and the delivery note on the next page. They all relate to the same transaction. Can you spot any discrepancies? The answers are set out at the bottom of the page. (Note that a ream of paper is 500 sheets.)

───────────── INVOICE ─────────────

Stourford Office Supplies
Unit 12, Avon Industrial Estate, Stourford, SF5 6TD
Tel 01807 765434 Fax 01807 765123 Email stourford@stourford.co.uk
VAT Reg GB 0745 4001 76

Invoice to

Martley Machine Rental Limited	
67 Broadgreen Road	
Martley	
MR6 7TR	

invoice no	**652771**
account	**MAR435**
your reference	**47780**
date/tax point	**31 03 20-3**

deliver to

as above

Product code	Description	Quantity	Price	Unit	Total	Discount %	Net
3564748	80gsm white Supalaser	15	3.50	ream	52.00	0.00	52.00

terms

Net monthly

Carriage paid

E & OE

GOODS TOTAL	52.00
VAT	10.04
TOTAL	41.96

The purchase order and delivery note agree, but the invoice has a number of discrepancies:

- the order reference differs (47700 and 47780)
- the product code differs (3564749 and 3564748)
- the product description differs (100 gsm and 80 gsm)
- the price differs (£4.00 and £3.50 per ream)

Martley Machine Rental

PURCHASE ORDER

67 Broadgreen Road
Martley
MR6 7TR
Tel 01908 546321   Fax 01908 546335
VAT REG GB 0745 8383 56

Stourford Office Supplies Unit 12 Avon Industrial Estate Stourford SF5 6TD	purchase order no **47700** date **13 03 20-3**

product code	quantity	description
3564749	**15 reams**	**100gsm white Supalaser paper @ £4.00 per ream**

AUTHORISED   signature...*C Farmer*............   date ....*13 March 20-3*..................

catalogue number	quantity	order specifications	purchase order reference number

───── DELIVERY NOTE ─────

Stourford Office Supplies

Unit 12, Avon Industrial Estate, Stourford, SF5 6TD

Tel 01807 765434 Fax 01807 765123 Email stourford@stourford.co.uk

VAT Reg GB 0745 4001 76

Martley Machine Rental Ltd 67 Broadgreen Road Martley MR6 7TR	delivery note no 26754 delivery method **Puma Express** your order **47700** date **27 03 20-3**

product code	quantity	description
3564749	**15 reams**	**100gsm white Supalaser paper**

Received

signature...*G Hughes*............   print name (capitals)...*G HUGHES*.........date ....*31.03 20-3*.................

details to check on the purchase order and delivery note

CHECKING THE CALCULATIONS ON THE INVOICE

Another important step is for the accounts department to check the calculations on the invoice. If any one of these calculations is incorrect, the final total will be wrong, and the invoice will have to be queried with the supplier, so accurate checking is essential. The checks to be made are:

quantity x unit price

The quantity of the items multiplied by the unit price must be correct. The result – the total price or 'price extension' – is used for the calculation of any trade discount applicable.

trade or bulk discount

Any trade or bulk discount – allowances given to approved trade customers or for bulk purchases – must be deducted from the total price worked out. Trade or bulk discount is calculated as a percentage of the total price, eg a trade discount of 20% on a total price of £150 is calculated:

$$£150 \text{ x } \frac{20}{100} = £30$$

The net price charged (before VAT) is therefore

£150 – £30 = £120 = net total

prompt payment discount

Any prompt payment discount (PPD) – an allowance sometimes given for quick payment – should be calculated and deducted from the full amount due on the invoice by the purchaser after the invoice has been received and within the time limit stipulated. No deductions will have been made from the invoice by the seller. The invoice will show the full amount due and any reduction will then be documented by a credit note issued by the seller. Page 35 explains the PPD process in more detail.

VAT

Value Added Tax (a sales tax) in this book is calculated at 20%. To calculate VAT, the total after the deduction of any bulk or trade discount is treated as follows:

$$\text{Total x } \frac{20}{100} = \text{VAT amount}$$

Use a calculator and multiply the total by 0.2 to give the VAT, which is then added to the total.

Note that fractions of a penny are ignored. If the total price is £55.78, the VAT will be:

£55.78 x 0.2 = £11.156

£11.156 then loses the last digit – the fraction of a penny – to become £11.15.

date and terms of payment The terms of payment are usually stated on the invoice, eg 'net monthly' – which means payment is done within one month of the invoice. The accounts department needs to know the terms so that payment can be made in that time – see Chapter 8 for processing payments to suppliers.

For the purpose of your studies you must assume that the calculations on all invoices must be checked. In practice, invoicing using a digital bookkeeping system performs the calculations automatically, and should be correct.

Now check the calculations on the invoice on page 164. You should be able to detect a number of errors:

- quantity x unit price should be £52.50, not £52.00

- the VAT is wrongly calculated £52.00 x 0.2 = £10.40, not £10.04 (it would be £10.50 on £52.50)

- the VAT has been deducted instead of added: the total should be £52.50 + £10.50 = £63.00

GOODS RETURNS – CHECKING CREDIT NOTES

A purchaser will sometimes have to return faulty or incorrect goods or claim for prompt payment discount. In these cases the purchaser will request a credit note from the seller to reduce the amount owed. In no circumstances should the invoice itself be changed.

If faulty or incorrect goods are sent back, they are normally sent with a **goods returns note** which sets out the details of the goods. See the example on the next page.

Trends
4 Friar Street
Broadfield
BR1 3RF
Tel 01908 761234   Fax 01908 761987
VAT REG GB 0745 8383 56

GOODS RETURNS NOTE

Cool Socks Limited
Unit 45 Elgar Estate,
Broadfield,
BR7 4ER

returns note no   **2384**

date   **08 10 20-3**

product code	quantity	description
45B	**10 pairs**	**Blue Toebar socks**

RETURNS FOR RETURN: *faulty goods, credit requested*

SIGNATURE   *R SINGH*   DATE   *10 10 20-3*

When the goods are received back by the seller and checked, a **credit note** will be issued to reduce the amount owing. The credit note from the Cool Socks Case Study is illustrated on the next page.

CHECKING THE CREDIT NOTE

When the **credit note** is received by the purchaser it will have to be checked carefully to make sure that the quantity of goods, the price, discount and VAT are calculated correctly. It will be checked against the **goods received note** if one has been issued (not all businesses do), or the **goods returns note** or other internal records to make sure that the discrepancy has been properly resolved – eg has full credit been given for damaged/missing/incorrect goods? In the case of the example below, it is £28.32 for damaged socks.

If the credit note is correct, the document will be entered into the accounting system and then filed with the copy purchase order, delivery note, invoice, GRN or copy returns note, awaiting the arrival of the statement.

CREDIT NOTE

COOL SOCKS LIMITED

Unit 45 Elgar Estate, Broadfield, BR7 4ER

Tel 01908 765314 Fax 01908 765951 Email toni@cool.u-net.com

VAT REG GB 0745 4672 76

to

Trends
4 Friar Street
Broadfield
BR1 3RF

credit note no	**12157**
account	**3993**
your reference	**47609**
our invoice	**787923**
date/tax point	**13 10 20-3**

Product code	Description	Quantity	Price	Unit	Total	Discount %	Net
45B	Blue Toebar socks	10	2.36	pair	23.60	0.00	23.60

Reasons for credit

10 pairs of socks received damaged

(Your returns note no. R/N 2384)

GOODS TOTAL	23.60
VAT	4.72
TOTAL	28.32

Trends		GOODS RECEIVED NOTE	

Supplier

Cool Socks Limited Unit 45 Elgar Estate, Broadfield, BR7 4ER	GRN no	**1871**
	date	**05 10 20-3**

quantity	description	order number
100 pairs	**Blue Toebar socks**	**47609**

carrier   **Lynx Parcels**   consignment no   **8479347**

received by   *V Williams*   checked by   *R Patel*

condition of goods	good condition	**Copies to**	
(please tick and comment)	damaged ✓ (10 pairs) shortages	Buyer	✓
		Accounts	✓
		Stockroom	✓

goods received note – details to check

If you compare the **credit note** on the opposite page and the **goods received note** shown above you will see that the following details can be checked:

- the identity of the goods returned – here it is blue Toebar socks

- the quantity returned – ten pairs of socks in this case

- the purchase order reference number – here it is 47609

As you will see, all is correct and so it is in order for Trends to make payment for this transaction on the due date.

The processes of paying for purchases is dealt with in Chapter 8.

CODING PURCHASES INVOICES AND CREDIT NOTES

the need to code

When a business processes invoices and credit notes received from suppliers, it will usually code them so that they can be entered into the accounting system quickly and easily. This will be very useful, for example, if a digital bookkeeping system is used. Normally two different sets of codes will be used:

- a **supplier account** code which will identify the supplier of the goods or services – this code may be alphabetical, alpha-numerical or numerical; if letters are involved they usually relate to the first few letters of the name of the supplier

- a **general ledger account** code which will identify the account to be used in the accounting system – it normally relates to the type of purchases made or expenses paid; it may be alpha-numerical or numerical

You will see from the purchases invoice and credit note on the next page that the codes may be entered in boxes imprinted onto the document by a rubber stamp used by the buyer (see the grey arrows indicating the boxes).

using the account code lists

The business will keep account lists so that accounts staff can look up the appropriate code. As noted above, these will be for:

- supplier accounts

- general ledger accounts, eg categories of purchases

Extracts from these two types of account lists are shown below. Note that the account names are listed in alphabetical order:

Supplier	Supplier code
Jarma Supplies	JA006
John Taylor Limited	JO004
Labtech Limited	LA001
Liverpool Kitware	LI001

Item	General Ledger code
Shades	5045
T-shirts	5060
Trainers	5100
Trousers	5210

The **invoice** on the next page has therefore been given the following codes:

Supplier code JA006 for Jarma Supplies

General ledger code 5060 for Max T-shirts purchased

The **credit note** on the next page has been given the following codes:

Supplier code LA001 for Labtech Limited

General ledger code 5045 for Monaco shades purchased

INVOICE

JARMA SUPPLIES
Advent House, Otto Way
New Milton, SR1 6TF
Tel 01722 295875 Fax 01722 295611 Email sales@johnsonthreads.co.uk
VAT Reg GB 01982 6865 06

Invoice to

RT Fashionware 34, Tennyson High Road Maidstone ME4 5EW	

Invoice no	**7736**
account	**94122**
your reference	**675**
date/tax point	**01 04 20-7**

description	quantity	price	unit	total
Max T-shirts (red)	200	3.00	each	600.00

terms
30 days
Carriage paid
E & OE

supplier a/c reference	general ledger a/c number
JA006	5060

GOODS TOTAL	600.00
VAT	120.00
TOTAL	720.00

coding details entered on sellers' documents by the purchaser, RT Fashionware

CREDIT NOTE

LABTECH LIMITED
Unit 7 Roughway Estate, Martley Road, Cookford, CO1 9GH
Tel 01843 265432 Fax 01843 265439 Email accounts@fabtech.co.uk
VAT Reg GB 0877 9333 06

to

RT Fashionware 34, Tennyson High Road Maidstone ME4 5EW	

credit note no	**976**
account	**94122**
your reference	**47601**
date/tax point	**12 04 20-7**

description	quantity	price	unit	total
Monaco shades 2744	5	30.00	each	150.00

reason for credit:
lenses damaged

supplier a/c reference	general ledger a/c number
LA001	5045

GOODS TOTAL	150.00
VAT	30.00
TOTAL	180.00

- A business ordering goods or services needs to obtain the best price for the goods and services, either from catalogues and online price lists or by requesting a quotation.

- When a business places orders for goods or services on credit, it may do so using a paper-based system or by ordering online.

- When a business orders goods on credit using a manual paper-based system, it is likely to deal with a number of financial documents: quotation, purchase order, delivery note, goods received note, purchase invoice, goods returns note, credit note.

- It is important that a series of checks are made on the financial documents to ensure that the goods or services provided are the correct ones, charged at the right price. The checks will involve calculations and references.

- If a discrepancy is found, it should be noted and the seller contacted so that the account of the purchaser can be credited and the amount owing reduced accordingly.

- Purchases invoices and credit notes should be coded with the supplier account and general ledger account codes for types of purchases so that they can easily be entered into the accounting system.

Key Terms	**quotation**	requested by the purchaser and issued by the seller stating the cost of goods or services to be provided
	purchase order	issued and authorised by the buyer of goods and services, sent to the seller, indicating the goods or services required
	delivery note	lists and accompanies the goods sent to the purchaser
	goods received note	used by purchasers to record receipt of goods and documenting any returns made
	purchases invoice	issued by the seller of goods or services to the purchaser indicating the amount owing and the required payment date
	goods returns note	sent to the supplier with faulty goods
	credit note	issued by the seller of goods or services to the purchaser reducing the amount owing

Activities

6.1 State which type of business document would normally be used when goods are bought on credit:

(a) to order the goods from the seller

(b) to accompany goods sent from the seller

(c) to record the receipt and any discrepancies relating to the goods at the buyer's premises

(d) to advise the buyer in the first instance of the amount of money due

(e) to advise the buyer that a reduction is being made in the buyer's account for faulty goods supplied

6.2 Distinguish between a delivery note and a goods received note.

6.3 Which documents would normally be checked by the buyer against the purchase order? Select **one** option.

(a)	The delivery note and the invoice	
(b)	The invoice and the returns note	
(c)	The goods received note and the returns note	
(d)	The returns note and the delivery note	

6.4 What document would a buyer expect to receive from a seller if goods which were delivered in a damaged condition have been returned to the seller?

6.5 Eduservice, an educational consultancy business, ordered memory sticks from Compusupply Limited on purchase order 53659 for the IT Department at Martley College in Broadfield. The goods were delivered to the Eduservice office at 45 The Ridings, Broadfield on 3 February.

You work for Eduservice as an accounts assistant. Part of your job is to deal with all the documents.

You have today (5 February 20-3) received an invoice from Compusupply. You are not happy with the service you are receiving from this company and are thinking of going elsewhere for a supplier.

Shown on the next two pages are:

• an extract from an email from Compusupply agreeing the level of trade discount given

• the original purchase order

• the invoice you receive

You are to write the text of an email to Compusupply setting out the errors that have been made. Address the email to sales@compusupply.co.uk and use your own name as an accounts assistant. The date is 5 February 20-3.

Extract of email dated 1 November 20-2 from Compusupply to Eduservice

"In view of our long-standing trading relationship we are happy to increase the trade discount we allow your company from 10% to 15% from 1 November 20-2.

Kind regards

James Watts
Credit Controller
Compusupply"

EDUSERVICE

45 The Ridings
Broadfield
BR2 3TR
Tel 01908 333691

PURCHASE ORDER

To

Compusupply Limited
Unit 17 Elgar Estate,
Broadfield, BR7 4ER

purchase order no   **53659**

date   **27 January 20-3**

Product code	Quantity	Description
4573	1 box	Opus 128GB memory sticks @ £95 per box of ten Please deliver to: J Wales, IT Department Martley College, Fairacre, Broadfield BR5 7YT

Authorised signature ....*J Wales*....................................date............*27.1.20-3*...............

INVOICE

COMPUSUPPLY LIMITED
Unit 17 Elgar Estate, Broadfield, BR7 4ER
Tel 01908 765756 Fax 01908 765777 Email sales@compusupply.co.uk
VAT Reg GB 0745 4689 13

invoice to

Eduservice	
45 The Ridings	
Broadfield	
BR2 3TR	

invoice no	**20424**
account	**242**
your reference	**53659**
date/tax point	**30 01 20-3**

deliver to

as above

Product code	Description	Quantity	Price	Unit	Total	Discount %	Net
4574	Opus 256GB memory sticks	1	125.00	box	125.00	10	112.50

GOODS TOTAL	112.50
VAT	22.50
TOTAL	135.00

terms
Net monthly
Carriage paid
E & OE

6.6 **(a)** John Smith & Co, a stationery shop, ordered 20 boxes of gel pens from Helicon Stationery Supplies on purchase order 17643 (see below).

The goods were delivered to John Smith & Co on 4 December 20-4, but the order was short by 2 boxes and only 18 boxes were delivered. This was noted in a goods received note (see the next page). The problem was advised to Helicon Supplies by email on 4 December and a credit note requested. The credit note was issued on 10 December and sent to John Smith & Co. (on page 181).

You are to check the three documents and write the text of an email from John Smith & Co to Helicon pointing out any discrepancies you find. Use your own name. The date is 12 December.

(b) John Smith & Co code all purchase invoices and credit notes with a supplier code and a general ledger code. Extracts from the two coding lists are shown below.

You are to state the supplier and general ledger codes which are to be used on the credit note on the next page.

Supplier	Supplier code
French & Co	FR002
Gemax Supplies	GE004
Helicon Stationery	HE001
JSTAT Ltd	JS001

Item	General Ledger code
Paper	5005
Pens	5010
Pension costs	5201
Power costs	7210

John Smith & Co   PURCHASE ORDER

7 Buttermere Road

Broadfield BR6 3TR

Tel 01908 761234 Fax 01908 761987

email info@johnsmith&co.co.uk

VAT REG GB 0745 8383 56

| Helicon Stationery Supplies
91 High Street,
Broadfield, BR7 4ER | purchase order no | **17643** |
| | date | **25 11 20-4** |

Product code	Quantity	Description
919BK	20 boxes of 10	Gel Pens (Black)

AUTHORISED signature ....*D Smith*...................................date…...…........................... *25/11/20-4*.......

John Smith & Co   GOODS RECEIVED NOTE

GRN no.   302

Supplier   Helicon Stationery Supplies

Date   4 December 20-4

Order ref	Quantity	Description
17643	20 boxes of 10	Gel Pens (Black)

received by ......*D Patel*...checked by .....*R T Fraser*...............................

condition of goods condition – *good*

damages – *none*

shortages ✓ *18 out of 20 boxes received*

CREDIT NOTE

HELICON STATIONERY SUPPLIES
91 HIGH STREET, BROADFIELD, BR7 4ER
Tel 01908 129426 Fax 01908 129919
email sales@heliconstationery.co.uk
VAT REG GB 0622 838370

to

John Smith & Co
7 Buttermere Road
Broadfield BR6 3TR

credit note no	**234672**
account	**2984**
your reference	**17644**
date/tax point	**10 December 20-4**

Product code	Description	Quantity	Price	Unit	Total	Discount %	Net
909BK	Rollerball pens (black)	3	8.00	box	24.00	10	19.20

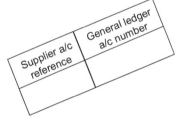

GOODS TOTAL	19.20
VAT @ 20%	3.84
TOTAL	23.04

reason for credit

Shortages

6.7 Identify which document would be received from a supplier for each of the purposes below.

Purpose	Document
Document stating the cost of goods or services to be provided	
Document stating the amount owing and the terms of payment	
Document listing and accompanying the goods	
Document reducing the amount owing	

For the documents, choose from the following options (use each once only):

Delivery note
Invoice
Credit note
Quotation

6.8 You are the bookkeeper at Golding Traders Limited. The following documents relate to incorrect goods supplied by Ballard Limited.

Golding Traders Ltd
Goods Returns Note
To: Ballard Ltd
1 May 20-7

10 x Product 27
Returned as faulty
£15 net each
Credit requested

Ballard Ltd
Credit note: CN68
To: Golding Enterprises Ltd
Date: 1 May 20-7

	£
20 x Product 27	150.00
VAT @ 20%	30.00
Total	120.00

Identify **three** discrepancies in the credit note:

Discrepancy	✓
Buyer details	
Quantity of goods	
Date of credit note	
Net amount	
VAT amount	
Total amount	

7 Accounting for purchases, returns, and discounts

this chapter covers...

This chapter focuses on using the accounting system to record the details of purchases, purchases returns, and discounts received (using the credit note system – see pages 35-37).

Having looked in the previous chapter at the documents and procedures involved in buying on credit, we will now take the financial documents of purchases invoices and credit notes for purchases returns and discounts received and record them in books of prime entry (day books) and in the bookkeeping system of general ledger and payables ledger.

We will be using three books of prime entry:

- *purchases day book*
- *purchases returns day book*
- *discounts received day book*

Information from these day books will then be transferred into the bookkeeping system using accounts in general ledger and payables ledger.

In this chapter we focus on accounting for credit purchases, purchases returns, and discounts received. Cash purchases transactions will be seen when we study the cash book in Chapter 9.

THE ACCOUNTING SYSTEM

We have seen in Chapter 1 (page 4) that the accounting system comprises a number of stages of recording and presenting financial transactions:

- financial documents
- books of prime entry (eg day books)
- double-entry bookkeeping
- trial balance

In this chapter we look at how financial documents for credit purchases, purchases returns, and discounts received transactions are recorded in the books of prime entry, together with the entries to be made in the double-entry bookkeeping accounts. Books of prime entry are used in manual bookkeeping systems, or they can be set up in a computer spreadsheet. They are not used in digital bookkeeping because these systems automatically update as financial documents are entered.

ACCOUNTING FOR CREDIT PURCHASES, PURCHASES RETURNS, AND DISCOUNTS RECEIVED

In accounting, the term 'purchases' means **the purchase of goods with the intention that they should be resold at a profit.**

This means that an office stationery shop will record as purchases those items – such as photocopier paper, ring binders – which it buys with the intention of resale at a profit. Such purchases, together with the running costs of the business (eg wages, heating and lighting, telephone), are described as **revenue expenditure**. Other asset items purchased in connection with the running of the business – eg buildings, shop fittings – are recorded not as purchases but, instead, are accounted for as the purchase of an asset. Such expenditure is described as **capital expenditure**.

'Purchases returns' are when goods previously bought on credit are returned by the buyer to the supplier.

'Discounts received' (or **prompt payment discount**) is a discount offered by a supplier to customers in order to encourage customers to settle up straightaway or in a short time from the invoice date; it is discounts received in the accounting system of the buyer.

The diagram on the next page shows the order in which the accounting records are prepared for credit purchases, purchases returns, and discounts received transactions. You will see that the steps are:

■ start with a **financial document** – either a purchases invoice (for purchases) or a credit note received (for purchases returns and discounts received)

■ enter it in the appropriate **book of prime entry** (the first accounting book in which the financial document is recorded and summarised), purchases day book, purchases returns day book, or discounts received day book

■ transfer the information from the book of prime entry into the double-entry accounts in the **general ledger**

■ transfer the information from the book of prime entry into the subsidiary accounts of trade payables in the **payables ledger** (also known as **purchases ledger)**

accounting for credit purchases and purchases returns transactions

financial documents

- purchases invoices

- credit notes received for purchases returns and discounts received

books of prime entry

- purchases day book

- purchases returns day book

- discounts received day book

general ledger

double-entry accounts

- purchases account

- purchases returns account

- discounts received account

- purchases ledger control account

- Value Added Tax account

Payables ledger (purchases ledger)

subsidiary accounts

- accounts of trade payables (suppliers)

We will now look in more detail at the use of the books of prime entry and the double-entry bookkeeping system for credit purchases, purchases returns, and discounts received. These are very similar to the system already used for credit sales, sales returns, and discounts allowed in Chapter 4 and you may wish to refer to the sections of Chapter 4 which cover books of prime entry (pages 95-96), and methods of coding in accounting systems (pages 111-112).

ACCOUNTING SYSTEM FOR CREDIT PURCHASES

The accounting system for credit purchases fits together in the following way:

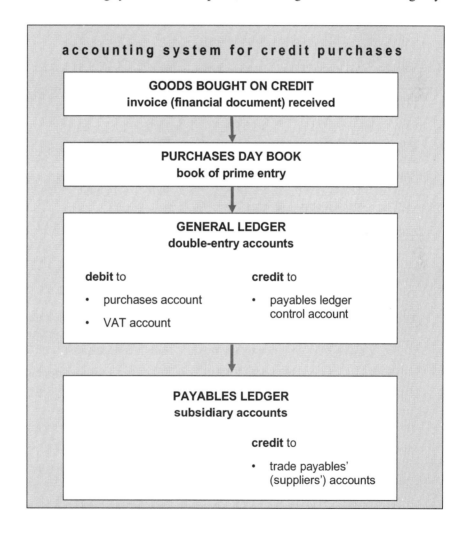

We will now look in more detail at the purchases day book and the accounting system for credit purchases.

In the examples which follow we will assume that the business is registered for Value Added Tax and that VAT is charged on invoices received from suppliers.

The VAT rate used in the examples is 20%.

PURCHASES DAY BOOK

The purchases day book is a collection point for accounting information on the credit purchases of a business and is set out in the following way (with sample entries shown):

Purchases Day Book					PDB57	
Date	**Supplier name**	**Invoice number**	**Account code**	**Total**	**VAT***	**Net**
20-4				£	£	£
5 Jan	P Bond Ltd	1234	PL125	96	16	80
9 Jan	D Webster	A373	PL730	144	24	120
16 Jan	P Bond Ltd	1247	PL125	48	8	40
20 Jan	Sanders & Sons	5691	PL495	192	32	160
31 Jan	Totals for month			480	80	400
				GL2350	GL2200	GL5100

* VAT = 20%

Notes:

- purchases day book is prepared from financial documents – purchases invoices received from suppliers. The invoice number used is either that of the supplier's invoice (as above) or is a unique number given to each invoice by the buyer's accounts department

- the code 'PDB57' is used for cross-referencing to the bookkeeping system: here it indicates that this is page 57 of the purchases day book (PDB)

- the **account code** column cross-references here to 'PL' – the Payables Ledger – followed by the account number of the trade payable (supplier)

- the **total** or **gross** column records the amount of each financial document, ie after VAT has been included

- the code 'GL' beneath the totals amounts refers to the account numbers in General Ledger

- purchases day book is totalled at appropriate intervals – daily, weekly or monthly (as here) – and the total of the **net** column tells the business the amount of credit purchases for the period

- the amounts from purchases day book are recorded in the ledger accounts

In order to prepare the purchases day book, we take purchases invoices – that have been checked and authorised – for the period and enter the details:

- date of invoice

- supplier name

- purchase invoice number, using either the supplier's invoice number, or a unique number given to each invoice by the buyer's accounts department

- cross-reference to the supplier's account number in the payables ledger, eg 'PL125'

- enter the total amount of the invoice into the 'total' column

- enter the VAT amount shown on the invoice – don't be concerned with any adjustments to the VAT for the effect of any settlement (cash) discounts, simply record the VAT amount shown

- enter the net amount of the invoice (often described as 'goods total'), before VAT is added

BOOKKEEPING FOR CREDIT PURCHASES

After the purchases day book has been written up and totalled, the information from it is transferred to the double-entry system in the general ledger. The accounts in the general ledger to record the transactions from the purchases day book on the previous page are as follows:

GENERAL LEDGER

Dr		Value added tax account (GL2200)		Cr
20-4		£	20-4	£
31 Jan	Purchases Day Book			
	PDB57	80		

Dr		Payables ledger control account (GL2350)		Cr
20-4		£	20-4	£
			31 Jan	Purchases Day Book
			PDB57	480

Dr		Purchases account (GL5100)		Cr
20-4		£	20-4	£
31 Jan	Purchases Day Book			
	PDB57	400		

Note that from the purchases day book:

■ total of the total column, £480, has been credited to payables ledger control account (which records the liability to trade payables)

■ the total of the VAT column, £80, has been debited to VAT account

■ the total of the net column, £400, has been debited to purchases account

■ each entry in general ledger is cross-referenced back to the page number of the purchases day book; here the reference is to 'PDB57'

The last step is to record the amount of purchases made from each individual trade payable. We do this by recording the purchases invoices in the payables ledger as follows:

PAYABLES LEDGER

Dr		P Bond Limited (PL125)		Cr
20-4	£	20-4		£
		5 Jan	Purchases PDB57	96
		16 Jan	Purchases PDB57	48

Dr		Sanders & Sons (PL495)		Cr
20-4	£	20-4		£
		20 Jan	Purchases PDB57	192

Dr		D Webster (PL730)		Cr
20-4	£	20-4		£
		9 Jan	Purchases PDB57	144

Notes:

■ the purchases day book incorporates a reference column, used to cross-reference each transaction to the account of each supplier in the payables ledger (PL); this enables a particular transaction to be traced from financial document (invoice received), through the book of prime entry (purchases day book), to the supplier's account

■ each entry in the payables ledger is cross-referenced back to the page number of the purchases day book; here the reference is 'PDB57'

subsidiary accounts/memorandum accounts

The accounts in payables ledger are prepared following the principles of double-entry bookkeeping. However, they are **subsidiary accounts** which means they are used to provide a note of how much each trade payable is owed by the business.

Subsidiary accounts are not part of double-entry but are represented in the general ledger by payables ledger control account. This means that, here, the £480 credit entry is split up in the payables ledger between the three suppliers' subsidiary accounts. Note that subsidiary accounts are often referred to as **memorandum accounts**.

ACCOUNTING SYSTEM FOR PURCHASES RETURNS

Purchases returns (or returns out) are when goods previously bought on credit are returned by the business to its suppliers. A credit note (see page 30) is requested and, when received, it is entered in the accounting system to reduce the amount owing to the trade payable.

The accounting procedures for purchases returns involve:

- **financial documents** – credit notes received from suppliers

- **book of prime entry** – purchases returns day book

- **double-entry accounts** – general ledger (purchases returns account, which records the total net amount of credit notes received; Value Added Tax account, which records the VAT amount of purchases returns; and payables ledger control account, which records the liability to trade payables)

- **payables ledger** – the subsidiary accounts for each individual trade payable of the business

The way in which the accounting system for purchases returns fits together is shown in the diagram on the next page.

accounting system for purchases returns

GOODS RETURNED TO THE SUPPLIER
credit note (financial document) received from supplier

PURCHASES RETURNS DAY BOOK
book of prime entry

GENERAL LEDGER
double-entry accounts

debit to

- payables ledger
  control account

credit to

- purchases returns
  account

- VAT account

PAYABLES LEDGER
subsidiary accounts

debit to

- trade payables'
  (suppliers') accounts

We will now look in more detail at the purchases returns day book and the double-entry accounts for purchases returns. Note that the business is registered for Value Added Tax.

PURCHASES RETURNS DAY BOOK

The purchases returns day book uses virtually the same layout as the purchases day book seen earlier in this chapter. It operates in a similar way, storing up information about purchases returns transactions until such time as a transfer is made into the double-entry accounts system. The prime documents for purchases returns day book are credit notes received from suppliers.

The purchases returns day book is written up as follows, with sample entries:

Purchases Returns Day Book						PRDB3
Date	**Supplier name**	**Credit note no**	**Account code**	**Total**	**VAT***	**Net**
20-4				£	£	£
20 Jan	D Webster	123	PL730	48	8	40
27 Jan	Sanders & Sons	406	PL495	96	16	80
31 Jan	Totals for month			144	24	120
				GL2350	GL2200	GL5110

* VAT = 20%

Notes:

- the purchases returns day book is prepared from credit notes received from suppliers. The credit note number used is either that of the supplier's credit note (as above) or is a unique number given to each credit note by the buyer's accounts department

- the day book is totalled at appropriate intervals – weekly or monthly

- the VAT-inclusive amounts from the total column are debited to the trade payables' individual accounts in the payables ledger

- the total of the VAT column is transferred to the credit of the VAT account in the general ledger

- the total of the net column tells the business the amount of purchases returns for the period. This amount is transferred to the credit of purchases returns account in the general ledger

- the total or gross column records the amount of each credit note received, ie after VAT has been included. This amount is transferred to the debit of payables ledger control account in general ledger

BOOKKEEPING FOR PURCHASES RETURNS

After the purchases returns day book has been written up and totalled, the information from it is transferred into the double-entry system. The accounts in the general ledger to record the transactions from the above purchases returns day book (including any other transactions already recorded on these accounts) are as follows:

GENERAL LEDGER

Dr			Value added tax account (GL2200)		Cr
20-4		£	20-4		£
31 Jan	Purchases Day		31 Jan	Purchases Returns	
	Book PDB57	80		Day Book PRDB3	24

Dr			Payables ledger control account (GL2350)		Cr
20-4		£	20-4		£
31 Jan	Purchases Returns		31 Jan	Purchases Day	
	Day Book PRDB3	144		Book PDB57	480

Dr			Purchases returns account (GL5110)		Cr
20-4		£	20-4		£
			31 Jan	Purchases Returns	
				Day Book PRDB3	120

The last step is to record the amount of purchases returns made to each trade payable. We do this by recording the purchases returns in the subsidiary accounts for each trade payable in the payables ledger as follows:

PAYABLES LEDGER

Dr			Sanders & Sons (PL495)		Cr
20-4		£	20-4		£
27 Jan	Purchases				
	Returns PRDB3	96	20 Jan	Purchases PDB57	192

Dr			D Webster (PL730)		Cr
20-4		£	20-4		£
20 Jan	Purchases				
	Returns PRDB3	48	9 Jan	Purchases PDB57	144

ACCOUNTING SYSTEM FOR DISCOUNTS RECEIVED

We have already seen, on pages 35-36, the two methods permitted by HM Revenue & Customs to account for the Value Added Tax when a prompt payment discount (PPD) is offered by the supplier.

In this section we see how the accounting for PPD in the customer's (buyer's) books, ie discounts received, is carried out using the method where a credit note is issued by the supplier. Note that this method is used by AAT to assess PPD transactions.

When accounting for discounts received by using credit notes, a Discounts Received Day Book (DRDB) is used to record credit notes issued by the supplier for PPD and received by the customer. The accounting system is shown below.

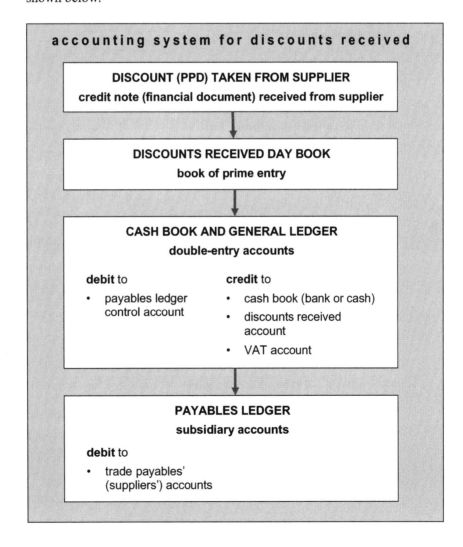

We will now look in detail at the discounts received day book and the double-entry accounts to record prompt payment discount in the books of the customer (buyer). Note that the business is registered for Value Added Tax.

DISCOUNTS RECEIVED DAY BOOK

Discounts received day book (DRDB) uses virtually the same layout as the purchases day book seen on page 188.

In order to see how the discounts received day book and the bookkeeping entries are recorded we will use the following purchases invoice received by Lea Ltd from the supplier, Bialas & Co:

INVOICE

Number 2120

From Bialas & Co   4 April 20-4

To Lea Ltd

	£
Goods Net	500.00
VAT	100.00
Total	600.00

Terms: 5% prompt payment discount for payment within ten days

---

Note: if the supplier is paid after ten days, the payment will be for £600 and no PPD entries will be required.

If the supplier is paid within ten days, the payment will be net £475, VAT £95, total £570. The supplier will issue a credit note for £30 (ie £25 + VAT £5) which will be recorded by the customer in the discounts received day book as follows:

Discounts Received Day Book						DRDB1
Date	Supplier name	Credit note no	Account code	Total	VAT	Net
20-4				£	£	£
10 April	Bialas & Co	CN42*	PL204	30	5	25
30 April	Totals for month			30	5	25
				GL2350	GL2200	GL3490

*Note that the credit note received from the supplier is recorded here as a CN, using the supplier's credit note number – 'CN 42' used as an example.

Notes:

- the discounts received day book is prepared from credit notes for PPD received from suppliers

- the day book is totalled at appropriate intervals – weekly or monthly (only one transaction in the example on the previous page)

- the VAT-inclusive amounts from the total column are debited to the trade payables' individual subsidiary accounts in the payables ledger

- the total of the VAT column is transferred to the credit of the VAT account in the general ledger

- the total of the net column tells the business the amount of discounts received for the period. This amount is transferred to the credit of discounts received account in the general ledger

- the total column records the amount of each credit note received, ie after VAT has been included. This amount is transferred to the debit of payables ledger control account in the general ledger

BOOKKEEPING FOR DISCOUNTS RECEIVED

After the discounts received day book has been written up and totalled, the information from it is transferred into the double-entry system as follows:

Cash Book* (credit side)								CB025
Date	Details	Account code	Cash	Bank	VAT	Cash purchases	Trade payables	Other expenses
20-4			£	£	£	£	£	£
10 April	Bialas & Co	PL204		570			570	

*The layout of the cash book is explained fully in Chapter 9

GENERAL LEDGER

Dr	Discounts received account (GL3490)		Cr
20-4	£	20-4	£
		10 April Discounts Received Day Book DRDB1	25

Dr	Value added tax account (GL2200)		Cr
20-4	£	20-4	£
		10 April Discounts Received Day Book DRDB1	5

Dr		Payables ledger control account (GL2350)		Cr
20-4		£	20-4	£
10 April	Bank CB025	570		
10 April	Discounts Received			
	Day Book DRDB1	30		

The last step is to record the amount of discounts received in the subsidiary account of the trade payable in the payables ledger as follows:

PAYABLES LEDGER

Dr		Bialas & Co (PL204)				Cr
20-4		£	20-4			£
10 April	Bank CB025	570	4 April	Purchases	PDB	600
10 April	Discounts Received					
	Day Book DRDB1	30				

THE USE OF ANALYSED PURCHASES DAY BOOKS

Businesses use analysed day books whenever they wish to analyse purchases and purchases returns between different categories of purchases:

- goods bought for resale, often split between types of goods purchased, eg in a clothes shop between ladies wear and mens wear

- purchases made by different departments, eg within a department store

For example, a business with two different types of purchases – purchases type 1 and purchases type 2 – will write up its purchases day book as follows:

Purchases Day Book								PDB86
Date	Supplier name	Invoice number	Account code	Total	VAT*	Net	Purchases type 1	Purchases type 2
20-4				£	£	£	£	£
2 Sep	Fashions Limited	1401	PL087	144	24	120	70	50
4 Sep	Eastern Telephones	1402	PL061	240	40	200	–	200
8 Sep	Mercian Models	1403	PL102	336	56	280	280	–
12 Sep	Media Advertising	1404	PL092	720	120	600	–	600
15 Sep	Style Limited	1405	PL379	480	80	400	100	300
19 Sep	Wyvern Motors	1406	PL423	192	32	160	–	160
30 Sep	Totals for month			2,112	352	1,760	450	1,310
				GL2350	GL2200		GL5160	GL5190

* VAT = 20%

Analysed purchases day books and purchases returns day books can be adapted to suit the particular needs of a business. Thus there is not a standard way in which to present the books of prime entry – the needs of the user of the information are all important. By using analysed day books, the owner of the business can see how much has been bought by types of purchases, or by departments.

Notes:

■ in this purchases day book, each purchases invoice has been given a unique number (starting at 1401) by the buyer's accounts department

■ the account code column is to 'PL' (Payables Ledger) and the supplier's account number

■ the code 'GL' beneath the totals amounts refers to the account numbers in General Ledger

■ the analysis columns – here purchases type 1 and purchases type 2 – show the amount of purchases net of VAT (ie before VAT is added)

■ the analysis columns analyse the net amount – by type of expenditure – from purchases invoices

Case
Study

WYVERN TRADERS – PURCHASES AND RETURNS

This Case Study shows how credit purchases and purchases returns are recorded in the accounting system of a business. The Case Study makes use of:

- **books of prime entry**
  - purchases day book
  - purchases returns day book

- **general ledger accounts**
  - purchases account
  - purchases returns account
  - Value Added Tax account
  - payables ledger control account

- **payables ledger accounts**

  - trade payables' subsidiary accounts

The Chapter Summary (pages 203-205) includes diagrams which summarise the procedures for recording credit purchases and purchases returns transactions in the accounting system.

situation

Wyvern Traders is a wholesaler of stationery and office equipment. The business is registered for VAT. The VAT rate is 20%. The following are the credit purchases and purchases returns transactions for April 20-4:

20-4	
1 Apr	Purchased goods from Midland Supplies, £120.00 + VAT, its invoice no 12486
9 Apr	Returned goods to Midland Supplies, £40.00 + VAT, credit note no 104 received
14 Apr	Purchased goods from Swan Equipment, £80.00 + VAT, its invoice no P076
26 Apr	Purchased goods from Swan Equipment, £160.00 + VAT, its invoice no P102
30 Apr	Returned goods to Swan Equipment, £80.00 + VAT, credit note no X102 received

solution

The day books, general ledger and purchases ledger accounts are illustrated on the next two pages: arrows indicate the transfers from the day books to the individual accounts. Note that some accounts have been repeated on both pages in order to show, on the same page, the accounts relating to a particular day book: in practice a business would keep all the transactions together in one account.

Purchases Day Book						PDB19
Date	Supplier name	Invoice number	Account code	Total	VAT	Net
20-4				£	£	£
1 Apr	Midland Supplies	12486	PL045	144	24	120
14 Apr	Swan Equipment	P076	PL112	96	16	80
28 Apr	Swan Equipment	P102	PL112	192	32	160
30 Apr	Totals for month			432	72	360
				GL2350	GL2200	GL5100

General Ledger

Dr	Payables ledger control account (GL2350)					Cr
Date	Details	£	Date	Details		£
20-4			20-4			
			30 Apr	Purchases Day Book PDB19		432

Dr	Value added tax account (GL2200)					Cr
Date	Details	£	Date	Details		£
20-4 30 Apr	Purchases Day Book PDB19	72	20-4			

Dr	Purchases account (GL5100)					Cr
Date	Details	£	Date	Details		£
20-4 30 Apr	Purchases Day Book PDB19	360	20-4			

Payables Ledger

Dr	Midland Supplies (PL045)					Cr
Date	Details	£	Date	Details		£
20-4			20-4			
			1 Apr	Purchases PDB19		144

Dr	Swan Equipment (PL112)					Cr
Date	Details	£	Date	Details		£
20-4			20-4			
			14 Apr	Purchases PDB19		96
			28 Apr	Purchases PDB19		192

Purchases Returns Day Book						PRDB7
Date	Supplier name	Credit note number	Reference	Total	VAT	Net
20-4				£	£	£
9 Apr	Midland Supplies	104	PL045	48	8	40
30 Apr	Swan Equipment	X102	PL112	96	16	80
30 Apr	Totals for month			144	24	120
				GL2350	GL2200	GL5110

General Ledger

Dr	Payables ledger control account (GL2350)					Cr
Date	Details	£	Date	Details		£
20-4			20-4			
30 Apr	Purchases Returns Day Book PRDB7	144	30 Apr	Purchases Day Book PDB19		*432

Dr	Value added tax account (GL2200)					Cr
Date	Details	£	Date	Details		£
20-4			20-4			
30 Apr	Purchases Day Book PDB19	*72	30 Apr	Purchases Returns Day Book PRDB7		24

Dr	Purchases returns account (GL5110)					Cr
Date	Details	£	Date	Details		£
20-4			20-4			
			30 Apr	Purchases Returns Day Book PRDB7		120

Payables Ledger

Dr	Midland Supplies (PL045)					Cr
Date	Details	£	Date	Details		£
20-4			20-4			
9 Apr	Purchases Returns PRDB7	48	1 Apr	Purchases PDB19		*144

Dr	Swan Equipment (PL112)					Cr
Date	Details	£	Date	Details		£
20-4			20-4			
30 Apr	Purchases Returns PRDB7	96	14 Apr	Purchases PDB19		*96
			28 Apr	Purchases PDB19		*192

*transactions entered previously

Chapter Summary

The diagrams on the next two pages summarise the material we have studied in this chapter. They show the procedures for recording transactions in the accounting system for credit purchases, purchases returns, and discounts received.

Further chapter summary points follow on page 206.

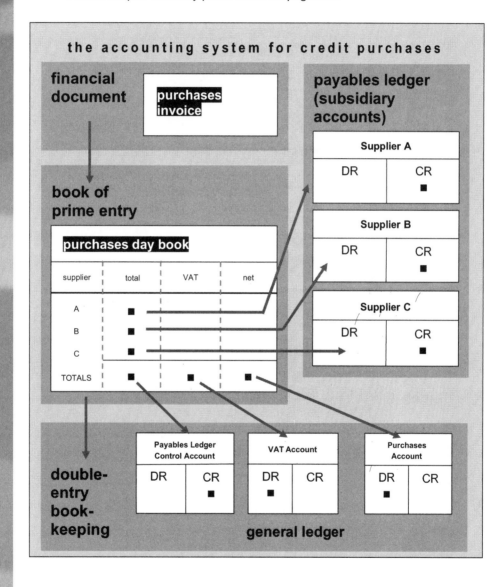

the accounting system for credit purchases

the accounting system for purchases returns

financial document

credit note

payables ledger (subsidiary accounts)

Supplier A	
DR	CR
■	

Supplier B	
DR	CR
■	

book of prime entry

purchases returns day book

supplier	total	VAT	net
A	■		
B	■		
TOTALS	■	■	■

double-entry book-keeping

Payables Ledger Control Account	
DR	CR
■	

VAT Account	
DR	CR
	■

Purchases Returns Account	
DR	CR
	■

general ledger

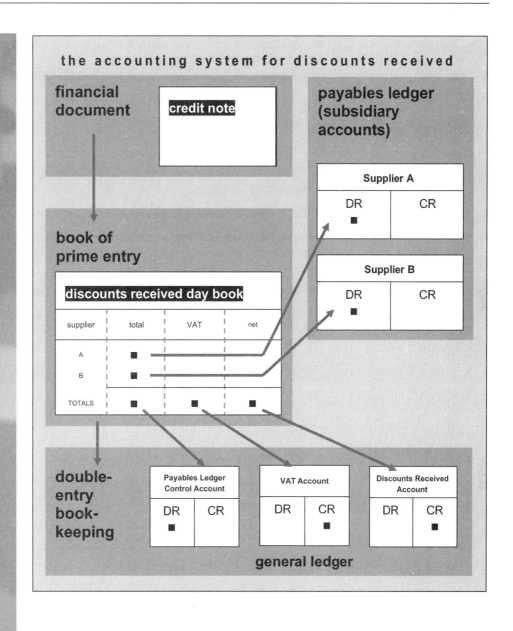

the accounting system for discounts received

- The accounting system comprises a number of specific stages of recording and presenting financial transactions:

  – financial documents

  – books of prime entry (eg day books)

  – double-entry bookkeeping

  – trial balance

- The financial documents relating to credit purchases are:

  – purchases invoices

  – credit notes for purchases returns and discounts received

- Purchases day book is the book of prime entry for credit purchases. It is prepared from purchases invoices received from suppliers.

- Purchases returns day book is the book of prime entry for purchases returns. It is prepared from credit notes received from suppliers.

- Discounts received day book is the book of prime entry for discounts received. It is prepared from credit notes for prompt payment discount received from suppliers.

- Analysed purchases and purchases returns day books are used when a business wishes to analyse its purchases between different types of expenditure.

- Recording credit purchases in the double-entry system uses:

  – financial documents, purchases invoices

  – book of prime entry, purchases day book

  – double-entry accounts in the general ledger

  – subsidiary accounts in the payables ledger

- Recording purchases returns in the double-entry system uses:

  – financial documents, credit notes for purchases returns received from suppliers

  – book of prime entry, purchases returns day book

  – double-entry accounts in the general ledger

  – subsidiary accounts in the payables ledger

- Recording discounts received in the double-entry system uses:

  – financial documents, credit notes for prompt payment discount received from suppliers

  – book of prime entry, discounts received day book

  – double-entry accounts in the general ledger

  – subsidiary accounts in the payables ledger

Key Terms		
	purchases	the purchase of goods with the intention that they should be resold at a profit
	revenue expenditure	the cost of purchases and running costs of the business
	capital expenditure	the cost of asset items other than for resale, purchased in connection with the running of the business, eg buildings, shop fittings
	purchases day book	book of prime entry prepared from purchases invoices
	purchases returns	goods purchased on credit which are returned to the supplier
	discounts received	prompt payment discount offered by a supplier to customers in order to encourage customers to settle up straightaway or in a short time from the invoice date; it is discounts received in the accounting system of the buyer
	purchases returns day book	book of prime entry prepared from credit notes received from suppliers
	discounts received day book	book of prime entry prepared from credit notes for prompt payment discount received from sellers
	analysed day books	day books which incorporate analysis columns, for example between
		– goods bought for resale, often split between different types of goods
		– purchases made by different departments
	general ledger	ledger section which includes
		– purchases account
		– purchases returns account
		– discounts received account
		– payables ledger control account
		– Value Added Tax account
	payables ledger	subsidiary ledger section which contains the subsidiary accounts of the trade payables (suppliers)
	subsidiary account (memorandum account)	a subsidiary ledger (eg payables ledger) account which provides a record of individual amounts (eg owing by the business to trade payables)

Activities

7.1 Which **one** of the following is a book of prime entry?

(a)	Purchases account	
(b)	Value Added Tax account	
(c)	Purchases returns day book	
(d)	Payables ledger account of M Ostrowski	

7.2 Which **one** of the following is in the right order?

(a)	Purchases returns day book; payables ledger control account; credit note issued; purchases returns account; VAT account; supplier's account	
(b)	Purchases returns account; VAT account; supplier's account; payables ledger control account; purchases returns day book; credit note issued	
(c)	Purchases returns day book; purchases returns account; VAT account; payables ledger control account; supplier's account; credit note issued	
(d)	Credit note issued; purchases returns day book; purchases returns account; VAT account; payables ledger control account; supplier's account	

7.3 Which **one** of the following is the correct general ledger entries for a discounts received transaction?

(a)	Debit payables ledger control; debit VAT; credit discounts received	
(b)	Debit payables ledger control; credit discounts received; credit VAT	
(c)	Debit discounts received; debit VAT; credit payables ledger control	
(d)	Debit discounts received; credit payables ledger control; credit VAT	

7.4 Explain in note format:

(a) The principles of recording a credit purchases transaction in the accounting system.

(b) The principles of recording a purchases returns transaction in the accounting system.

For Activities 7.5 and 7.6:

- work in pounds and pence, where appropriate

- the rate of Value Added Tax is to be calculated at 20% (when calculating VAT amounts, you should ignore fractions of a penny, ie round down to a whole penny)

- use a coding system incorporating the following:

purchases day book	– PDB36	general ledger account numbers	
purchases returns day book	– PRDB11	payables ledger control account	– GL2350
payables ledger account numbers		purchases account	– GL5100
AMC Enterprises	– PL520	purchases returns account	– GL5110
S Green	– PL574	Value Added Tax account	– GL2200
I Johnstone	– PL604		
Mercia Manufacturing	– PL627		
L Murphy	– PL659		
Severn Supplies	– PL721		

7.5 During April 20-5, Wyvern Wholesalers had the following credit transactions:

20-5

2 Apr   Purchased goods from Severn Supplies £250 + VAT, invoice no 6789

5 Apr   Purchased goods from I Johnstone £210 + VAT, invoice no A241

9 Apr   Purchased goods from L Murphy £185 + VAT, invoice no 2456

15 Apr   Purchased goods from Mercia Manufacturing £180 + VAT, invoice no X457

19 Apr   Purchased goods from AMC Enterprises £345 + VAT, invoice no AMC 456

26 Apr   Purchased goods from S Green £395 + VAT, invoice no 2846

You are to:

(a) Record the above transactions in Wyvern Wholesaler's purchases day book for April 20-5, using the format shown on the next page.

(b) Record the accounting entries in Wyvern Wholesaler's general ledger and payables ledger.

(Note that you will need to retain these ledger accounts for use with Activity 7.6)

Purchases Day Book						PDB36
Date	Supplier name	Invoice number	Account code	Total £	VAT £	Net £

7.6 The following are the purchases returns of Wyvern Wholesalers for April 20-5. They are to be:

(a) Recorded in the purchases returns day book for April 20-5, using the format shown below.

(b) Recorded in the general ledger and payables ledger (use the ledgers already prepared in the answer to Activity 7.5).

20-5

7 Apr   Returned goods to Severn Supplies £50 + VAT, credit note no 225 received

14 Apr   Returned goods to L Murphy £80 + VAT, credit note no X456 received

21 Apr   Returned goods to AMC Enterprises £125 + VAT, credit note no 3921 received

29 Apr   Returned goods to S Green £68 + VAT, credit note no SG247 received

Purchases Returns Day Book						PRDB11
Date	Supplier name	Credit note number	Account code	Total £	VAT £	Net £

7.7 You are employed by Hussein Limited as an accounts assistant. The business has a manual accounting system. Double-entry takes place in the general ledger; individual accounts of trade payables are kept as subsidiary accounts in the payables ledger. The VAT rate is 20%.

Notes:

- show your answer with a tick, words or figures, as appropriate

- coding is not required

(a) The following credit transactions all took place on 30 April 20-4 and have been recorded in the purchases day book as shown below. No entries have yet been made into the ledger system.

Purchases day book

Date 20-4	Supplier name	Invoice number	Total £	VAT £	Net £
30 April	Seng Ltd	4517	1,152	192	960
30 April	Peall & Co	2384	2,832	472	2,360
30 April	Knightons	A761	4,176	696	3,480
30 April	Galeazzi plc	7248	1,488	248	1,240
	Totals		9,648	1,608	8,040

What will be the entries in the general ledger?

General ledger

Account name	Amount £	Debit	Credit

What will be the entries in the payables ledger?

Payables ledger

Account name	Amount £	Debit	Credit

(b) The following credit transactions all took place on 30 April 20-4 and have been entered into the purchases returns day book as shown below. No entries have yet been made into the ledger system.

Purchases returns day book

Date 20-4	Supplier name	Credit note number	Total £	VAT £	Net £
30 April	Martin & Co	381	1,056	176	880
30 April	Wentworth Stores	C48	672	112	560
	Totals		1,728	288	1,440

What will be the entries in the general ledger?

General ledger

Account name	Amount £	Debit	Credit

What will be the entries in the payables ledger?

Payables ledger

Account name	Amount £	Debit	Credit

(c)   The following discounts received transactions all took place on 30 April 20-4 and have been recorded in the discounts received day book as shown below. No entries have yet been made into the ledger system.

Discounts received day book

Date 20-4	Supplier name	Credit note number	Total £	VAT £	Net £
30 April	Kumar Ltd	CN070	12	2	10
30 April	Prior & Co	CN594	60	10	50
	Totals		72	12	60

What will be the entries in the general ledger?

General ledger

Account name	Amount £	Debit	Credit

What will be the entries in the payables ledger?

Payables ledger

Account name	Amount £	Debit	Credit

7.8 The following is taken from the coding lists used at a business called Fashion Trading.

Supplier	Purchases ledger account code
Bingham Fashions	BIN001
Bourne Stores	BOU002
Elite Trading	ELI001
Green Dragon	GRE001
Guest & Co	GUE002
High Society	HIG001
Modes Ltd	MOD001
Myers Trading	MYE002
Treetop Stores	TRE001
Wragby Ltd	WRA001
Zeta & Co	ZET001

You are to set up the payables ledger account codes for the new suppliers shown below.

Supplier	Payables ledger account code
Bridon Ltd	
Foster & Co	
Hirst & Co	

7.9 Purchases invoices have been prepared and partially recorded in the purchases day book, as shown below.

(a) Complete the entries in the purchases day book by inserting the appropriate figures for each invoice.

(b) Total the last five columns of the purchases day book.

Purchases day book

Date 20-4	Supplier name	Invoice number	Total £	VAT £	Net £	Purchases type 1 £	Purchases type 2 £
30 June	Canoy Ltd	C350	1,608		1,340	1,340	
30 June	McVeigh & Co	5148		390			1,950
30 June	Robinsons	R/862	2,952			2,460	
	Totals						

7.10 You are the bookkeeper at Grey's Retail Ltd and are processing supplier invoices. The following invoice has been received:

Coffee Supplies	
Invoice no: 96348	

To: Grey's Retail Ltd
Date: 28 April 20-6

	£
6 coffee machines at £55.60 each	333.60
VAT @ 20%	66.72
TOTAL	400.32

Payment by BACS preferred

(a) You are to record the invoice in the digital bookkeeping system by:

- selecting the correct daybook

- making the appropriate entries on the available line in the day book

- totalling the total, VAT and net columns

Daybook	
Sales day book	
Purchases returns day book	
Purchases day book	
Discounts received day book	

Date 20-6	Name	Invoice number	Total £	VAT £	Net £
5 Apr	Razaq Ltd	2470	650.82	108.47	542.35
12 Apr	Coffee Supplies	96331	433.74	72.29	361.45
22 Apr	Francis Fashions	FF/274	993.48	165.58	827.90
24 Apr	Etter Trading	691	209.54	34.92	174.62
	TOTALS				

(b) Identify how the total amount you have calculated for the total column will be recorded in the general ledger.

as a debit entry to receivables ledger control account	
as a debit entry to payables ledger control account	
as a credit entry to receivables ledger control account	
as a credit entry to payables ledger control account	

(c) Identify how the total of the VAT column will be recorded in the general ledger account for VAT.

as a debit entry	
as a credit entry	

7.11 This task is about transferring data from the books of prime entry.

The totals of the purchases returns day book at the end of the month are as follows:

Details	Total £	VAT £	Net £
Total for month	732	122	610

(a) Show the entries to be made in the general ledger.

Account name	Amount £	Debit	Credit

An entry in the discounts received day book is for a credit note received from Bisain Ltd for £45 plus VAT.

(b) Show the entry in the payables ledger.

Account name	Amount £	Debit	Credit

7.12 This task is about totalling and balancing ledger accounts.

The following supplier's account is in the payables ledger at the close of the financial year on 31 May 20-1:

20-1	Details	Amount £	20-1	Details	Amount £
12 May	Bank	1,054	1 May	Balance b/f	2,109
18 May	Purchases Returns	218	24 May	Purchases	1,727
				Total	

Complete the account by:

- inserting the balance carried down, together with date and details

- inserting the totals

- inserting the balance brought down together with date and details

Note:

- for details, choose from: Balance b/d, Balance c/d, Difference

- for date, choose from: 1 May, 31 May, 1 June, 30 June

8 Process payments to suppliers

this chapter covers...

In Chapter 6 'Financial documents for purchases' we described the financial documents dealt with by a purchaser of goods and services on credit.

In this chapter we describe the next stage – processing the documentation needed when payment is to be made for the goods or services purchased.

The chapter covers the following areas:

- *a brief review of the purchasing process*

- *checking a statement of account received from a supplier against the transactions in the account of the supplier in the payables ledger*

- *identifying any discrepancies between a statement of account and transactions in the account of the supplier in the payables ledger*

- *calculating the amount due to each supplier on the correct payment date*

- *preparing remittance advices for making payment by cheque or by electronic bank transfer (eg BACS or Faster Payment)*

This chapter will not go into detail about the various bank payment systems. These are fully explained in the Osborne Books text 'Principles of Bookkeeping Controls Tutorial'.

A REVIEW OF THE PURCHASING PROCESS

When a business makes a purchase of goods on credit, it deals with a number of financial documents. These were covered in Chapter 5 and include:

- **purchase order** – issued by the buyer ordering the goods
- **delivery note** – sent with the goods by the supplier
- **goods received note** – details of goods received and any discrepancies
- **purchase invoice** – received from the supplier, setting out what is owed
- **purchase credit note** – any refund to the buyer's account for missing, damaged or incorrect goods or any mistakes on the invoice

The next stage – dealt with in this chapter – is:

- the receipt of the supplier's **statement of account** setting out what is owed; the transactions on the statement should be checked against the supplier's account in the payables ledger of the buyer
- the preparation of a **remittance advice** by the buyer, advising the supplier that payment is being made and the method of payment

This stage, and its place in the process, is shown at the bottom of the diagram on the next page.

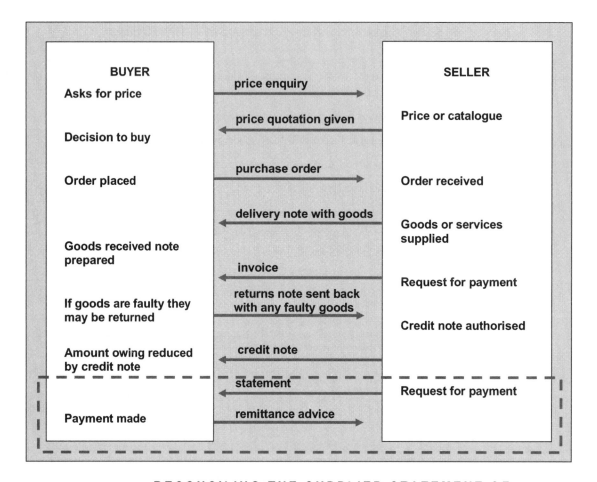

RECONCILING THE SUPPLIER STATEMENT OF ACCOUNT

Chapter 6 described the processes of checking all the purchases documentation to identify and deal with any discrepancies. The documents involved in the checking process are:

- delivery note and the actual goods received (possibly using a goods received note)

- supplier invoices and credit notes for calculation errors

- supplier invoices and credit notes against the purchase order

- credit notes for prompt payment discount (PPD)

By the time that all these checks have been made and the invoices and credit notes have been authorised, the buyer should settle up and pay the **supplier's account in the payables ledger**. This account contains details of all the transactions – invoices for purchases, credit notes for purchases returns and prompt payment discount (PPD), and payments made. The account should in fact mirror all the items which will appear in the supplier's statement of account. See the next page for an example of a **statement of account** and the supplier account in the payables ledger. This process of **reconciliation** – which basically means 'tying up' the transactions – is illustrated in the Case Study which follows.

Case Study

KNITWICK – SUPPLIER STATEMENT RECONCILIATION

situation

Knitwick Traders is a clothing company which specialises in fashion wear. It has a regular trading relationship with Medici Importers which supplies it with Italian clothes.

Medici Importers sends statements of account to Knitwick at the end of each month and Knitwick normally settles the account at the beginning of the next month. During the month of November 20-5 the following documents were sent by Medici Importers to Knitwick. They were checked by Knitwick and were found to be correct.

2 invoices:	8 November	Ref 4312	£850.00
	14 November	Ref 4367	£120.00
1 credit note:	20 November	Ref 534	£85.00

In addition, Knitwick sent £674.50 in settlement of October's account to Medici Importer's bank account by electronic bank transfer in the first week of November.

In the first week of December, Knitwick received the statement of account shown on the next page. You have been asked to reconcile the statement with the payables ledger account for Medici Importers also shown on the next page.

STATEMENT OF ACCOUNT

MEDICI IMPORTERS

8 San Marco Avenue, Broadfield, BR2 8DC

Tel 01908 765101 Fax 01908 765109 Email info@medicimporters.co.uk

VAT REG GB 0532 4672 21

TO

Knitwick Traders Unit 14 Landseer Estate Hull HU9 6CV	account	**2894**
	date	**30 11 20-5**

Date	Details	Debit £		Credit £		Balance £
01 11 20-5	Balance b/f	674.50	✓			674.50
05 11 20-5	BACS payment			674.50	✓	00.00
08 11 20-5	Invoice 4312	850.00	✓			850.00
14 11 20-5	Invoice 4367	120.00	✓			970.00
20 11 20-5	Credit note 534			85.00	✓	885.00
Electronic bank transfer: pay Medici Importers at National Bank, Account 76528607, Sort code 54 12 36				**TOTAL**		885.00

Debit		Payables Ledger: Medici Importers Account						Credit	
20-5	Details		£	p	20-5	Details		£	p
5 Nov	Bank	✓	674	50	1 Nov	Balance b/d	✓	674	50
20 Nov	Purchases returns	✓	85	00	8 Nov	Purchases	✓	850	00
					14 Nov	Purchases	✓	120	00

solution

Knitwick will compare the two documents and tick off the items which appear in both documents. These are shown here in the two different grey frames for purposes of illustration only.

All the transactions are accounted for – there are no unticked amounts which might indicate some form of discrepancy.

This means that the two documents have now been 'reconciled' – ie they both tie up with each other – and payment of the account, the £885.00 owing, can be authorised and made on the due date.

DEALING WITH DISCREPANCIES

The Case Study on the previous two pages has shown a situation where all the documentation is correct and has been reconciled; all is well and payment can then be authorised and paid on the due date in accordance with the terms of payment, eg 'Net monthly'.

It is assumed here that the relevant financial documents – eg invoices and credit notes – have already been checked for accuracy and are free from any discrepancies.

But there may sometimes be discrepancies between the **supplier's statement of account** and the supplier's account kept in the buyer's **payables ledger**. These will need to be resolved before payment can be made.

These problems may be dealt with at accounts assistant level, or if the problem is more serious, by the accounts supervisor. Examples include:

- **an invoice or credit note which appears on the supplier's statement, but for the incorrect amount**

  – the document will be held by the buyer and the amount can be verified, so this is likely to be an error made by the supplier when entering the amount in the accounts; it will need to be queried by the buyer and investigated and put right by the supplier

- **an invoice or credit note is on the supplier's statement and not in the buyer's payables ledger, ie there are incorrect details**

  – this could be an invoice or credit note not entered in the buyer's payables ledger, or to the wrong supplier's account; this should be investigated and, if there is an error by the buyer, included in the payment of account

- **an invoice or credit note is in the buyer's payables ledger and not on the supplier's statement, ie there is a missing transaction**

  – this could be an invoice or credit note not entered in the supplier's accounts, or to the wrong customer account; this item should be queried by the buyer and, if there is an error made by the supplier, included in the payment of account

- **an invoice or credit note which appears twice on the supplier's statement, ie there is a duplicated transaction**

  – this is an obvious duplication of an invoice or credit note by the supplier; the supplier should be notified of the error and the amount not included in the payment of account

■ **timing differences**

– these often occur at the end of a month when, for example, a seller issues an invoice but it is not recorded in the buyer's payables ledger until the first day or two of the new month

■ **under/over payments**

– it is always a good idea to check that payments made earlier (for example at the previous month end) have been recorded correctly on the statement of account received from the supplier; the check is from the supplier's account in payables ledger through the bank account (see next chapter) to the statement of account

■ **prompt payment discount (PPD)**

– a check should be made to ensure that a credit note on the statement of account for PPD is the same as that recorded on the supplier's account in the payables ledger; this should have been checked as part of the purchases documents, but it is always safe to double check

Accurate reconciliation of the supplier statement and payables ledger account is very important: if a payment is made and there is an undetected discrepancy, it can be very difficult to put things right.

INVOICE AUTHORISATION AND DISPUTED INVOICES

statement or no statement?

When statements are issued, businesses generally pay on receipt of the statement, as this is an easy way of calculating payment. This is the situation set out in the Case Study earlier in this chapter (see pages 221-222).

In practice, however, **statements are not always sent out by suppliers**. Some suppliers rely instead on each customer making payment of invoices when they are due, adjusting for any credit notes issued.

Whatever method is used by a buyer for making payment, certain principles remain the same:

■ invoices should be paid within the agreed payment terms, as set out on the invoice

■ invoices should be **checked** and **authorised for payment** before the payment date

invoice authorisation

In most businesses, invoices that have been checked are passed on for payments to suppliers. These invoices will then have to be **authorised** for payment.

When an invoice is checked and found to be correct, the person carrying out the check will usually mark the document and **authorise** it for payment. This authorisation can take a number of forms:

■ the checker initials and dates the invoice, and ticks it or writes 'pay' as an authorisation

■ the business may have a rubber stamp which can be used in the authorisation process. This stamp may also provide space for **coding**, eg the cost code (the account number for the type of purchase) and the purchase order reference number, which can be entered in the purchases day book and also used for internal filing purposes; it may also contain the signature or initials of the person who has authority to authorise the invoice for payment

This procedure of authorisation helps the efficiency of the business:

■ the checker's initials will be there in case of any future query on the invoice, eg an undetected error

■ the invoice will be in the system for payment on the due date in accordance with the terms of payment

disputed invoices

In this chapter so far we have assumed that a business:

■ will pay the total amount shown on the statement

■ will pay all the invoices that are due and authorised for payment

There are times, however, when a buyer might decide that an invoice on a statement should not be paid. Normally in an accounts department you will be able to see this on the statement because the invoice will not be ticked, or you may get a note from the accounts supervisor telling you not to pay certain items. The reason for this is that the invoice may be **disputed** with the supplier: for example, your business may claim that the goods supplied are incorrect.

Now read the following Case Study which explains how to calculate a payment which involves a disputed invoice.

ALDERSGATE SUPPLIES – PAYMENT OF ACCOUNT

situation

You work in the Accounts Department of Krumm & Co which is supplied with electrical equipment by Aldersgate Supplies.

It is your job to prepare the payments for suppliers at the beginning of each month. The latest statement from Aldersgate Supplies is shown on the next page and an email dated 4 December from your supervisor is set out below.

The ticks on the statement indicate the items that are recorded in the payables ledger and are to be taken into account when payment is made.

email	
from	henry@krumm.co.uk
subject	Aldersgate Supplies account - disputed invoice
date	4 December 20-5 12:01:11 GMT
to	a.student@krumm.co.uk

Hi Kasia

Please note that Invoice 16700 for £450 is in dispute. Aldersgate clearly misread our purchase order and sent the wrong equipment, but still claim that they sent us the right stuff. On no account should this invoice be paid until the dispute is settled. Thanks.

Regards

Henry

STATEMENT OF ACCOUNT
ALDERSGATE SUPPLIES
10 Aldersgate Street, London EC1A 7GH
Tel 0207 7051017 Fax 0207 7051231 Email sales@aldersgatesupplies.co.uk
VAT REG GB 6733 8372 99

TO

Krumm & Co		
56 Eccles Road	account	**26742**
Bolton		
BL7 4DF	date	**30 11 20-5**

Date	Details	Debit £	Credit £	Balance £
01 11 20-5	Balance b/f	1250.70 ✓		1250.70
04 11 20-5	BACS payment		1250.70 ✓	00.00
08 11 20-5	Invoice 16700	450.00		450.00
14 11 20-5	Invoice 16810	790.00 ✓		1240.00
20 11 20-5	Credit note 534		79.00 ✓	1161.00
27 11 20-5	Invoice 16985	800.00 ✓		1961.00
Electronic bank transfer: pay Aldersgate Supplies at HRBC Bank, Account 79001875, Sort code 41 22 01	**TOTAL**			1961.00

solution

The payment amount is worked out as follows:

		calculation (£)
1	The first two items represent the balance outstanding at the beginning of November and then the payment made by Krumm & Co. They are the same amount (a debit and a credit) and therefore cancel each other out.	0
2	Invoice 16700 for £450 is in dispute and so is not included	0
3	Invoice 16810 for £790 is added	+ 790.00
4	Credit note 534 for £79 is deducted	− 79.00
5	Invoice 16985 for £800 is added	+ 800.00
	The total payment to be made to Aldersgate Supplies	= £1511.00

The next step is to prepare a remittance advice note to advise Aldersgate Supplies of the payment being made by electronic bank transfer – see page 230.

PREPARING REMITTANCE ADVICES

allocating amounts correctly

When making payment to a supplier, it is important to allocate the amount correctly to the outstanding – or open – items in the supplier's account in the payables ledger. By allocating we mean the process of matching payments made to the outstanding items. The general rule is that payments are allocated to older transactions first, in the following order:

- opening balance

- invoices, in full or part payment

- credit notes, utilised in full or part against invoices

As we have seen, if there is an unresolved dispute on an invoice then payment may not be made on that item – which will remain outstanding – until the dispute is resolved. Where items are not paid, they will total to the balance carried forward on the supplier's account in payables ledger.

definition of a remittance advice

As we saw in Chapter 5, a **remittance advice** is a document which states that a certain amount of money is being sent by a credit customer to a supplier in settlement of an account. A remittance advice is used:

- **to accompany a cheque** – a practice which is becoming less common as fewer cheques are now used to make payment

- to advise the sending of a payment **direct to the seller's bank account** through **BACS** or **Faster Payments** electronic bank transfer systems

completing the remittance advice

A remittance advice normally takes one of two forms:

- **a list of all the items which make up the payment**

    This is very useful for the supplier as it will enable the supplier's accounts department to reconcile the incoming payment with the customer's account in the receivables ledger by ticking off all the items. Sometimes, if the account is very active the remittance advice may contain hundreds of items and take up a number of pages. Always take care to ensure that the right amount is paid without any underpayments or overpayments.

■ **notification of the total amount**

This is the simplest form of remittance advice: it sets out the fact that a payment for a certain amount is being made by cheque or electronically.

A cheque remittance advice listing individual transactions is shown below.

An explanation of the details that have to be completed on a remittance advice for an electronic bank transfer is given on the next page.

REMITTANCE ADVICE

TO   FROM

Cool Socks Limited
Unit 45 Elgar Estate,
Broadfield,
BR7 4ER

31 October 20-3

Trends
4 Friar Street
Broadfield
BR1 3RF

date	Your reference	Our reference	Payment amount
01 10 20-3	INVOICE 787923	47609	283.20
10 10 20-3	CREDIT NOTE 12157	47609	(28.32)
		CHEQUE TOTAL	254.88

Case Study

ALDERSGATE SUPPLIES – REMITTANCE ADVICE

situation – continued

You work in the Accounts Department of Krumm & Co which has a supplier, Aldersgate Supplies. You are asked to complete the remittance advice advising that a Faster Payments transfer is being sent direct to the bank account of Aldersgate Supplies.

solution

The completed document is shown below.

REMITTANCE ADVICE

FROM:

Krumm & Co

TO:
1
Aldersgate Supplies
10 Aldersgate Street, London EC1A 7GH

56 Eccles Road

Bolton BL7 4DF

3 12 20-5 **2**

date **3**	your reference **4**	our reference **5**	**6** payment amount £
17 11 20-5	Invoice 16810	PO98756	790.00
24 11 20-5	Credit note 534	PO98756	(79.00)
30 11 20-5	Invoice 16985	PO98792	800.00
FASTER PAYMENTS TOTAL		**7**	1511.00

8 THIS AMOUNT HAS BEEN PAID BY FASTER PAYMENTS TRANSFER DIRECTLY INTO YOUR BANK ACCOUNT AT HRBC BANK ACCOUNT NO 79001875 SORT CODE 41 22 01

The following details have been completed by Krumm & Co:

1   at the top left, the name and address of the supplier – Aldersgate Supplies
2   at the top right, the date of the transfer of the money – 3 December 20-5
3   'date' – the dates of each of the documents listed
4   'your reference' – the description and supplier reference numbers of the invoices and credit note listed
5   'our reference' – Krumm & Co's purchase order numbers relating to the listed documents
6   'payment amount' – the amounts of the invoices and the credit note; note that the credit note amount is in brackets because it is deducted
7   'total' – the amount being transferred to Aldersgate Supplies' bank account
8   at the bottom – details of the bank account number and sort code number of Aldersgate Supplies' bank (HRBC)

Chapter Summary

■ When a business ordering goods on credit from a supplier has checked the invoice and credit note, it will be in a position to settle up the supplier's account in payables ledger.

■ A common practice is for the supplier to issue a **statement of account** to each customer, listing all the transactions – sales, returns, payments – which will then be recorded in the **payables ledger account.**

■ It is important for the customer to check that the items on the supplier's statement of account 'tie up' with the items in the supplier's account in payables ledger. This process is known as **reconciliation**.

■ If there are any **discrepancies** between the supplier's statement of account and the payables ledger account, they must be identified and investigated. Such items will affect the amount of money that will be paid to the supplier.

■ When payment of the account is made by the buyer, the amount is calculated by totalling **authorised invoices** due for payment and deducting any **authorised credit notes** and **discrepancies** that have been found.

■ Payment on the due date is advised to the supplier by completing and sending a **remittance advice**, with details of an electronic bank transfer made to the supplier's bank account, or by enclosing a cheque.

■ Payments are allocated to the outstanding items on the supplier's account in payables ledger.

Key Terms		
	statement of account	issued by a supplier listing all the payments, invoices and credit notes on the account, and giving a total of the amount due
	payables ledger account	the account of the supplier in the accounting records of the buyer; it will also list the transactions on the account
	reconciliation	a comparison and 'tying up' of transactions in two documents – in this case the statement of account and payables ledger – in order to check for any discrepancies
	discrepancy	a difference between the transactions recorded in two separate documents, such as between the supplier's statement of account and the supplier's account in the buyer's payables ledger
	remittance advice	an advice for the supplier advising the sending of an amount of money, either by cheque or direct to their account using an electronic bank transfer
	allocation of payments	process of matching payments made to outstanding items on the supplier's account in payables ledger

Activities

8.1 The two documents that have to be reconciled to calculate the amount owing to a supplier are:

(a)	The invoice and the remittance advice	
(b)	The supplier statement and the remittance advice	
(c)	The supplier statement and the supplier's payables ledger account in the books of the buyer	
(d)	The remittance advice and the supplier's payables ledger account in the books of the buyer	

Which **one** of these options is correct?

8.2 The following must be checked and authorised for payment before a supplier payment can be prepared by a business that has received goods on credit terms:

(a)	Supplier invoice	
(b)	Delivery note	
(c)	Remittance advice	
(d)	Supplier account in the payables ledger	

Which **one** of these options is correct?

8.3 If you found two purchases invoices for £250 with the same date and invoice number listed on a supplier statement you would need to query it and:

(a)	Add £250 to the amount owing to the supplier as shown on the statement	
(b)	Deduct £250 from the amount owing to the supplier as shown on the statement	
(c)	Enter the invoice amount in the supplier's account in the payables ledger	
(d)	Pay the total amount owing as shown on the supplier statement	

Which **one** of these options is correct?

8.4 A remittance advice is used:

(a)	Instead of a cheque when paying a supplier	
(b)	Instead of an electronic bank transfer when paying a supplier	
(c)	To accompany a cheque when paying a supplier	
(d)	To request payment when returning goods	

Which **one** of these options is correct?

8.5 You work in the accounts department of Hemsley Ltd. One of your routine tasks is to reconcile the supplier statements of account with the supplier accounts in the payables ledger.

You are to reconcile the statement of account and payables ledger account of your supplier Luxon Traders shown below. If you find any discrepancies:

- explain what the error could be

- suggest what you would do to resolve the problem

- state the amount you think the payment should be

STATEMENT OF ACCOUNT

LUXON TRADERS
56 High Street, Fowey, Cornwall, TR4 9DS
info@luxontraders.co.uk

TO:

Hemsley Limited
6 Enterprise Park
Luton
LU7 3BN

account   **9133**

date   **31 03 20-1**

Date	Details	Debit £	Credit £	Balance £
01 03 20-1	Balance b/f	156.00		156.00
05 03 20-1	BACS payment		156.00	00.00
08 03 20-1	Invoice 76333	150.00		150.00
08 03 20-1	Invoice 76333	150.00		300.00
20 03 20-1	Credit note 923		50.00	250.00
			TOTAL	250.00

Debit	Payables Ledger: Luxon Traders Account				Credit		
20-1	Details	£	p	20-1	Details	£	p
5 Mar	Bank	156	00	1 Mar	Balance b/d	156	00
20 Mar	Purchases returns	50	00	8 Mar	Purchases	150	00

8.6 You work in the accounts department of R J Powell Ltd. One of your routine tasks is to reconcile the supplier statements of account with the supplier accounts in the payables ledger.

You are to reconcile the statement of account and payables ledger account of your supplier A Krauss Limited shown below. If you find any discrepancies:

- explain what the error could be

- suggest what you would do to resolve the problem

- state the amount you think the payment should be

STATEMENT OF ACCOUNT

A Krauss Limited

213 Farringdon Road, Latcham, LA4 5FG
sales@akrausstrading.co.uk

TO:

R J Powell Limited

48 Heathside Street

Broadheath

WR2 8NB

| account | **32123** |
| date | **30 04 20-1** |

Date	Details	Debit £	Credit £	Balance £
01 04 20-1	Balance b/f	990.00		990.00
07 04 20-1	BACS payment		990.00	00.00
09 04 20-1	Invoice 12856	233.25		233.25
19 04 20-1	Invoice 12932	109.50		342.75
			TOTAL	342.75

Debit	Payables Ledger: A Krauss Limited Account						Credit	
20-1	**Details**	£	p	**20-1**	**Details**	£	p
7 Apr	Bank	990	00	1 Apr	Balance b/d	990	00
22 Apr	Purchases returns	72	90	9 Apr	Purchases	233	25
				19 Apr	Purchases	109	50

8.7 Complete the remittance advice on the bottom of the page, using the details and the ticked items on the statement shown below. The purchase order number for the invoices are PO85262 and PO85271, and for the credit note PO85248. The bank details are on the advice. The date is 3 October.

STATEMENT OF ACCOUNT
ALDERSGATE SUPPLIES

10 Aldersgate Street, London EC1A 7GH
Tel 0207 7051017 Fax 0207 7051231 Email sales@aldersgatesupplies.co.uk
VAT REG GB 6733 8372 99

TO:

Hetherington Limited Unit 23 Wessex Estate Langborne Road Seatown SE8 5VZ	account	**26742**
	date	**30 09 20-5**

Date	Details	Debit £		Credit £		Balance £
01 09 20-5	Balance b/f	550.00	✓			550.00
04 09 20-5	BACS payment			550.00	✓	00.00
08 09 20-5	Invoice 10945	120.75	✓			120.75
14 09 20-5	Invoice 10963	380.25	✓			501.00
20 09 20-5	Credit note 109			46.00	✓	455.00
Electronic bank transfer: pay Aldersgate Supplies at HRBC Bank, Account 79001875, Sort code 41 22 01		**TOTAL**				455.00

BACS REMITTANCE
ADVICE

TO:

FROM:

Hetherington Limited
Unit 23 Wessex Estate
Langborne Road
Seatown SE8 5VZ

date:

date	your reference	our reference	payment amount £
		TOTAL	

THIS AMOUNT HAS BEEN PAID BY FASTER PAYMENTS TRANSFER DIRECTLY INTO YOUR BANK ACCOUNT AT HRBC BANK ACCOUNT NO 79001875, SORT CODE 41 22 01

8.8 Hetherington Limited also sends out cheques with some remittance advices.

Complete the cheque remittance advice and cheque set out below. You should not sign the cheque as only a director has authority to do so. The settlement details are as follows:

Date: 5 June 20-5

Supplier: Sutherland & Co, 67 Great March Street, Eastwick, EA3 9JN

Invoice 7856 for £345.90 dated 23 May 20-5, purchase order 472984

Credit note 4562 for £87.50 dated 29 May 20-5, purchase order 472975

REMITTANCE ADVICE

FROM:

Hetherington Limited
Unit 23 Wessex Estate
Langborne Road
Seatown SE8 5VZ

TO:

date:

date	your reference	our reference	payment amount £
		CHEQUE TOTAL	

Southern Bank PLC

Mereford Branch

16 Broad Street, Mereford MR1 7TR

date _____ 97-76-54

Pay _____ Account payee only only

£

HETHERINGTON LTD

123456   97 76 54   68384939   Director

8.9 You are the bookkeeper at Rannie Limited. It is the policy of Rannie Limited to check statements of account when they are received and to include in the payment only those transactions from the statement that are shown in the supplier's account in payables ledger.

The following is the supplier account activity from the digital bookkeeping system for Ribeiro & Co:

Supplier activity report: Ribeiro & Co			
Date **20-9**	**Details**	**Debit** **£**	**Credit** **£**
1 May	Balance b/f		4,085
2 May	Credit note CN 34	236	
6 May	Bank payment	4,085	
12 May	Invoice 4176		1,215
18 May	Invoice 4218		2,608
25 May	Invoice 4265		964

(a) The statement of account from the supplier is below. You are to identify the **three** items in the statement of account that should not be included in the payment because they are missing from the supplier activity report.

Ribeiro & Co Hillier Road, Rimmington, RM2 5TP STATEMENT OF ACCOUNT: Rannie Ltd				
Date **20-9**	**Document** **number**	**Details**	**Amount** **£**	**✓**
2 May	CN 34	Goods returned	–236	
12 May	4176	Goods	1,215	
15 May	4198	Goods	878	
18 May	4218	Goods	2,608	
25 May	4265	Goods	964	
28 May	CN 45	Goods returned	–147	
31 May	4310	Goods	1,876	

(b) Payment to Ribeiro & Co will be made on 6 June 20-9.

Complete the remittance advice, below, for the payment.

Rannie Ltd BACS Remittance Advice To:		
Date	**Your reference**	**Amount** **£**
	TOTAL	

8.10 You are the bookkeeper at Kimber Limited. A statement of account for June 20-7 has been received from a supplier, Fairhead Limited.

The following is an extract from your digital bookkeeping system of the June purchases from Fairhead Limited and its statement of account:

June purchases list: Fairhead Ltd

Date 20-7	Details	Amount £
3 June	Invoice 5621	2,310
7 June	Credit note 105	−225
15 June	Invoice 5722	1,804
18 June	Credit note 109	−151
20 June	Invoice 5794	976

Statement of account: Fairhead Ltd
To: Kimber Ltd
30 June 20-7

Date 20-7	Details	Amount £
3 June	Invoice 5621	2,300
15 June	Invoice 5722	1,804
18 June	Credit note 901	−151
30 June	Invoice 5794	976
	TOTAL	4,929

You are to identify the discrepancies (if any) between the transactions from the purchases list and the transactions on the statement of account.

20-7	Details	£	Discrepancies
3 June	Invoice 5621	2,310	
7 June	Credit note 105	−225	
15 June	Invoice 5722	1,804	
18 June	Credit note 109	−151	
20 June	Invoice 5794	976	

For the discrepancies column, choose from the following options (use each once only):

No discrepancy
Incorrect amount
Not on statement
Incorrect date
Incorrect credit note number

9 Cash book

this chapter covers...

Cash book records the money transactions of the business, such as receiving payments from customers, and making payments to suppliers and for other expenses. Such money transactions are received and paid either in cash, by cheque, debit or credit card, and Faster Payments.

In this chapter:

- *we look at how financial transactions are recorded in a two column cash book with money columns for bank and cash*
- *we extend the money columns of the cash book to include analysis between VAT, trade receivables, trade payables, cash sales, cash purchases, income and expenses*
- *we see how cash book is written up from financial transactions, is totalled and balanced*

The cash book of a business is usually controlled by the cashier. Entries made in cash book must be transferred to the general ledger, receivables ledger and payables ledger.

There are two Case Studies in this chapter. The first is for a business that is just setting up using a two column cash book; the second is for an established business using an analysed cash book. In both Case Studies we examine how the financial transactions are transferred from cash book to the ledgers.

The recording of entries in a cashbook is carried out easily using digital bookkeeping systems such as:

- *spreadsheet templates, appropriate for small businesses*
- *online tools such as apps and cloud-based accounting software, appropriate for small to medium businesses*
- *desktop finance software, appropriate for medium to large businesses*

CASH BOOK IN THE ACCOUNTING SYSTEM

Cash book is used to record the money transactions of the business – both in cash and through the bank. It is the book of prime entry for bank receipts and payments. There are two ways in which cash book is used in the accounting system:

- either the cash book combines the roles of the book of prime entry and double-entry bookkeeping

- or the cash book is the book of prime entry only and a separate bank account is kept in general ledger in order to complete double-entry bookkeeping

These two methods will be examined in detail later in this chapter.

Note that, as well as the cash book, businesses often have a petty cash book which is used for low-value cash payments for purchases and expenses. We will study petty cash book in Chapter 10.

USES OF THE CASH BOOK

The cash book records the money transactions of the business, such as:

receipts
- from cash sales
- from trade receivables (customers)
- loans from the bank
- VAT refunds
- capital introduced by the owner

payments
- for cash purchases
- to trade payables (suppliers)
- for expenses
- for bank loan repayments
- for VAT payments
- for the purchase of assets, eg vehicles, office equipment
- for drawings (money taken by the owner of the business for personal use)

Note that the cash book is the record kept by the business of its bank transactions – the bank will keep its own records, and **bank statements** (see page 262) will either be sent regularly or will be available online through internet banking.

The cash book is controlled by the cashier who:

■ records receipts and payments through the bank

■ makes payments, and prepares cheques and bank transfers for signature by those authorised to sign

■ pays cash and cheques received into the bank

■ has control over the business cash – in a cash till, cash box or safe

■ issues cash to the petty cashier who operates the petty cash book (see Chapter 10)

■ checks the accuracy of the cash and bank balances at regular intervals

It is important to note that transactions passing through the cash book must be supported by documentary evidence. In this way a link is established that can be followed through the accounting system to ensure that it is complete. This link runs through:

■ financial document

■ book of prime entry

■ double-entry accounts

This linking of the transactions is required both as a security feature within the business (to help to ensure that false and fraudulent transactions cannot be made), and also for taxation purposes.

The cashier has an important role to play within the accounting function of a business – most business activities will, at some point, involve a money transaction of either a receipt or a payment. The cash book and the cashier are therefore at the hub of the accounting system. In particular, the cashier is responsible for:

■ issuing receipts for cash (and sometimes bank transfers) received

■ making authorised payments in cash and by cheque/bank transfer against documents received (such as invoices and statements) showing the amounts due

At all times, payments can only be made by the cashier when authorised to do so by the appropriate person within the business, eg the accounts supervisor or the purchasing manager.

With so many transactions passing through the cash book, accounting procedures must include:

■ security – of cash, cheque books and internet banking, the correct authorisation of payments

■ confidentiality – that all cash/bank transactions, including cash and bank balances, are kept confidential

If the cashier has any queries about any transactions, they should be referred to the accounts supervisor.

LAYOUT OF THE TWO COLUMN CASH BOOK

Although a cash book can be set out in many formats to suit the requirements of a particular business, a common format is the two column cash book – so called because it has two money columns on each side. This is set out in the same way as a double-entry account, with debit and credit sides, but with two money columns on each side, as shown below:

Dr								Cash Book		Cr
Date	Details	Account code	Cash £	Bank £	Date	Details	Account code	Cash £	Bank £
		money in					money out		

Note the following points:

■ this layout includes both the bank account and the cash account (used for cash kept on the business premises)

■ the cash and bank columns on the debit side are used for money in, ie receipts

■ the cash and bank columns on the credit side are used for money out, ie payments

■ the account code column is used to code or cross-reference to the other entry in the ledger system

The Case Study which follows shows the use of the cash and bank columns of a two column cash book, and also how data is transferred from cash book into the double-entry bookkeeping system.

CASH BOOK FOR A NEW BUSINESS

situation

Jayne Hampson sets up a new business on 1 June 20-8. The following transactions of her business take place during the first month and are to be entered in her two column cash book:

1 June	Started in business with capital of £10,000 paid into the bank
4 June	Bought a delivery van for £7,500 paying by cheque
7 June	Paid rent for the month of £500 by cheque
12 June	Transferred £1,000 from bank to cash
18 June	Paid wages £500 in cash
20 June	Received a loan from the bank of £2,000
26 June	Jayne Hampson took drawings of £200 in cash

Note that Jayne Hampson's business is not registered for Value Added Tax.

solution

The cash book entries are recorded as follows.

Dr					Cash Book					CB52	Cr
Date	Details	Account code	Cash £	Bank £	Date	Details	Account code	Cash £	Bank £		
20-8					20-8						
1 Jun	Capital	GL3100		10,000	4 Jun	Delivery van	GL0750		7,500		
12 Jun	Bank	C	1,000		7 Jun	Rent	GL6350		500		
20 Jun	Bank loan	GL2140		2,000	12 Jun	Cash	C		1,000		
					18 Jun	Wages	GL6380	500			
					26 Jun	Drawings	GL3200	200			
					30 Jun	Balances c/d		300	3,000		
			1,000	12,000				1,000	12,000		
1 Jul	Balances b/d		300	3,000							

Notes:

- money in – eg capital introduced – is recorded on the debit side, ie the business has received money

- money out – eg rent and wages paid – is recorded on the credit side, ie the business has paid out money

- the balance of the cash and bank columns has been calculated as the difference between money in and money out (receipts minus payments equals the balance). Balancing of accounts is usually carried out at the end of each month when the balances are carried down (c/d) to the first day of the next month where they are brought down (b/d). We will look in more detail at balancing the cash book later in this chapter.

From the completed cash book, we need to transfer the data into the double-entry system. To do this we need to:

- identify on which side of the cash book the transaction has been recorded – debit (money in), or credit (money out)

- record the other double-entry transaction on the opposite side of the appropriate account

The other accounts from this cash book can now be recorded and, over the next few pages, we will look at each transaction and see how each is recorded in the double-entry bookkeeping system. Note that the transaction on 12 June (transferred £1,000 from bank to cash) involves both a receipt and a payment within the cash book; it is usual to indicate both of them in the account code column with a 'C' – this stands for 'contra' and shows that both parts of the transaction are in the same book, ie no further accounting transactions are needed.

The page of the cash book is coded CB52 and this will be the cross-reference for the other ledger accounts.

TRANSFERS TO THE DOUBLE-ENTRY SYSTEM

capital

Capital (also referred to as equity) is the amount of money invested in the business by the owner. A capital account records the amount paid into the business; the accounting entries are:

- debit cash book bank or cash column

- credit capital account

The capital transaction from Jayne Hampson's cash book is entered in capital account as follows:

GENERAL LEDGER

Dr				**Capital account (GL3100)**		Cr
20-8			£	20-8		£
				1 Jun	Bank	CB52	10,000

Note: the introduction of capital into a business is often the very first business transaction entered into the double-entry system.

non–current assets

Non-current assets are items purchased by a business for use on a long-term basis. Examples are premises, vehicles, machinery and office equipment.

When non-current assets are purchased, a separate account for each type of non-current asset is used in general ledger, eg premises account, vehicles account, machinery account, etc. The bookkeeping entries are:

– debit non-current asset account (using the appropriate account)

– credit cash book bank or cash column

The non-current asset transaction in Jayne Hampson's cash book is entered in vehicles account as follows:

GENERAL LEDGER

Dr				Vehicles account (GL0750)		Cr
20-8			£	20-8		£
4 Jun	Bank	CB52	7,500			

payments for expenses

Businesses pay various day-to-day expenses – revenue expenditure – such as rent, wages, electricity, telephone, vehicle running expenses, etc. A separate account is used in general ledger for each main class of revenue expenditure, eg rent paid account, wages account, etc.

The accounting entries are:

– debit expense account (using the appropriate account)

– credit cash book bank or cash column

The two expenses transactions in Jayne Hampson's cash book are entered in the expenses accounts as follows:

GENERAL LEDGER

Dr				Rent paid account (GL6350)		Cr
20-8			£	20-8		£
7 Jun	Bank	CB52	500			

Dr				Wages account (GL6380)		Cr
20-8			£	20-8		£
18 Jun	Cash	CB52	500			

loans

loan received

When a business receives a loan, eg from the bank, it is the bank column of cash book which is debited, while a loan account (in the name of the lender) is credited:

– debit cash book bank column

– credit loan account (in the name of the lender)

The loan transaction from Jayne Hampson's cash book is entered in loan account as follows:

GENERAL LEDGER

Dr				**Bank loan account (GL2140)**				Cr
20-8			£	20-8				£
				20 Jun	Bank	CB52	2,000	

loans repaid

A loan repayment, on the other hand (not shown in the Case Study), is recorded the opposite way round to a loan received because money is being paid from the bank to repay the lender. Therefore loan account is debited and the bank column of cash book is credited:

– debit loan account

– credit cash book bank column

Note that loans are not usually received or repaid in cash, so it is the cash book bank column that records the transaction.

drawings

Drawings is the term used when the owner takes money from the business for personal use. A drawings account is used to record such amounts; the accounting entries for withdrawal of money are:

– debit drawings account

– credit cash book bank or cash column

The transaction in Jayne Hampson's cash book is entered in drawings account as follows:

GENERAL LEDGER

Dr				**Drawings account (GL3200)**		Cr
20-8			£	20-8		£
26 Jun	Cash	CB52	200			

BALANCING THE CASH BOOK

The cash book – like the other accounts in the double-entry system – needs to be balanced in order to show the running total of the account. For cash book, the cash and bank columns are separately balanced in order to show:

- the amount of cash held by the business

- the amount of money in the bank or an overdraft

The cash book is balanced in the following way (using the cash book from the Case Study on page 246, as an example).

cash columns

- add the two cash columns and subtotal in pencil (ie £1,000 in the debit column, and £700 in the credit column); remember to erase the subtotals afterwards

- deduct the lower total from the higher (payments from receipts) to give the balance of cash remaining (ie £1,000 – £700 = £300)

- the higher total is recorded at the bottom of both cash columns in a totals 'box' (£1,000)

- the balance of cash remaining (£300) is entered as a balancing item above the totals box (on the credit side), and is brought down underneath the total on the debit side as the opening balance for next month (£300)

bank columns

- add the two bank columns and sub-total in pencil giving £12,000 on the debit side and £9,000 on the credit side

- deducting the lower from the higher total gives £12,000 – £9,000 = £3,000

- the bank balance of £3,000 is entered on the side with the lower sub-total – here the credit side – as balance carried down and then brought down on the debit side, below the totals line, to indicate money in the bank

Note that a cash balance can be brought down on the debit side only, indicating the amount of cash held. A bank balance can be brought down on either debit or credit side – a debit balance indicates money in the bank, while a credit balance indicates a bank overdraft.

It is very important to appreciate that the bank columns of cash book represent a business's own records of bank transactions and the balance at bank. The bank keeps its own records of the business's bank transactions – as shown by the bank statement.

ANALYSED CASH BOOK

Many businesses use an analysed cash book to provide more information. As well as the columns for cash and bank which we have seen earlier in this chapter, an analysed cash book divides receipts and payments between a number of analysis columns, such as:

■ receipts

- cash sales

- VAT on cash sales and other income

- receipts from trade receivables (customers) in the receivables ledger

- other income

■ payments

- cash purchases

- VAT on cash purchases and other expenses

- payments to trade payables (suppliers) in the payables ledger

- other expenses

A business will use whatever analysis columns suit it best: the cash book should be adapted to meet the needs of the business in the best possible way.

Case Study

ANALYSED CASH BOOK

situation

Wyvern Auto Spares buys car parts from manufacturers, and sells to local garages and to members of the public. The business is registered for VAT.

The business uses a cash book which analyses receipts and payments as follows:

RECEIPTS	PAYMENTS
bank	bank
cash	cash
VAT	VAT
cash sales	cash purchases
trade receivables	trade payables
other income	other expenses

The following transactions are to be received for the first week of December 20-7:

1 Dec	Balances from previous week: cash £255, bank £875
1 Dec	Sales for cash £240 + VAT
1 Dec	Commission received by cheque, £40 + VAT
1 Dec	A customer, Main Street Garage, settles an invoice for £195, paying by bank transfer
2 Dec	Paid rent on premises £325 (no VAT) by cheque
2 Dec	Sales for cash £192, including VAT
2 Dec	Paid an invoice for £250 from Boxhall Supplies Ltd (a supplier) by bank transfer for £240, £10 being deducted for prompt payment discount*
3 Dec	Transferred £500 of cash into the bank
3 Dec	Paid for office stationery in cash, £40 + VAT
3 Dec	A45 Service Station, settles an invoice for £143, paying £140 by cheque and is allowed £3 for prompt payment discount*
4 Dec	Sales £320 + VAT, received half in cash, and half by cheque
4 Dec	Paid for urgently needed spares in cash, £96, including VAT
5 Dec	Paid an invoice for £150 from Vord Supplies (a supplier) by bank transfer
5 Dec	Sales for cash £200 + VAT
5 Dec	Paid wages £385 in cash
5 Dec	Balanced the cash book at the end of the week

As cashier to Wyvern Auto Spares Limited, you are to:

- prepare the analysed cash book for the week commencing 1 December 20-7
- balance the cash book at 5 December 20-7

The rate of Value Added Tax is 20%. All cheques are banked on the day of receipt.

*Prompt payment discount (PPD) for the transactions on 2 December and 3 December is not recorded in cash book; instead, a credit note will be issued by the supplier to the customer (see Chapters 4 and 7).

For calculating VAT amounts from net and total figures, please refer to page 37.

solution

Dr (Receipts)

Date	Details	Account code	Cash	Bank	VAT	Cash sales	Trade receivables	Other income
			£	£	£	£	£	£
20-7								
1 Dec	Balances b/d		255	875				
1 Dec	Sales	GL	288		48	240		
1 Dec	Commission	GL		48	8			40
1 Dec	Main Street Garage	RL		195			195	
2 Dec	Sales	GL	192		32	160		
3 Dec	Cash	C		500				
3 Dec	A45 Service Station	RL		140			140	
4 Dec	Sales	GL	192	192	64	320		
5 Dec	Sales	GL	240		40	200		
			1,167	1,950	192	920	335	40
6 Dec	Balances b/d		138	1,235				

Cr (Payments)

Date	Details	Account code	Cash	Bank	VAT	Cash purchases	Trade payables	Other expenses
			£	£	£	£	£	£
20-7								
2 Dec	Rent paid	GL		325				325
2 Dec	Boxhall Supplies Ltd	PL		240			240	
3 Dec	Bank	C	500					
3 Dec	Office stationery	GL	48		8			40
4 Dec	Purchases	GL	96		16	80		
5 Dec	Vord Supplies	PL		150			150	
5 Dec	Wages	GL	385					385
5 Dec	Balances c/d		138	1,235				
			1,167	1,950	24	80	390	750

Note the following points:

- the analysed cash book analyses each receipt and payment between a number of headings. A business will adapt the cash book and use whatever analysis columns suit it best

- for transactions involving receipts from trade receivables and payments to trade payables, no amount for VAT is shown in the VAT columns. This is because VAT has been charged on invoices issued and received and was recorded in the VAT account (via the day books) when the sale or purchase was made

- the cash and bank columns are balanced as described earlier (page 250)

- the column for account codes indicates the ledger section for completing double-entry. The transaction on 3 December of the transfer of cash to bank is coded 'C' and is shown on both sides of the cash book – no further entries need to be made

LEDGER TRANSFERS FROM THE ANALYSED CASH BOOK

Set out over the next few pages are the entries from the analysed cash book in the Case Study of Wyvern Auto Spares as they are transferred to the double-entry system. These transfers are for:

- VAT
- cash sales
- cash purchases
- receipts from trade receivables
- payments to trade payables
- other income
- other expenses

The entries for general ledger, receivables ledger and purchases ledger are as follows:

Dr		Receivables ledger control account			Cr
20-7		£	20-7		£
			5 Dec	Cash Book	*335

Dr		Payables ledger control account			Cr
20-7		£	20-7		£
5 Dec	Cash Book	*390			

*Note how only the total of the analysis column for trade receivables and trade payables from the cash book is entered in the appropriate control account.

Dr		Sales account			Cr
20-7		£	20-7		£
			5 Dec	Cash Book	**920

Dr		Purchases account			Cr
20-7		£	20-7		£
5 Dec	Cash Book	**80			

**Total of the analysis column from the analysed cash book

Dr		Value added tax account		Cr
20-7		£	20-7	£
5 Dec	Cash Book	***24	5 Dec Cash Book	***192

*** Total of the analysis column from the analysed cash book.

Dr		Commission received account		Cr
20-7		£	20-7	£
			1 Dec Bank	40

Dr		Rent paid account		Cr
20-7		£	20-7	£
2 Dec	Bank	325		

Dr		Office stationery account		Cr
20-7		£	20-7	£
3 Dec	Cash	40		

Dr		Wages account		Cr
20-7		£	20-7	£
5 Dec	Cash	385		

Note that, in the above accounts, the term 'Cash Book' is used as the cross-reference when the total of an analysis column is recorded. This is because transactions will often be a mix of cash and bank items. Where the receipt or payment can be identified to 'Cash' or 'Bank' – as with the income and expenses here – then the cross-reference is to the appropriate word.

RECEIVABLES LEDGER

Dr		Main Street Garage		Cr
20-7		£	20-7	£
			1 Dec Bank	195

Dr		A45 Service Station		Cr
20-7		£	20-7	£
			3 Dec Bank	140

PAYABLES LEDGER

Dr		Boxhall Supplies Ltd		Cr
20-7		£	20-7	£
2 Dec	Bank	240		

Dr		Vord Supplies		Cr
20-7		£	20-7	£
5 Dec	Bank	150		

Note that the transactions recorded in receivables ledger and payables ledger are – as totals – recorded in receivables ledger control account and payables ledger control account.

PROCESSING RECURRING RECEIPTS AND PAYMENTS

As well as dealing with transactions as they occur on a day-by-day basis, a cashier needs to process recurring – regular – receipts and payments through the cash book. This will involve ensuring that:

■ regular receipts – such as rent received, income from service contracts – are received into the cash book at the right time and for the correct amount

■ regular payments – such as rent paid, business rates, electric and gas bills – are paid from the cash book at the right time and for the correct amount

Some of these receipts and payments can be made directly from the bank account by methods such as standing orders and direct debits. These methods are explained in detail in Chapter 1 of *Principles of Bookkeeping Controls Tutorial*. However, for all recurring receipts and payments, the cashier needs to keep a record and to ensure that each is processed, ie check that the correct amount has been received or paid and is recorded in the cash book. This can be done by having a schedule for cash book receipts and cash book payments – as shown in the Case Study on the next page. Such schedules can be recorded manually or digitally – the latter can be set to provide prompts when receipts or payments are due.

Case Study

RECURRING RECEIPTS AND PAYMENTS

situation

Amy Shah is the cashier at Elmhurst Services, a VAT-registered business. She has a recurring receipt and a recurring payment to set up today, 1 September 20-7.

Recurring receipt

Elmhurst Services has contracted to provide administrative support for another business, Elmhurst Traders, which will pay £60 per week plus VAT, initially for a year. Payments will be made by standing order into Elmhurst Services' bank account.

Recurring payment

Elmhurst Services pays rent to the owner of the building for the floor area of the office block that it occupies. The cost is £1,000 per month (no VAT) for the year commencing 1 September 20-7, and payments will be made by standing order.

Show how these recurring items are to be recorded on a schedule to be held by Amy Shah, the cashier.

solution

Recurring receipt

Cash book – receipts				
Date	**Details**	**Total**	**Frequency**	**Recurrences**
1 Sep	Admin support	£72* * £60 + £12 VAT	Weekly	52

Recurring payment

Cash book – payments				
Date	**Details**	**Total**	**Frequency**	**Recurrences**
1 Sep	Rent paid	£1,000	Monthly	12

HOW THE CASH BOOK FITS INTO THE ACCOUNTING SYSTEM

We have looked at a number of bank and cash receipts and payments which are recorded firstly in the cash book and secondly in the ledger system of the general ledger, receivables ledger and payables ledger. As the cash book is the first place in the accounting system to record bank transactions, it is the **book of prime entry** for bank and cash receipts and payments.

There are two ways in which the cash book can fit into the accounting system:

- as well as being a book of prime entry, the cash book can perform the function of being a double-entry account, ie a debit entry made in cash book is recorded on the credit side of another double-entry account

- the cash book is treated solely as a book of prime entry, in which case separate double-entry accounts – called **cash account** and **bank account** – are used in the general ledger

The diagram on the next page shows how the cash book performs the functions of a book of prime entry and a double-entry account. The diagram shows the flow involving:

- financial documents – primary records for bank receipts and payments

- the cash book as a book of prime entry

- double-entry bookkeeping, involving the cash book and other ledgers

In accounting systems where the cash book is used as a book of prime entry only, separate accounts for cash and bank are used in the general ledger. These are shown on page 260.

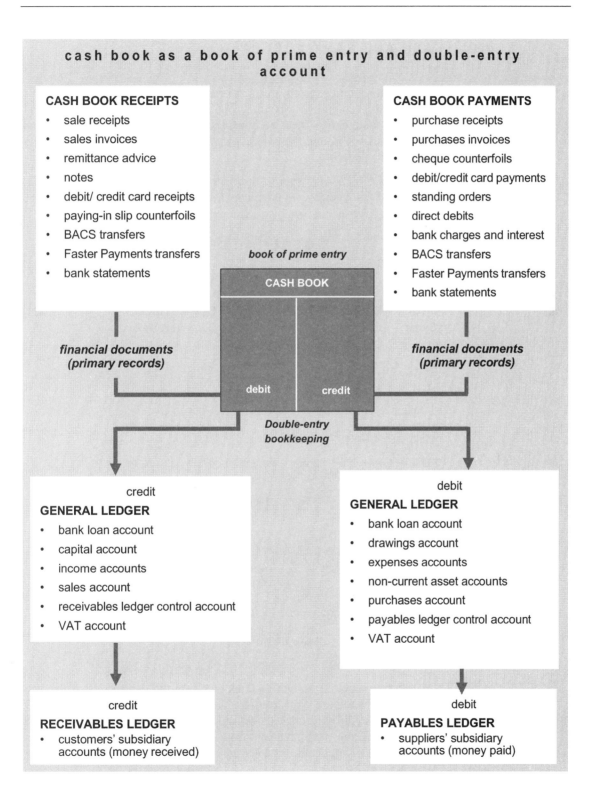

cash book as a book of prime entry and double-entry account

CASH BOOK RECEIPTS

- sale receipts
- sales invoices
- remittance advice
- notes
- debit/ credit card receipts
- paying-in slip counterfoils
- BACS transfers
- Faster Payments transfers
- bank statements

CASH BOOK PAYMENTS

- purchase receipts
- purchases invoices
- cheque counterfoils
- debit/credit card payments
- standing orders
- direct debits
- bank charges and interest
- BACS transfers
- Faster Payments transfers
- bank statements

book of prime entry

CASH BOOK

debit | credit

Double-entry bookkeeping

financial documents (primary records)

financial documents (primary records)

credit
GENERAL LEDGER

- bank loan account
- capital account
- income accounts
- sales account
- receivables ledger control account
- VAT account

debit
GENERAL LEDGER

- bank loan account
- drawings account
- expenses accounts
- non-current asset accounts
- purchases account
- payables ledger control account
- VAT account

credit
RECEIVABLES LEDGER
- customers' subsidiary accounts (money received)

debit
PAYABLES LEDGER
- suppliers' subsidiary accounts (money paid)

CASH AND BANK ACCOUNT

Where an accounting system treats the cash book solely as a book of prime entry, a cash account and a bank account are used in the general ledger to complete double-entry. These accounts show the total receipts and payments made in cash or through the bank during the period, together with opening and closing balances.

From the cash book of Wyvern Auto Spares, in the Case Study on page 253, the totals of the receipts and payments from the cash and bank columns are recorded in cash account and bank account as shown below.

GENERAL LEDGER

Dr			Cash account			Cr
20-7		£	20-7			£
1 Dec	Balance b/d	255	5 Dec	Cash Book		**1,029
5 Dec	Cash Book	*912	5 Dec	Balance c/d		138
		1,167				1,167
6 Dec	Balance b/d	138				

* £288 + £192 + £192 + £240

** £500 + £48 + £96 + £385   see cash book on page 253

Dr			Bank account			Cr
20-7		£	20-7			£
1 Dec	Balance b/d	875	5 Dec	Cash Book		**715
5 Dec	Cash Book	*1,075	5 Dec	Balance c/d		1,235
		1,950				1,950
6 Dec	Balance b/d	1,235				

*£48 + £195 + £500 + £140 + £192

**£325 + £240 + £150   see cash book on page 253

Note that the amounts shown as Cash Book on the debit sides of the two accounts are the total receipts from the cash book, excluding balances brought down (and, if applicable, carried down). Likewise, the amounts shown on the credit sides are the total payments from the cash book, excluding balances brought down (if applicable) and carried down.

CHECKING THE CASH BOOK

As the cash book forms such an integral part of a business double-entry system, it is essential that transactions are recorded accurately and that balances are calculated correctly at regular intervals, eg weekly or monthly, depending on the needs of the business. How can the cash book be checked for accuracy?

cash columns

To check the cash columns is easy. It is simply a matter of counting the cash in the cash till, cash box, or safe, and agreeing it with the balance shown by the cash book. In the example from the cash book of Wyvern Auto Spares, in the Case Study on page 253, there should be £138 in the cash till at 6 December 20-7. If the cash cannot be agreed in this way, the discrepancy needs to be investigated urgently.

bank columns

How are these to be checked? We could, perhaps, enquire at the bank and ask for the balance at the month-end; or we could arrange for a bank statement (see below) to be sent to us, or use internet banking to print off a statement. However, the balance of the account at the bank may well not agree with that shown by the bank columns of the cash book. There are several reasons why there may be a difference: for example, a cheque that has been written out recently to pay a bill may not yet have been recorded on the bank statement, ie it has been entered in the cash book, but is not yet on the bank statement. To agree the bank statement and the bank columns of the cash book, it is usually necessary to prepare a bank reconciliation statement, and this topic is dealt with fully in Chapter 3 of *Principles of Bookkeeping Controls Tutorial.*

bank statement

A bank sends statements – or they are available electronically – to its customers at regular intervals, very much in the same way that a business issues statements of account to its customers. An example of a bank statement is shown at the top of the next page.

The bank statement shows three money columns:

- **payments**, such as cheques paid out, bank transfers made (BACS, Faster Payments), standing orders and direct debits paid, bank charges and interest

- **receipts**, such as cash and cheques paid in, bank transfers received (BACS, Faster Payments)

■ **balance**, in the form of a running balance (a new balance shown after each transaction made), and indicating whether it is Debit (Dr) – an overdraft, or Credit (Cr) – money in the bank

National Bank plc Bartown Branch		Account title	Severn Trading Company
		Account number	67812318
		Statement number	45

Date	Details	Payments	Receipts	Balance
20-1		£	£	£
2 Feb	Balance brought forward			1340.50 Cr
7 Feb	Credit		208.50	1549.00 Cr
10 Feb	Cheque 123456	675.25		873.75 Cr
17 Feb	Credit		278.30	1152.05 Cr
17 Feb	Cheque 123457	125.00		1027.05 Cr
24 Feb	Credit		162.30	1189.35 Cr
24 Feb	BACS J Jarvis Ltd		100.00	1289.35 Cr
26 Feb	Cheque 123458	421.80		867.55 Cr
26 Feb	Direct debit A-Z Finance	150.00		717.55 Cr
27 Feb	Credit		353.95	1071.50 Cr
27 Feb	Bank charges	10.00		1061.50 Cr

It is important to note that a bank statement is prepared from the bank's viewpoint: thus a credit balance shows that the bank has a liability to its customer, while a debit balance shows that the bank has an asset due from its customer.

In the customer's own cash book, a debit balance indicates money in the bank (a credit balance on the bank statement – which demonstrates the principles of double-entry bookkeeping) while a cash book credit balance indicates an overdraft at the bank (a debit balance on the bank statement).

There is more on banking and bank statements in Chapters 1, 2 and 3 of *Principles of Bookkeeping Controls Tutorial*.

Chapter Summary

- The cash book records the money transactions of the business in the form of cash and bank receipts and payments.

- Receipts are recorded on the debit side; payments are recorded on the credit side.

- A common form of cash book is the two column cash book with columns for cash and bank.

- Transactions recorded in the cash book include:

  - cash sales

  - cash purchases

  - receipts from credit customers

  - payments to credit suppliers

  - other payments and receipts, eg non-current assets, expenses paid, loans received and repaid

- An analysed cash book provides more information and divides receipts and payments between a number of columns.

- Analysis columns for receipts include:

  - cash sales

  - VAT on cash sales and other income

  - receipts from trade receivables

  - other income

- Analysis columns for payments include:

  - cash purchases

  - VAT on cash purchases and other expenses

  - payments to trade payables

  - other expenses

- In the accounting system, cash book can combine the roles of:

  - the book of prime entry for bank and cash receipts and payments

  - the double-entry account for cash and bank

- When the cash book is used solely as the book of prime entry, a cash account and a bank account are used in general ledger to complete double-entry bookkeeping.

- Bank statements are sent out/available electronically to customers at regular intervals.

Key Terms

cash book	records cash and bank receipts and payments; can combine the roles of the book of prime entry for bank receipts and payments and the double-entry account for cash and bank, or can be a book of prime entry only
two column cash book	cash book with columns for cash and bank
capital	the amount of money invested in the business by the owner
non-current assets	items purchased by a business for use on a long-term basis
drawings	when the owner takes money from the business for personal use
cash sales	where a customer buys goods or services and pays in full immediately
cash purchases	where a business buys goods or services from a supplier and pays in full immediately
analysed cash book	a cash book which divides receipts and payments between a number of columns
receipts analysis columns	for example: – cash sales – VAT on cash sales and other income – receipts from trade receivables – other income
payments analysis columns	for example: – cash purchases – VAT on cash purchases and other expenses – payments to trade payables – other expenses
cash account and bank account	double-entry accounts in the general ledger used when the cash book is treated solely as the book of prime entry; they show the total receipts and payments made in cash or through the bank during the period, together with the opening and closing balances
bank statement	shows bank receipts and payments together with the bank balance or overdraft

Activities

9.1   The cash book is:

(a)	A financial document	
(b)	The account kept by the bank of its customer's bank receipts and payments	
(c)	A part of double-entry bookkeeping only	
(d)	The book of prime entry for bank receipts and payments	

Which **one** of these options is correct?

9.2   The following cash book shows a number of transactions of a new business set up by Hannah Wyrembak on 30 April 20-7:

Dr					Cash Book				CB70	Cr
Date	**Details**	**Account code**	**Cash £**	**Bank £**	**Date**	**Details**	**Account code**	**Cash £**	**Bank £**	
20-7					20-7					
30 Apr	Capital		2,000	8,000	30 Apr	Rent paid			1,000	
30 Apr	Loan from bank			5,000	30 Apr	Wages		800		
					30 Apr	Drawings			500	
					30 Apr	Vehicle			10,000	
					30 Apr	Balances c/d		1,200	1,500	
			2,000	13,000				2,000	13,000	
1 May	Balances b/d		1,200	1,500						

Note that Hannah Wyrembak's business is not registered for Value Added Tax.

You are to transfer the data from the cash book into the double-entry system of Hannah Wyrembak.

Note: full account codes are not required.

9.3 The following cash book shows a number of transactions of Teme Traders which all took place on 30 April 20-5:

Dr								Cash Book		CB32	Cr
Date	Details	Account code	Cash £	Bank £	Date	Details	Account code	Cash £	Bank £
20-5					20-5				
30 Apr	Balances b/d		275	2,080	30 Apr	Mereford Mills (trade payables)			3,200
30 Apr	Cash sales		40		30 Apr	Cash purchases			96
30 Apr	Commission received			48	30 Apr	Office equipment			2,600
30 Apr	Lindum Ltd (trade receivable)			2,400	30 Apr	Wages			1,550
30 Apr	Loan from bank			2,000	30 Apr	General expenses		80	
30 Apr	Balance c/d			918	30 Apr	Balance c/d		235	
			315	7,446				315	7,446
1 May	Balance b/d		235		1 May	Balance b/d			918

Note that Teme Traders' business is not registered for Value Added Tax.

(a) The balance brought down of £2,080 on 30 April shows that, according to the cash book, the business has money in the bank. True or false?

(b) The balance brought down of £918 on 1 May shows that, according to the cash book, the business has money in the bank. True or false?

(c) You are to transfer the data from the cash book into the general ledger of Teme Traders.

(d) Show the entries in the receivables ledger and payables ledger of Teme Traders.

Note: full account codes are not required.

9.4 Which **one** of the following transactions will not be recorded on the payments side of cash book?

(a)	Purchase of a vehicle for £10,000 paid for by cheque	
(b)	Cash purchase for £150	
(c)	Bank transfer from a trade receivable for £1,350	
(d)	BACS transfer to a supplier for £2,200	

9.5 Which **one** of the following transactions will not be recorded on the receipts side of cash book?

(a)	Cheque to a trade payable for £870	
(b)	Bank transfer from a trade receivable for £3,250	
(c)	Debit card payment by a customer for £580	
(d)	Cash sales of £195	

9.6 Indicate whether the following statements are true or false by putting a tick in the relevant column of the table below.

		True	False
(a)	Cash book is the book of prime entry for bank and cash receipts and payments		
(b)	Cash book can be the double-entry account for bank and cash		
(c)	The VAT column total on the receipts side of an analysed cash book is debited to VAT account in general ledger		
(d)	The trade receivables column total from an analysed cash book is credited to receivables ledger control account in general ledger		

9.7 David Lewis runs a shop selling carpets to the public on cash terms and to trade customers on credit terms. He buys his carpets direct from manufacturers, who allow him credit terms.

David Lewis' business is registered for VAT. The VAT rate is 20%. He uses an analysed cash book, which is a book of prime entry and a double-entry account.

The following transactions take place during the week commencing 12 May 20-7 (all cheques are banked on the day of receipt):

12 May	Debit balances from previous week: cash £205, bank £825
12 May	Cash sales £600 (including VAT), cheque received
12 May	Paid shop rent by bank transfer £255 (no VAT)
13 May	Cash sales £150 + VAT, cash received
13 May	A trade receivable, T Jarvis, settles an invoice for £155 by bank transfer
13 May	Paid an invoice for £363 from Terry Carpets (a trade payable) by cheque
14 May	Cash sales £720 (including VAT), cheque received
14 May	Paid an invoice for £145 from Trade Supplies (a trade payable), paying by cheque
14 May	Purchases paid for in cash, £36 (including VAT)
15 May	Transferred £250 of cash into the bank
15 May	Cash sales £288 (including VAT), cash received
15 May	Paid an invoice for £291 from Longlife Carpets (a trade payable), by bank transfer
16 May	Cash purchases of £200 + VAT, paid by BACS
16 May	A trade receivable, Wyvern Council, settles an invoice for £560, paying by BACS

You are to:

(a) Enter the transactions from the previous page in the analysed cash book of David Lewis shown below.

(b) Balance the cash book at 16 May 20-7, bringing down the balances at 17 May 20-7.

(c) Show the cash book transactions in the following accounts:

receivables ledger	–	T Jarvis	
	–	Wyvern Council	
payables ledger	–	Terry Carpets	
	–	Trade Supplies	
	–	Longlife Carpets	

Note: full account codes are not required.

Dr (Receipts)

Date	Details	Account code	Cash	Bank	VAT	Cash sales	Trade receivables	Other income
			£	£	£	£	£	£

Cr (Payments)

Date	Details	Account code	Cash	Bank	VAT	Cash purchases	Trade payables	Other expenses
			£	£	£	£	£	£

9.8 You are an accounts assistant at Trafalgar Limited. One of your duties is to write-up the cash book.

There are five payments to be entered in Trafalgar Limited's cash book.

Receipts for cash payments

Received cash with thanks for goods bought.	
From Trafalgar Ltd, a customer without a credit account.	
Net	£25
VAT	£5
Total	£30
Knowles & Co	

Received cash with thanks for goods bought.	
From Trafalgar Ltd, a customer without a credit account.	
Net	£80
VAT	£16
Total	£96
S Goulding	

Bank payments

Liyan Ltd
(Payables ledger account PL320)
£920

Nelson Street Garage
(No credit account with this supplier)
£132 including VAT

Sandhu & Co
(Payables ledger account PL540)
£645

(a) Record the details from the two receipts for cash payments and the three bank payments into the credit side of the cash book shown below and total each column.

Cash book – credit side

Details	Cash	Bank	VAT	Trade payables	Cash purchases	Vehicle expenses
	£	£	£	£	£	£
Balance b/f						
Knowles & Co						
S Goulding						
Liyan Ltd						
Nelson Street Garage						
Sandhu & Co						
Totals						

There are three amounts received to be entered in Trafalgar Limited's cash book.

Bank receipts from credit customers:

Watkin Ltd	£429
P Pandya	£1,522

Cash received:

£235 received from Matt Martin for rent of parking spaces (no VAT)

(b) Record the above details into the debit side of the cash book and total each column.

Cash book – debit side

Details	Cash £	Bank £	Trade payables £	Other income £
Balance b/f	254	1,598		
Watkin Ltd				
P Pandya				
Matt Martin				
Totals				

(c) Using your answers to (a) and (b) above, calculate the cash balance.

£ [   ]

(d) Using your answers to (a) and (b) above, calculate the bank balance.

£ [   ]

(e) Will the bank balance calculated in (d) above be a debit or credit balance?

Debit	
Credit	

9.9 You are the bookkeeper at Weston Stores Ltd and are processing receipts and payments.

The amount shown below has been received from customers and the transaction is ready to be entered into the cash book module of your digital bookkeeping system.

Receipt 684
10 May 20-9
Cash sales from customers:
Total £4,589.04 including VAT

(a) Make the necessary entries in the cash book by:

- selecting the correct side of the cash book

- choosing the description for the details column of the cash book

- making the entry in the cash book

Cash book	✓
Cash book – receipts	
Cash book – payments	

Description for details column	✓
Total	
VAT	
Trade receivables	
Sales	

Date 20-9	Details	Total £	VAT £	Net £

(b) Identify which document you will refer to for details of payments to be recorded in the cash book.

Information required	Document
Details of payments made to credit suppliers	
Details of regular payments made through the bank account	

Select your document from the following list: Cash sales receipts, Internet banking payments schedule, Paying-in slip counterfoils, Sales invoices, Standing order and direct debit schedule.

9.10 You are the cashier at Akzel Ltd. Today, 1 June 20-8, you are setting up a recurring payment in the digital bookkeeping system.

Standing order and direct debit schedule/;

> Akzel Ltd has signed a contract for a year to pay £138, including VAT, each month to OfficeFast Ltd for the maintenance of office equipment. Date of first payment: 1 June 20-8.

Show the necessary entries in the cash book by:

- selecting the correct side of the cash book

- recording the entry in the cash book

Cash book	
Cash book – receipts	
Cash book – payments	

Date 20-8	Details	Total £	VAT £	Net £	Frequency	Recurrences

10 Petty cash book

this chapter covers...

In this chapter we look at the petty cash book, which is used to record low-value cash payments for small purchases and expenses incurred by a business. Examples of these payments include the purchase of office stationery items, and the payment of travel expenses.

The way that the petty cash book works is that an amount of cash is handed by the cashier to a member of staff, the petty cashier, who:

- *is responsible for security of the petty cash money*
- *makes cash payments against authorised petty cash vouchers*
- *records the payments made, and analyses them, in a petty cash book*
- *reconciles the petty cash book with the amount of cash held*

We look at the layout of the petty cash book, with columns for expenses, and see how it is written up by the petty cashier from authorised petty cash vouchers.

We see how a petty cash book is balanced and how the petty cashier claims reimbursement from the cashier of amounts of money paid out.

Towards the end of the chapter, we will see how a petty cash book fits into the accounting system as the book of prime entry for low-value cash payments and as part of the double-entry system.

The recording of entries in a cashbook is carried out easily using digital bookkeeping systems such as:

- *spreadsheet templates, appropriate for small businesses*
- *online tools such as apps and cloud-based accounting software, appropriate for small to medium businesses*
- *desktop finance software, appropriate for medium to large businesses*

THE PETTY CASH BOOK IN THE ACCOUNTING SYSTEM

The petty cash book is used to record low-value cash payments for purchases and expenses – such as small items of stationery, postages, etc. Items like these are not appropriate to enter in the cash book because they would 'clutter' it up with lots of small amounts. Instead a member of staff is given the responsibility of being the petty cashier.

Petty cash book is the book of prime entry for low-value cash payments.

USES OF THE PETTY CASH BOOK

The petty cash book records the low-value cash payments for purchases and expenses of the business, such as:

– stationery items

– small items of office supplies

– window cleaning

– bus, rail and taxi fares incurred on behalf of the business

– meals and drinks incurred on behalf of the business

– post office (for postages)

– tips and donations

Petty cash payments are usually for amounts up to a maximum value, for example, up to £25 for any one expense item. The petty cashier of a business will be told the maximum amount that can be paid out on any one voucher.

As well as payments, there may, from time to time, be small receipts of cash to be recorded. For example, if a member of staff purchases items such as postage stamps or stationery, they will pay the petty cashier who issues a cash receipt to record the details and the amount of money received.

The petty cash book is the responsibility of the petty cashier who:

■ receives an amount of money (known as the petty cash float) from the cashier to be used for petty cash payments

■ is responsible for security of the petty cash money

■ makes cash payments against authorised petty cash vouchers

■ records the payments made, and analyses them to expenses columns in a petty cash book

- receives and records any small amounts of income, eg postage stamps sold to staff for their private use

- balances the petty cash book at regular intervals, usually weekly or monthly

- tops up the petty cash float by claiming reimbursement from the cashier of amounts paid out

- passes the completed petty cash book to the bookkeeper so that data can be transferred into the ledger system

THE IMPREST SYSTEM

Petty cash books usually operate using the **imprest system**. With this system, the petty cashier starts each week (or month) with a certain amount of money – the imprest amount. As payments are made during the week (or month) the amount of money will reduce and, at the end of the period, the cash will be made up by a payment from bank account to restore the imprest amount. For example:

Started week with imprest amount	£100.00
Total of petty cash amounts paid out during week	£80.00
Cash held at end of week	£20.00
Amount drawn from bank to restore imprest amount	£80.00
Cash at start of next week, ie imprest amount	£100.00

If, at any time, the imprest amount proves to be insufficient, further amounts of cash can be drawn from the cashier. Also, from time to time, it may be necessary to increase the imprest amount so that regular shortfalls of petty cash are avoided.

In contrast, the **non-imprest system** is where the petty cash supply is not topped up to the same value each time but only when the cash runs low.

PETTY CASH VOUCHERS – PURPOSE AND CONTENT

The purpose of petty cash vouchers is to enable payments to be made out of petty cash. They are the financial documents used by the petty cashier to write up the petty cash book.

Petty cash vouchers contain the following:

- the date, details and amount of expenditure
- the signature of the person making the claim and receiving the money
- the signature of the person authorising the payment – normally the petty cashier, or a manager if the amount is higher than the authorisation limit

Additionally:

- most petty cash vouchers are numbered, so that they can be controlled
- relevant documentation, such as a cash receipt from a shop or post office etc, is attached to the petty cash voucher

An example petty cash voucher is as follows:

petty cash voucher		Number *47*
		Date *5 April 20-4*

description		£	p
Photocopier paper		*3*	*20*
VAT at 20%		*0*	*64*
Total		*3*	*84*

signature ....*T Harris*...

authorised ....*R Singh*...

LAYOUT OF THE PETTY CASH BOOK

Petty cash book is usually set out as follows:

Petty cash book

Date 20-4	Details	Amount £	Date 20-4	Details	Amount £	VAT £	Motor expenses £	Office expenses £

The layout shows that:

- there are columns showing the date and details of all receipts and payments
- receipts are shown in the debit column on the left
- the amount column on the credit side records the amount paid out on each petty cash voucher
- then follow columns which analyse by expense each transaction entered in the amount column

A business will use whatever expenses columns are most suitable for it and, indeed, there may be more columns than shown in the example. It is important that expenses are recorded in the correct columns so that petty cash book shows a true picture of petty cash expenditure.

PETTY CASH AND VAT

Value Added Tax is charged by VAT-registered businesses on their taxable supplies. Therefore, there will often be VAT included as part of the expense paid out of petty cash. Often the indication of the supplier's VAT registration number on a receipt or invoice will tell you that VAT has been charged on the items purchased.

Where VAT has been charged, the amount of tax might be indicated separately on the receipt or invoice. However, for small money amounts it is quite usual for a total to be shown without indicating the amount of VAT. An example of a receipt which does not show the VAT content is illustrated below. The receipt is for a box of envelopes purchased from Wyvern Stationers. It shows:

- the name and address of the retailer

- the date and time of the transaction

- the VAT registration number of the retailer

- the price of the item, £4.80

- the amount of money given, a £10 note

- the amount of change given, £5.20

Wyvern Stationers	
25 High St Mereford	
08 10 -4 16.07	
VAT Reg 454 7106 34	
Salesperson Rashid	
Stationery	4.80
TOTAL	4.80
CASH	10.00
CHANGE	5.20

What the receipt does not show, however, is the VAT content of the purchase price – it only shows the price after the VAT has been added on.

How do we calculate the purchase price before the VAT is added on?

The formula is:

$$\frac{amount\ paid\ x\ 100}{100 + VAT\ rate} = price\ before\ VAT\ is\ added\ on$$

With a VAT rate of 20%, the calculation is:

$$\frac{£4.80\ x\ 100}{100 + 20} = \frac{£480}{120} = £4.00$$

The VAT content is therefore:

£4.80 minus £4.00 = 80p

In this case £0.80 will be entered in the VAT column in the petty cash book, £4.00 in the appropriate expense column, and the full £4.80 in the total amount column.

Remember when calculating VAT amounts that fractions of a penny are ignored, ie the tax is rounded down to a whole penny.

PETTY CASH BOOK

This Case Study shows how a petty cash book is prepared by the petty cashier from authorised petty cash vouchers. The petty cash float is reimbursed at the end of the week and the petty cash book is balanced. Voucher numbers have been recorded in the details column – note that in AAT Assessments, voucher numbers may not need to be shown.

situation

You work in the accounts department of Wyvern Traders. One of your tasks is to keep the petty cash book, which is operated using the imprest system. There are a number of transactions which have been authorised (all transactions, unless otherwise indicated, include VAT at 20%) to be entered for the week in the petty cash book (PCB30):

20-4

5 Apr	Started the week with an imprest amount of £100.00
5 Apr	Envelopes £3.84 on voucher no 47
5 Apr	Taxi fare £5.76 on voucher no 48
6 Apr	Received £10 in cash from Jo Lee for postage stamps purchased (cash receipt no 122 issued)
6 Apr	Post office £2.75 (no VAT) on voucher no 49
7 Apr	Taxi fare £9.60 on voucher no 50
7 Apr	Paid J Jones, a trade payable (PL054), £15.00 (no VAT shown in petty cash book – amount will be on VAT account already) on voucher no 51
8 Apr	Marker pens £7.20 on voucher no 52
8 Apr	Post office £5.85 (no VAT) on voucher no 53
9 Apr	Taxi fare £12.00 on voucher no 54

The petty cash book is to be balanced on 9 April with reimbursement of the imprest amount from cash book (CB55). The balance is to be brought down on 10 April.

solution

The following petty cash book is prepared by the petty cashier of Wyvern Traders for the week ended 9 April 20-4 as follows:

Petty Cash Book											PCB30
Date 20-4	Details	Amount £	Date 20-4	Details		Amount £	VAT £	Postages £	Stationery £	Travel £	Ledger £
5 Apr	Balance b/d	100.00									
			5 Apr	Envelopes	47	3.84	0.64		3.20		
			5 Apr	Tax fare	48	5.76	0.98			4.80	
6 Apr	J Lee 122 (postages)	10.00									
			6 Apr	Post office	49	2.75		2.75			
			7 Apr	Taxi fare	50	9.60	1.60			8.00	
			7 Apr	J Jones (PL054)		15.00					15.00
			8 Apr	Marker pens	52	7.20	1.20		6.00		
			8 Apr	Post office	53	5.85		5.85			
			9 Apr	Taxi fare	54	12.00	2.00			10.00	
						62.00	6.40	8.60	9.20	22.80	15.00
							GL2200	GL6330	GL6360	GL6370	GL2350
9 Apr	Bank CB55	52.00									
			9 Apr	Balance c/d		100.00					
		162.00				162.00					
10 Apr	Balance b/d	100.00									

Notes:

- this petty cash book has been prepared for the week, but it is for a business to decide how often petty cash book is to be totalled and balanced – generally, though, this will be done either weekly or monthly

- this cash book starts each new week with a cash float of £100 – this is the imprest amount. The amount of the float at the start is for the business to decide based on the level of expenses regularly paid out in petty cash – £100 may be sufficient, but larger floats may be needed. In any case, if the petty cashier runs out of cash during the week or month, a top-up can be made from cash book

- the expenses columns are for a business to decide what is suitable for their circumstances. The ledger column is used for payments from petty cash to trade payables who have accounts in payables ledger – these suppliers are more usually paid through the bank but, if the amount is small, they may be paid in cash from petty cash

We will now see in the main text below how the data is transferred into the double-entry bookkeeping system.

Note that the page of the petty cash book is coded PCB30 and this will be the cross-reference for the other ledger accounts.

BALANCES

5 Apr Balance b/d

The week commences with a petty cash book float of £100, described as 'balance b/d', ie brought down from the previous page of the petty cash book. (Note that this may also be written as 'balance b/f', ie brought forward from the previous page.) The imprest amount for this petty cash book is £100.

9 Apr Balance c/d

The petty cashier has claimed reimbursement from the cashier of £52.00, ie petty cash paid out £62.00 less £10 received from Jo Lee for postage stamps. This restores the cash float to £100 which is now recorded as the balance c/d on the credit (payments) side. The receipts and payments columns are then both totalled to £162.00.

10 Apr Balance b/d

To complete double-entry bookkeeping, the balance of £100 is brought down on the debit side. Note that, here, the date used is the day following the balance carried down – this shows that the cash float of £100 is ready for the next week's transactions.

TRANSFERRING THE EXPENSES COLUMNS

In order to complete double-entry, the total of each of the expenses columns is transferred into the double-entry bookkeeping system:

■ payment of an expense

  – debit expense account (using the appropriate account)

■ payment to a supplier (from the 'ledger' column)

  – debit payables ledger control account (in general ledger)

  – debit the trade payables' subsidiary account (in payables ledger)

From the Case Study the general ledger accounts will be entered as follows at the end of the week (9 April):

GENERAL LEDGER

Dr			Value added tax account (GL2200)		Cr
20-4		£	20-4		£
9 Apr	Petty cash book PCB30	6.40			

Dr			Postages account (GL6330)		Cr
20-4		£	20-4		£
9 Apr	Petty cash book PCB30	8.60	6 Apr	Petty cash book PCB30	*10.00

*cash received by the petty cashier from Jo Lee for postage stamps purchased

Dr			Stationery account (GL6360)		Cr
20-4		£	20-4		£
9 Apr	Petty cash book PCB30	9.20			

Dr			Travel expenses account (GL6370)		Cr
20-4		£	20-4		£
9 Apr	Petty cash book PCB30	22.80			

Dr			Payables ledger control account (GL2350)		Cr
20-4		£	20-4		£
9 Apr	Petty cash book PCB30	15.00			

The above £15 payment ledger transaction will also be debited to the account of the trade payable – here J Jones – in the payables ledger, as follows:

PAYABLES LEDGER

Dr			J Jones (PL054)		Cr
20-4		£	20-4		£
7 Apr	Petty cash book PCB30	15.00			

RESTORING THE CASH FLOAT

To restore the petty cash float to the imprest amount, the petty cashier completes a requisition form for a cash withdrawal from the bank. An example of a requisition is shown below:

CASH REQUISITION	
Amount	£52.00
Date	9 April 20-4
Details	Reimbursement of petty cash
Signature	Jane Watkins, petty cashier
Authorised by	Natalie Wilson, supervisor

The petty cashier will then withdraw the cash from the bank by means of either a debit card or by cheque.

The double-entry bookkeeping entries to record this reimbursement are:

– *debit* petty cash book

– *credit* cash book, ie the payments side

The amount of £52.00 cash paid from the bank to the petty cashier is recorded in the cash book as follows:

Dr								Cash Book			CB55	Cr
Date 20-4	Details	Account code	Cash	Bank	Date 20-4	Details	Account code	Cash	Bank
			£	£				£	£
					9 Apr	Petty cash	PCB30		52.00

After this reimbursement, the petty cash float is restored and the petty cash book has a balance brought down of £100.00 on 9 April. The petty cash book is now ready for next week's transactions.

CONTROL OF PETTY CASH

The petty cashier is usually responsible to the accounts supervisor for control of the petty cash and for correct recording of authorised petty cash transactions.

Most businesses set out in writing the procedures to be followed by the petty cashier. This is of benefit not only for the petty cashier to know the extent of his or her duties, but also to help the person who takes over at holiday or other times. The main procedures for the operation and control of petty cash are as follows:

1 On taking over, the petty cashier should check that the petty cash book has been balanced and that the amount of cash held agrees with the balance shown in the book. If there is any discrepancy, this should be referred to the accounts supervisor immediately.

2 The petty cashier should ensure that each week or month is started with the imprest amount of cash which has been agreed with the accounts supervisor.

3 The petty cash is to be kept securely in a locked cash box, and control kept of the keys.

4 Petty cash vouchers (in number order) are to be provided on request.

5 Petty cash is paid out against correctly completed petty cash vouchers after checking that:

   – the voucher is signed by the person receiving the money

   – the voucher is signed by the person authorising payment (the petty cashier or a manager)

   – a receipt (or other supporting evidence) is attached to the petty cash voucher, and that the receipt and petty cash voucher are for the same amount

   – the amount being claimed is within the authorised limit of the petty cashier

6 The petty cash book is prepared (to include calculation of VAT amounts when appropriate); it is important that the petty cash book is accurate.

7 Completed petty cash vouchers are stored safely – filed in numerical order. The vouchers will need to be kept for at least six years. They may be needed by the auditors or in the event of other queries. Completed petty cash books will also need to be retained.

8 A surprise check of petty cash will be made by the accounts supervisor – at any one time, the cash held plus amounts of petty cash vouchers should equal the imprest amount.

9 At the end of each week or month the petty cash book is to be balanced.

10 Details of the total of each expenses column are given to the person who looks after the double-entry accounts so that the amount of each expense can be entered into the double-entry system.

11 An amount of cash is drawn from the bank equal to the amount of payments made (less any sundry receipts), in order to restore the imprest amount.

12 The petty cash book and cash in hand are to be presented to the accounts supervisor for checking.

13 Any discrepancies are to be dealt with promptly; these may include:

– petty cash claims that have not been authorised

– insufficient supporting evidence (eg missing receipt) attached to the petty cash voucher

– amounts being claimed which exceed the authorised limit of the petty cashier

– a receipt and petty cash voucher total differing – the matter should be queried with the person who made the purchase

– a difference between the totals of the expenses columns and the amount of the total payments column in the petty cash book – check the addition of the columns, the figures against the vouchers, the VAT calculations (does the VAT plus the expense column amount equal the total amount?)

– a difference between the cash in the petty cash box and the balance shown in the petty cash book – if this is not an arithmetic difference, it may be a case of theft, and should be reported promptly to the accounts supervisor

– where discrepancies and queries cannot be resolved, they should be referred to the accounts supervisor

CHECKING THE CASH

An important aspect of petty cash, which has been noted in the previous section, is that the petty cashier must ensure that the amount of cash held is what it should be. This process – known as reconciling the petty cash book with cash in hand – takes place on different occasions, as follows:

- at the beginning of the weekly or monthly period of the petty cash book, the petty cashier should check that the amount of cash held agrees with the balance shown in the book – this is usually the imprest amount

- at any one time during the week or month, the amount of cash held plus the amounts of petty cash vouchers which have been paid out should be equal to the imprest amount – a surprise check may be made by the accounts supervisor

- at the end of the week or month, the amount paid out by the petty cashier will be reimbursed from the bank – this should restore the cash in hand to the imprest amount

Any difference in cash – whether a shortfall or a surplus – at any stage during the week or month should be investigated promptly and, if it cannot be resolved, should be referred to the accounts supervisor.

Case Study

CHECKING THE CASH

situation

Jameson Limited keeps an amount of petty cash in a locked box in the office. The imprest amount is £100 which is restored at the beginning of each month.

The following payments were made in April and have been recorded in the petty cash book:

6 April	**Stationery**	£12.50
10 April	**Taxi fare**	£10.00
14 April	**Post office**	£4.55
20 April	**Window cleaning**	£12.00
25 April	**Donation to charity**	£10.00

At 30 April the petty cash remaining in the locked box comprised:

1 x £10 note, 7 x £5 notes, 5 x £1 coins, 1 x 50p coin, 1 x 20p coin, 1 x 10p coin, 2 x 5p coins, 1 x 2p coin, 3 x 1p coins

solution

- total payments for April are £49.05
- therefore cash remaining should be £100.00 – £49.05 = £50.95
- actual cash remaining is:

	as at 30 April	
	number held	value £
£10 notes	1	10.00
£5 notes	7	35.00
£1 coins	5	5.00
50p coins	1	0.50
20p coins	1	0.20
10p coins	1	0.10
5p coins	2	0.10
2p coins	1	0.02
1p coins	3	0.03
TOTAL		50.95

- therefore, at 30 April, the petty cash book reconciles (agrees) with cash in hand

Notes on the Case Study:

- if there is a discrepancy, it should be investigated promptly and, if it cannot be resolved, should be referred to the accounts supervisor

- from a practical point of view, it is advisable to keep the cash in the form of lower denomination notes and a stock of coins – these will make it easier to pay out the amounts of petty cash claims (with less risk of error) than if larger denomination notes, such as £50 and £20, are used

HOW PETTY CASH BOOK FITS INTO THE ACCOUNTING SYSTEM

Over the last few pages we have seen how low-value cash payments for small purchases and expenses are recorded firstly in the petty cash book and secondly in the general ledger (and sometimes also in payables ledger). As the petty cash book is the first place in the accounting system to record these transactions, it is the book of prime entry for low-value cash payments.

In accounting systems the petty cash book is:

- either the book of prime entry for low-value cash payments and the double-entry account for petty cash (kept in general ledger)

- or the book of prime entry only, with a separate petty cash account (see page 291) kept in general ledger in order to complete double-entry bookkeeping

as a book of prime entry and double-entry account

The diagram below shows the petty cash book performing two functions within the accounting system:

- as the **book of prime entry** for low-value cash payments

- as **part of the double-entry** system

This diagram shows the flow involving:

- financial documents – petty cash vouchers

- the petty cash book as a book of prime entry

- double-entry bookkeeping, involving petty cash and the other ledgers

petty cash payments in the accounting system

FINANCIAL DOCUMENTS

petty cash vouchers for low-value purchases and expenses payments

BOOK OF PRIME ENTRY – PETTY CASH BOOK

entries recording low-value purchases and expenses payments

DOUBLE-ENTRY BOOKKEEPING – PETTY CASH BOOK

debit   VAT account with total of VAT column

and

debit   appropriate expense account with total of each column

credit   petty cash book payments column

Note on the double-entry:

If payments are made to trade payables through petty cash book (eg to J Jones in the Case Study on page 280), the debits will be to:

–   payables ledger control account in the general ledger

–   trade payable's subsidiary account in the payables ledger

petty cash book solely as a book of prime entry

The alternative to the above is for the accounting system to treat petty cash book solely as a book of prime entry, in which case a separate double-entry account – **petty cash account** – is used in the general ledger.

The use of a petty cash account, using the petty cash book of Wyvern Traders (from the Case Study), is shown below.

PETTY CASH ACCOUNT

Where an accounting system treats petty cash book solely as a book of prime entry, a **petty cash account** is used in general ledger to complete double-entry. From Wyvern Traders' petty cash book (on page 281) the totals of receipts and payments are entered in petty cash account (which has been given the account number GL0180) as follows:

GENERAL LEDGER

Dr				Petty cash account (GL0180)			Cr
20-4			£	20-4			£
5 Apr	Balance b/d		100.00	9 Apr	Petty cash book PCB30		62.00
9 Apr	Petty cash book PCB30		10.00	9 Apr	Balance c/d		100.00
9 Apr	Bank CB55		52.00				
			162.00				162.00
10 Apr	Balance b/d		100.00				

Notes:

- the debit 'balance b/d' on 5 April of £100.00 is the same as the opening balance in petty cash book – see page 281. This is the imprest amount for this petty cash book

- the credit entry for 'petty cash book PCB30' on 9 April of £62.00 is the total of the expenses columns from petty cash book. These amounts are debited to their respective accounts in general ledger, as already seen on pages 282-283

- the debit entry for 'petty cash book PCB30' on 9 April for £10.00 is the receipt of cash from Jo Lee – payment for the purchase of postage stamps. This amount is credited to the relevant account – here postages account – in general ledger, as already seen on page 283

■ the debit entry for 'bank CB55' on 9 April for £52.00 is the reimbursement of petty cash in order to restore the imprest amount. The requisition form for this is shown on page 284

■ the 'balance c/d' on 9 April (and brought down on 10 April) for £100.00 is the new balance on petty cash book, ready for next week's transactions

■ in petty cash account, the cross reference to petty cash book enables a transaction to be followed through the accounting system – from book of prime entry to double-entry account – to ensure that it is complete

Chapter Summary

■ The petty cash book records low-value cash payments for small purchases and expenses incurred by a business.

■ Petty cash receipts are recorded on the debit side; payments are recorded on the credit side.

■ Transactions recorded in the petty cash book include:

 – stationery items

 – small items of office supplies

 – window cleaning

 – bus, rail and taxi fares incurred on behalf of the business

 – meals and drinks incurred on behalf of the business

 – postages

 – tips and donations

■ The petty cash book is controlled by the petty cashier.

■ The petty cash book is kept using either the imprest system or the non-imprest system.

■ The petty cashier prepares the petty cash book from petty cash vouchers, which are analysed to various expense columns.

■ At regular intervals – weekly or monthly – the data from the completed petty cash book is transferred to general ledger where the total of each expenses column is debited to the relevant account.

■ The petty cash book is the book of prime entry for low-value cash payments.

■ The petty cash book may combine the roles of:

 – the book of prime entry for low-value cash payments

 – the double-entry account for petty cash

■ When the petty cash book is used as the book of prime entry only, a petty cash account in general ledger completes double-entry bookkeeping.

Key Terms

petty cash book	records low-value cash payments for small purchases and expenses; is the book of prime entry for low-value cash payments (and may also be the double-entry account for petty cash)
petty cashier	the person responsible for the petty cash book
petty cash voucher	financial document against which payments are made out of petty cash
imprest system	where the money held in the petty cash float is restored to the same amount for the beginning of each week or month
non-imprest system	where the petty cash supply is not topped up to the same value each time
petty cash float	amount of money held at any one time by the petty cashier
expenses columns	used in the petty cash book to record payments under various headings to suit the circumstances of the business
petty cash account	double-entry account in the general ledger used when the petty cash book is treated solely as the book of prime entry; it shows the total payments made by the petty cashier during the week or month, and records receipts from bank account, together with the opening and closing balances

Activities

10.1 The petty cash book:

(a)	Is a financial document	
(b)	Is a part of double-entry bookkeeping only	
(c)	Is the book of prime entry for low-value cash payments	
(d)	Records and analyses expenses payments on the debit side	

Which **one** of these options is correct?

10.2 A petty cash voucher:

(a)	Is a financial document against which payments are made out of petty cash	
(b)	Is used to draw cash from bank to top-up the petty cash float	
(c)	Is passed to the bookkeeper for posting to the general ledger expenses accounts	
(d)	Is used to restore the imprest amount of the cash float	

Which **one** of these options is correct?

10.3 Most petty cash books operate using the imprest system. This means that:

(a)	The petty cashier draws money from the cashier as and when required	
(b)	The cashier has to authorise each petty cash payment	
(c)	A copy has to be kept of each petty cash voucher	
(d)	The petty cashier starts each week or month with a fixed amount of money	

Which **one** of these options is correct?

10.4 When the total of a petty cash book's column for VAT is transferred to the VAT account in the general ledger, will it be recorded as a debit or credit entry in general ledger?

Debit	
Credit	

10.5 The petty cashier of the business where you work tops up the petty cash at the end of the month with £75 withdrawn from the bank. What will be the entries in the general ledger?

General ledger

Account name	Amount £	Debit	Credit

10.6 The business for which you work is registered for VAT. The following petty cash amounts include VAT at 20% and you are required to calculate the amount that will be shown in the VAT column and the appropriate expense column (remember that VAT amounts should be rounded down to the nearest penny):

(a) £9.60

(b) £4.80

(c) £2.40

(d) £2.46

(e) £5.60

(f) £3.48

(g) £8.76

(h) 96p

(i) 99p

(j) £9.43

10.7 The following petty cash book shows a number of transactions of Nelson and Company for March 20-9. The petty cash book is kept solely as a book of prime entry.

Petty Cash Book										PCB20
Date 20-9	Details	Amount £	Date 20-9	Details	Amount £	VAT £	Travel £	Post-ages £	Statio-nery £	Ledger £
1 Mar	Balance b/d	100.00								
			4 Mar	Taxi fare	6.72	1.12	5.60			
			6 Mar	Post office	6.80			6.80		
			9 Mar	Pens	4.80	0.80			4.00	
			11 Mar	Rail fare	5.46		5.46			
12 Mar	J Hart (postages)	8.50								
			16 Mar	Envelopes	2.88	0.48			2.40	
			18 Mar	P Andrews (PL)	13.50					13.50
			19 Mar	Rail fare	10.60		10.60			
			20 Mar	Post office	4.75			4.75		
			23 Mar	Tape	3.84	0.64			3.20	
			25 Mar	Post office	5.10			5.10		
			27 Mar	Taxi fare	9.12	1.52	7.60			
					73.57	4.56	29.26	16.65	9.60	13.50
31 Mar	Bank	65.07								
			31 Mar	Balance c/d	100.00					
		173.57			173.57					
1 Apr	Balance b/d	100.00								

(a) You are to transfer the data from the petty cash book into the general ledger accounts (including cash book) as at 31 March 20-9. Note that a petty cash account is required.

(b) Show the entry that will be recorded in the payables ledger as at 31 March 20-9.

Note: You can download blank account layouts at www.osbornebooks.co.uk

10.8 On returning from holiday, you are told to take charge of the petty cash book of Carr Trading. This is kept using the imprest system, the float being £150.00 at the beginning of each month. Expenses columns are used for VAT, travel, postages, stationery, meals, and miscellaneous.

There are a number of transactions for the month which have been authorised. All transactions, unless otherwise indicated, include VAT at 20%. Petty cash voucher numbers are not required.

20-3

1 Aug	Balance of cash £150.00
4 Aug	Taxi fare £9.60
6 Aug	Post office £5.50 (no VAT)
9 Aug	Marker pens £3.84
11 Aug	Rail fare £10.50 (no VAT)
12 Aug	Window cleaner £14.40
16 Aug	Large envelopes £4.80
18 Aug	Donation to charity £10.00 (no VAT)
19 Aug	Rail fare £10.60 (no VAT)
20 Aug	Post office £8.30 (no VAT)
23 Aug	Roll of packing tape £2.40
25 Aug	Post office £1.50 (no VAT)
27 Aug	Taxi fare £14.40

You are to:

• record the transactions for the month in the petty cash book (PCB42)

• total the expenses columns

• restore the imprest amount of petty cash book to £150.00 by transfer from the cash book

• balance the petty cash book at 31 August 20-3 and bring down the balance on 1 September

Note: You can download blank account layouts at www.osbornebooks.co.uk

10.9 Towan Limited keeps an amount of petty cash in a locked box in the office. The imprest amount is £150 which is restored at the beginning of each month.

The following payments were made in June and have been recorded in the petty cash book:

3 June	Post office	£5.85
7 June	Window cleaning	£12.50
10 June	Envelopes	£7.25
15 June	Meal allowance	£8.00
18 June	Donation to charity	£10.00
20 June	Pens	£9.47
24 June	Post office	£3.65

At 30 June the petty cash remaining in the locked box comprised:

3 x £10 notes, 8 x £5 notes, 15 x £1 coins, 11 x 50p coins, 6 x 20p coins, 11 x 10p coins, 5 x 5p coins, 6 x 2p coins, 11 x 1p coins

You are to complete the following:

(a)

Total of petty cash payments for June	£	
Cash remaining should be	£	
Actual cash remaining is:		
	as at 30 June	
	number held	value £
£10 notes		
£5 notes		
£1 coins		
50p coins		
20p coins		
10p coins		
5p coins		
2p coins		
1p coins		
TOTAL		
Amount of discrepancy (if any)	£	

(b) State what action should be taken when a petty cash book cannot be reconciled with cash in hand.

10.10   You are the bookkeeper at Chelton Supplies Ltd and you are dealing with the analysed petty cash book.

Today is 30 April 20-7 and there is one last petty cash payment for the month to be recorded: an amount of £26.82 including VAT has been paid for stationery.

(a)   Calculate the VAT and net amounts to be recorded in the petty cash book.

VAT £	Net £

Before the petty cash payment in (a) was recorded, the stationery analysis column totalled £78.36.

(b)   Calculate the total of the stationery analysis column after the payment in (a) is recorded.

£ [   ]

After all the April petty cash payments have been recorded, an amount of £35.84 was left in the petty cash float. On 30 April the petty cash float was topped up to the imprest amount of £300.

(c)   What will be the entry in the petty cash book to record this transaction?

Details	Amount £	Debit ✓	Credit ✓

Select your details from the following list: Bank, Cash receipt, Cash sales, Credit sales, Trade payables, Trade receivables.

11 The trial balance

this chapter covers...

At regular intervals – often at the end of each month – it is necessary for the bookkeeper to carry out an arithmetical check of the accuracy of the double-entry bookkeeping. This check is carried out by means of a trial balance, which is a summary of the balances of all the general ledger accounts at the end of the accounting period.

This chapter

■ *explains where the trial balance fits into the accounting system*

■ *defines a trial balance*

■ *summarises how accounts are balanced*

■ *shows how to prepare a trial balance*

■ *gives guidance on what to do when a trial balance fails to balance*

■ *explains the next steps in the accounting system*

THE TRIAL BALANCE

As we know, double-entry bookkeeping involves making two accounting entries for each business transaction – a debit entry and a credit entry. It therefore follows that, if the bookkeeping is accurate, the total of all the debit entries will equal the total of all the credit entries for any given period. To test this accuracy, the bookkeeper checks, often on a monthly basis, that the total of the debit entries equals the total of the credit entries by extracting a trial balance.

A trial balance is a list in two columns of the balances of all general ledger accounts, with debit balances on the left, credit balances on the right, and showing the total of each column.

Note that this definition refers to balances rather than entries in the accounts. The reason for this is that the bookkeeper balances and calculates the running total of each account before preparing the trial balance. It would clearly be cumbersome and time-consuming for the bookkeeper to enter every transaction in the trial balance. Balancing accounts is therefore regularly carried out both to speed up the preparation of the trial balance and also to provide the owner(s) of the business with valuable information about items such as sales, purchases, expenses and income.

BALANCING ACCOUNTS

The technique of balancing accounts is straightforward, and has already been seen on pages 72-77. The account below recaps how accounts are balanced.

Here is the account before it is balanced:

Dr			Vehicles account			Cr
20-1		£	20-1			£
10 Oct	Bank	15,000	15 Oct	Bank		5,000
25 Oct	Bank	20,000				

At the month-end, the bookkeeper balances the double-entry accounts, in preparation for the trial balance as follows:

Dr			Vehicles account			Cr
20-1		£	20-1			£
10 Oct	Bank	15,000	15 Oct	Bank		5,000
25 Oct	Bank	20,000	31 Oct	Balance c/d		30,000
		35,000				35,000
1 Nov	Balance b/d	30,000				

Only a manual bookkeeping system requires accounts to be balanced; when a digital bookkeeping system is in use, the balance of each account is available at any time.

BALANCE TERMINOLOGY

When balancing accounts in a manual bookkeeping system at the period end – eg month or year – always use the terms 'balance c/d' for the closing balance carried down into the next accounting period and 'balance b/d' for the balance brought down into the next accounting period as the opening balance. These terms are seen in the example account shown above.

From time to time, in manual bookkeeping, you may also see the terms 'balance c/f' (carried forward) and 'balance b/f' (brought forward). These are used for subtotalling money amounts, often at the bottom of a page where the figure is carried forward to the top of the next page where it is brought forward.

When balancing accounts in AAT Assessments, always use the terms 'balance c/d' for the end of the current accounting period and 'balance b/d' for the start of the new accounting period.

PREPARING THE TRIAL BALANCE

When all accounts within the general ledger are balanced, the bookkeeper can proceed to the trial balance in the form of two columns: debit balances on the left and credit balances on the right. If the bookkeeper has been accurate in the day-to-day recording of transactions – ie double-entry bookkeeping has been complied with – then the totals of the two columns will agree.

To understand the process of preparing a trial balance, examine the list of account balances of Sidbury Traders shown on the next page. You decide which are debit balances and which are credit balances by ticking the appropriate column.

Account balances of Sidbury Traders as at 31 December 20-1

Account name	£	Debit ✓	Credit ✓
Capital	20,000		
Bank (cash at bank)	13,000		
Cash	250		
Petty cash	100		
Vehicles	20,000		
Rent paid	3,000		
Wages	10,000		
Sales	60,000		
Purchases	32,000		
Sales returns	1,500		
Purchases returns	350		
Receivables ledger control	22,000		
Payables ledger control	18,000		
Value Added Tax (owing to HMRC)	3,500		

The trial balance is then set out with two money columns, debit and credit, with the list of account names set out to the left of the balances. The money columns are totalled to see if they agree.

Trial balance of Sidbury Traders as at 31 December 20-1

Account name	Debit £	Credit £
Capital		20,000
Bank (cash at bank)	13,000	
Cash	250	
Petty cash	100	
Vehicles	20,000	
Rent paid	3,000	
Wages	10,000	
Sales		60,000
Purchases	32,000	
Sales returns	1,500	
Purchases returns		350
Receivables ledger control	22,000	
Payables ledger control		18,000
Value Added Tax (owing to HMRC)		3,500
TOTALS	101,850	101,850

Note that all of the account names listed above have been used earlier within this book.

Here is guidance as to which accounts used in this book have debit balances and which have credit balances:

debit balances

Accounts with debit balances represent assets and expenses, and include:

- cash
- drawings
- expenses, eg discounts allowed, general expenses, rent paid, wages
- non-current assets, eg machinery, office equipment, premises, vehicles
- petty cash
- purchases
- receivables ledger control
- sales returns

credit balances

Accounts with credit balances represent liabilities, income and capital, and include:

- bank loan
- capital
- income, eg commission received, discounts received, rent received
- payables ledger control
- purchases returns
- sales

You should note that two accounts, bank and Value Added Tax, can have either debit or credit balances:

- bank
  - a debit balance when the business has money in the bank, ie an asset of the business
  - a credit balance when the business is overdrawn at the bank, ie a liability of the business
- Value Added Tax
  - a debit balance when VAT is due to the business by HM Revenue & Customs
  - a credit balance when the business owes VAT to HM Revenue & Customs

For a business that uses a digital bookkeeping system there is no need to balance accounts as the balance can be accessed as a report at any time. A trial balance is automatically generated and will always balance because the system only allows transactions that are in balance to be entered. However, a completed trial balance does not mean that the accounts are error-free – and this applies to both manual and digital bookkeeping systems. For example, not recording a transaction, recording the same transaction twice, or recording a transaction in the wrong account will all produce a seemingly balanced trial balance, but one that is incorrect. Errors not disclosed by the trial balance will be covered in detail in your later studies – see *Principles of Bookkeeping Controls Tutorial*, Chapter 7.

IF THE TRIAL BALANCE DOESN'T BALANCE

If the trial balance doesn't balance, the bookkeeper must locate the error as soon as possible, because the error may affect people with whom the business trades, for example trade receivables and trade payables. The procedure that should be adopted on finding a trial balance that doesn't balance is as follows:

- check the addition of the trial balance
- check that the balances have been entered correctly from the accounts
- check that all the general ledger balances have been entered
- find the difference between the differing totals
- look for the amount of the difference as an item in the accounts
- divide the difference by two: a transaction could have been entered as two debits or two credits

As noted earlier, some errors made by the bookkeeper in entering transactions into the accounts will not be shown by the trial balance and will often emerge in due course, either when a customer points out a mistake (charged too much, too little, or not at all), or when the accountant reviews the business transactions.

FINANCIAL STATEMENTS – NEXT STEPS

A business requires a trial balance to be prepared on a regular basis to confirm the arithmetical accuracy of the bookkeeping. It also uses the account balances as a basis for the production of its financial statements, normally once a year, but sometimes more frequently. The financial statements comprise:

- statement of profit or loss
- statement of financial position

These financial statements show the owner(s) how profitable the business is, what it owns, and how it is financed. The trial balance therefore is an important exercise in the bookkeeping process: it proves the arithmetical accuracy of the accounts and lists the balances which form the basis for the financial statements of the business. Financial statements will form an important part of your later AAT studies.

Chapter Summary	
■	A trial balance is a regular arithmetical check of the accuracy of the double-entry bookkeeping.
■	Balancing accounts is required in a manual bookkeeping system to calculate the balance of each account.
■	'Balance carried down (c/d)' and 'balance brought down (b/d)' are the descriptions used when balancing accounts.
■	Debit balances represent assets and expenses.
■	Credit balances represent liabilities, income and capital.
■	Bank account and Value Added Tax account could have either debit or credit balances, depending on the circumstances.
■	Some errors made by the bookkeeper will not be shown by the trial balance.
■	The account balances from the trial balance form the basis for the production of the business financial statements.

Key Terms		
	trial balance	a list in two columns of the balances of all general ledger accounts, listing debit balances on the left, credit balances on the right, and showing the total of each column
	c/d and b/d	carried down and brought down – used when balancing accounts at the period end
	c/f and b/f	carried forward and brought forward – used when subtotalling money amounts, often when a page is full
	financial statements	statement of profit or loss, and statement of financial position

Activities

11.1 This task is about totalling and balancing ledger accounts.

The following account is in the general ledger at the close of day on 30 June 20-1:

Value Added Tax

20-1	Details	Amount £	20-1	Details	Amount £
30 Jun	Purchases Day Book	1,245	1 Jun	Balance b/f	6,251
			30 Jun	Sales Day Book	1,579

- What is the balance brought down at 1 July on the account?
- Indicate whether the balance brought down is debit or credit.

Account name	Balance £	Debit ✓	Credit ✓
Value Added Tax			

11.2 Which **one** of the following best describes a trial balance?

(a)	A list of the money transactions of a business, distinguishing between receipts and payments, and showing the total for each.	
(b)	A list of the separate subsidiary accounts for each trade receivable and trade payable of a business, showing the total for each.	
(c)	A list of balances of all general ledger accounts, separated into columns for debit balances and credit balances, which shows the total of each column.	
(d)	A book of prime entry which is used to give totals to be entered into the accounts.	

11.3 Indicate whether the following accounts will have a debit balance or a credit balance:

Account name	Debit ✓	Credit ✓
Cash		
Sales		
Purchases returns		
Receivables ledger control		
Machinery		
Discounts received		
Rent paid		
Bank loan		

11.4   From the account balances below, prepare the trial balance of Brian Montagu as at 28 February
20-1 (use the trial balance layout provided).

	£
Cash	250
Sales	28,000
Bank (cash at bank)	1,350
Vehicles	12,300
Capital	7,150
Purchases	17,200
Payables ledger control	2,400
Receivables ledger control	3,600
Sales returns	450
Discounts received	150
Wages	2,550

Trial balance of Brian Montagu as at 28 February 20-1		
Account name	**Debit £**	**Credit £**
Cash		
Sales		
Bank (cash at bank)		
Vehicles		
Capital		
Purchases		
Payables ledger control		
Receivables ledger control		
Sales returns		
Discounts received		
Wages		
TOTALS		

11.5 From the account balances below, prepare the trial balance of Sara Greenwell as at 31 March 20-1 (use the trial balance layout provided). Her bookkeeper has omitted to open a capital account.

	£
Bank (overdraft)	650
Purchases	43,400
Petty cash	80
Sales	68,200
Purchases returns	150
Receivables ledger control	15,300
Office equipment	3,650
Drawings	5,840
Vehicles	19,500
General expenses	13,760
Payables ledger control	6,220
Value Added Tax (owing to HMRC)	720
Discounts allowed	330
Capital	?

Trial balance of Sara Greenwell as at 31 March 20-1		
Account name	**Debit £**	**Credit £**
Bank (overdraft)		
Purchases		
Petty cash		
Sales		
Purchases returns		
Receivables ledger control		
Office equipment		
Drawings		
Vehicles		
General expenses		
Payables ledger control		
Value Added Tax (owing to HMRC)		
Discounts allowed		
Capital		
TOTALS		

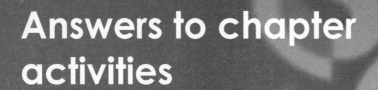

Answers to chapter activities

CHAPTER 1: THE ACCOUNTING SYSTEM

1.1	(b)	A sale with immediate payment
1.2	True	
1.3	(c)	Cash book, petty cash book, sales day book
1.4	(a)	Ledger accounts
1.5	(b)	A customer who owes money to a business
1.6	(c)	One debit and one credit
1.7	(b)	Suppliers
1.8	(a)	An amount owed by that business
1.9	**(a)**	£10,500
	(b)	£6,720
	(c)	£3,000
	(d)	£155,000
	(e)	Receivables ledger control account and payables ledger control accounts
1.10	(d)	Suppliers who sell goods and services on a credit basis
1.11	(c)	Income – Expenses = Profit
1.12	(a)	Assets – Liabilities = Capital

CHAPTER 2: FINANCIAL DOCUMENTS FOR SALES

2.1 **(a)** purchase order

  (b) delivery note

  (c) invoice

  (d) statement of account

  (e) credit note

2.2 **(a)** prompt payment discount

  (b) trade discount

  (c) bulk discount

2.3 £159.50 – £47.85 discount = £111.65 plus VAT of £22.33 (rounded down) = **£133.98**

2.4

	Total	Discount	Net total	VAT	Invoice total
	£	£	£	£	£
(a)	160.00	32.00	128.00	25.60	153.60
(b)	400.00	80.00	320.00	64.00	384.00
(c)	40.00	none	40.00	8.00	48.00
(d)	8,000.00	1,600.00	6,400.00	1,280.00	7,680.00

2.5 **(a)**

	Total	Discount	Net total	VAT	Invoice total
	£	£	£	£	£
1	100.00	20.00	80.00	16.00	96.00
2	1,650.00	330.00	1,320.00	264.00	1,584.00
3	2,500.00	500.00	2,000.00	400.00	2,400.00
4	10,900.00	2,180.00	8,720.00	1,744.00	10,464.00

  (b)

	Total	PPD	Net total
	£	£	£
1	96.00	4.80	91.20
2	1,584.00	79.20	1,504.80
3	2,400.00	120.00	2,280.00
4	10,464.00	523 20	9,940 80

  (c) Credit note

2.6 **(a)** Numerical coding – invoice & credit note: invoice 10982, credit note 2378

(b) Alphabetical coding – invoice & credit note: product code ASPS

(c) Alpha-numerical coding – account No HS234, postcode MR7 4EF or MR7 9JH

2.7 **(a)** Incorrect discount of 10% applied, wrong total. Corrected figures: goods total should be £76.00, VAT £15.20, final total £91.20.

(b) Total before discount should be £250.00. Corrected figures: goods total £225.00 (after deduction of 10% discount), VAT £45.00, final total £270.00.

2.8 Statement should be dated 31 July 20-3 and addressed to Mr Simpson.

The entries are:

20-3		Debit £	Credit £	Balance £
1 July	Balance b/f	58.75		58.75
4 July	Bank payment received		58.75	00.00
8 July	Invoice 10982	348.00		348.00
14 July	Credit note 2378		34.80	313.20
			TOTAL	313.20

2.9 **(a)**

Customer	£	Date
Merrow plc	*702.00	15 March 20-2
Barton Ltd	**2,116.80	19 March 20-2

* £600 – £15 PPD = £585 + £117 VAT = £702
** £1,800 – £36 PPD = £1,764 + £352.80 VAT = £2,116.80

(b) (b) Credit note

CHAPTER 3: DOUBLE-ENTRY AND THE ACCOUNTING EQUATION

3.1   (c)   Books of prime entry

3.2   (b)   Receivables ledger

3.3   (a)   Money in is a debit, money out is a credit

3.4

	Debit	Credit
Payment of wages		✓
Cash received from sales	✓	
Payment of an invoice by a credit customer	✓	
Payment of an insurance premium		✓
Loan received from a finance company	✓	
Loan repayment made		✓
Bank charges		✓

3.5

	Debit	Credit
Payment of wages	Wages	Bank
Payment of insurance	Insurance	Bank
Money received from sales	Bank	Sales
Purchases made	Purchases	Bank
Loan received from the bank	Bank	Loan
Loan repayment	Loan	Bank
Telephone bill paid	Telephone	Bank
Repairs bill paid	Repairs	Bank
Rent received from office space rented out	Bank	Rent received

3.6

Account	20-3	DR or CR	Details	Amount
Sales	1 May	Cr	Bank	975.00
	11 May	Cr	Bank	456.70
Telephone	6 May	Dr	Bank	265.00
Insurance	12 May	Dr	Bank	678.00
Bank Loan	14 May	Cr	Bank	5,000.00
Purchases	15 May	Dr	Bank	2,760.90

3.7   **Debit balances**: Purchases, Expenses, Customer Accounts, Assets

       Credit balances: Capital, Liabilities, Supplier Accounts, Sales, Income

3.8

	Debit	Credit
Asset bought by the business	✓	
Liability (eg bank loan taken out)		✓
Capital introduced by the owner		✓
Sales made by the business		✓
Purchases made by the business	✓	
Expenses of the business	✓	
Customer who owes the business money	✓	
Supplier who is owed money by the business		✓

3.9   (b)   Assets – Liabilities = Capital

3.10

Assets	Liabilities	Capital
£	£	£
120,000	45,000	75,000
156,000	61,000	95,000
265,500	86,500	179,000
88,000	38,000	50,000
127,500	37,500	90,000
345,700	136,700	209,000

3.11

Transaction	Debit	Credit
Increase in capital account		✓
Increase in liability account		✓
Decrease in asset account		✓
Decrease in liability account	✓	
Increase in asset account	✓	

3.12

Debit			Bank Account			Credit
Date	**Details**	**£**	**Date**	**Details**		**£**
20-4			20-4			
3 Feb	Capital	10,000	10 Feb	Purchases		750
4 Feb	Bank Loan	25,000	14 Feb	Business rates		450
6 Feb	Sales	1,340	15 Feb	Purchases		2,760
18 Feb	Sales	860	21 Feb	Advertising		138
25 Feb	Sales	2,640	28 Feb	Wages		3,560

Account	**20-3**	**DR or CR**	**Details**	**Amount £**
Capital	3 Feb	Cr	Bank	10,000
Bank loan	4 Feb	Cr	Bank	25,000
Sales	6 Feb	Cr	Bank	1,340
	18 Feb	Cr	Bank	860
	25 Feb	Cr	Bank	2,640
Purchases	10 Feb	Dr	Bank	750
	15 Feb	Dr	Bank	2,760
Business rates	14 Feb	Dr	Bank	450
Advertising	21 Feb	Dr	Bank	138
Wages	28 Feb	Dr	Bank	3,560

3.13 (a)

Dr		Solo Supplies Account (Payables Ledger)				Cr
20-3	**Details**	**£**	**20-3**	**Details**		**£**
31 Mar	Balance c/d	506.75	23 Mar	Purchases		248.00
			25 Mar	Purchases		78.75
			30 Mar	Purchases		180.00
		506.75				506.75
			1 Apr	Balance b/d		506.75

(b)

Dr						
20-3	**Details**	**£**	**20-3**	**Details**	**£**	

Dr	Atletico Supplies Account (Payables Ledger)					Cr
20-3	**Details**	**£**	**20-3**	**Details**	**£**
23 Mar	Purchases returns	80.00	24 Mar	Purchases	120.00
26 Mar	Purchases returns	70.00	27 Mar	Purchases	360.00
31 Mar	Balance c/d	500.00	30 Mar	Purchases	170.00
		650.00			650.00
			1 Apr	Balance b/d	500.00

(c)

Dr	Trajan Sports Account (Receivables Ledger)					Cr
20-3	**Details**	**£**	**20-3**	**Details**	**£**
23 Mar	Sales	450.00	24 Mar	Sales returns	80.00
26 Mar	Sales	70.00	30 Mar	Sales returns	70.00
27 Mar	Sales	180.00	31 Mar	Balance c/d	550.00
		700.00			700.00
1 Apr	Balance b/d	550.00			

(d)

Dr	Office Expenses Account (General Ledger)					Cr
20-3	**Details**	**£**	**20-3**	**Details**	**£**
4 Mar	Bank	75.20	31 Mar	Balance c/d	364.31
6 Mar	Bank	191.00			
8 Mar	Bank	34.65			
15 Mar	Bank	63.46			
		364.31			364.31
1 Apr	Balance b/d	364.31			

3.14

Statement	True	False
A digital bookkeeping system is always completely accurate		✓
An inaccurate entry in a manual bookkeeping system may lead to the owner of the business receiving wrong information	✓	
A digital bookkeeping system can import data from sources such as third-party software	✓	

3.15

Statement	Advantages	Disadvantages
The system is able to reconcile the receivables ledger to receivables ledger control account	✓	
The system automatically creates a trial balance	✓	
The system saves time with faster data entry	✓	
A change in the amount and/or frequency of recurring entries may not be identified		✓

3.16 Features of a digital bookkeeping system.

FOUR from:

- on-screen preparation of sales invoices, which can be sent electronically to the customer, with automatic updating of accounts in the receivables ledger

- electronic recording of purchases invoices, with automatic updating of accounts in the payables ledger

- electronic importing of transactions from bank records

- electronic payments to suppliers and for expenses

- automatic updating of general (nominal) ledger

- importing transactions from sources such as third-party software, csv (comma-separated values) files, and spreadsheets

CHAPTER 4: ACCOUNTING FOR SALES, RETURNS, AND DISCOUNTS

4.1   (a)   Sales day book

4.2   (a)   Sales invoice; sales day book; sales account; VAT account; receivables ledger control account; customer's account

4.3   (c)   Debit discounts allowed; debit VAT; credit receivables ledger control

4.4   **(a)**   • The financial documents for credit sales transactions are sales invoices that have been checked and authorised.

   • The details and amounts of the invoices are entered into sales day book. In the money columns of sales day book is recorded:

      – total column, the final total of each invoice

      – VAT column, the VAT amount shown on each invoice

      – net column, the net ('goods total') amount of each invoice

   • After sales day book has been prepared for the week or month, it is totalled and the information from it is transferred into the double-entry system.

   • The bookkeeping entries are:

      – the total of the total column is debited to receivables ledger control account in general ledger

      – the total of the VAT column is credited to VAT account in general ledger

      – the total of the net column is credited to sales account in general ledger

      – the amounts from the total column for each separate transaction are debited to the subsidiary accounts of the customers in receivables ledger

   (b)   • The financial documents for sales returns transactions are credit notes issued that have been checked and authorised.

   • The details and amounts of the credit notes are entered into sales returns day book. In the money columns of the sales returns day book is recorded:

      – total column, the final total of each credit note

      – VAT column, the VAT amount shown on each credit note

      – net column, the net ('goods total') amount of each credit note

   • After sales returns day book has been prepared for the week or month, it is totalled and the information from it is transferred into the double-entry system.

   • The bookkeeping entries are:

      – the total of the total column is credited to receivables ledger control account in general ledger

      – the total of the VAT column is debited to VAT account in general ledger

      – the total of the net column is debited to sales returns account in general ledger

      – the amounts from the total column for each separate transaction are credited to the subsidiary accounts of the customers in receivables ledger

4.5 **(a)**

Sales Day Book						SDB50
Date	Customer name	Invoice number	Account code	Total £	VAT £	Net £
20-5						
2 Apr	Malvern Stores	4578	RL110	66.00	11.00	55.00
5 Apr	Pershore Retailers	4579	RL145	78.00	13.00	65.00
7 Apr	E Grainger	4580	RL055	33.60	5.60	28.00
9 Apr	P Wilson	4581	RL172	69.60	11.60	58.00
12 Apr	M Kershaw	4582	RL090	91.20	15.20	76.00
14 Apr	D Lloyd	4583	RL095	79.20	13.20	66.00
19 Apr	A Cox	4584	RL032	39.60	6.60	33.00
22 Apr	Dines Stores	4585	RL048	122.40	20.40	102.00
23 Apr	Malvern Stores	4586	RL110	56.40	9.40	47.00
26 Apr	P Wilson	4587	RL172	42.00	7.00	35.00
29 Apr	A Cox	4588	RL032	98.40	16.40	82.00
30 Apr	Totals for month			776.40	129.40	647.00
				GL1200	GL2200	GL4100

(b)

GENERAL LEDGER

Dr		Receivables ledger control account (GL1200)			Cr
20-5			£ p	20-5	£ p
30 Apr	Sales Day Book SDB50		776.40		

Dr		Value added tax account (GL2200)			Cr
20-5		£ p	20-5		£ p
			30 Apr	Sales Day Book SDB50	129.40

Dr		Sales account (GL4100)			Cr
20-5		£ p	20-5		£ p
			30 Apr	Sales Day Book SDB50	647.00

RECEIVABLES LEDGER

Dr		Malvern Stores (RL110)			Cr
20-5			£ p	20-5	£ p
2 Apr	Sales	SDB50	66.00		
23 Apr	Sales	SDB50	56.40		

Dr		**Pershore Retailers (RL145)**				Cr	
20-5			£ p	20-5		£	p
5 Apr	Sales	SDB50	78.00				

Dr		**E Grainger (RL055)**				Cr	
20-5			£ p	20-5		£	p
7 Apr	Sales	SDB50	33.60				

Dr		**P Wilson (RL172)**				Cr	
20-5			£ p	20-5		£	p
9 Apr	Sales	SDB50	69.60				
26 Apr	Sales	SDB50	42.00				

Dr		**M Kershaw (RL090)**				Cr	
20-5			£ p	20-5		£	p
12 Apr	Sales	SDB50	91.20				

Dr		**D Lloyd (RL095)**				Cr	
20-5			£ p	20-5		£	p
14 Apr	Sales	SDB50	79.20				

Dr		**A Cox (RL032)**				Cr	
20-5			£ p	20-5		£	p
19 Apr	Sales	SDB50	39.60				
29 Apr	Sales	SDB50	98.40				

Dr		**Dines Stores (RL048)**				Cr	
20-5			£ p	20-5		£	p
22 Apr	Sales	SDB50	122.40				

4.6 **(a)**

Sales Returns Day Book						SRDB18
Date 20-5	Customer name	Credit note number	Account code	Total £	VAT £	Net £
8 Apr	Pershore Retailers	572	RL145	24.00	4.00	20.00
12 Apr	E Grainger	573	RL055	33.60	5.60	28.00
16 Apr	D Lloyd	574	RL095	39.60	6.60	33.00
28 Apr	Malvern Stores	575	RL110	24.00	4.00	20.00
30 Apr	A Cox	576	RL032	48.00	8.00	40.00
30 Apr	Totals for month			169.20	28.20	141.00
				GL1200	GL2200	GL4100

(b)

GENERAL LEDGER

Dr		Receivables ledger control account (GL1200)				Cr
20-5			£ p	20-5		£ p
30 Apr	Sales Day Book SDB50		776.40	30 Apr	Sales returns Day Book SRDB18	169.20

Dr		Value added tax account (GL2200)				Cr
20-5			£ p	20-5		£ p
30 Apr	Sales returns Day Book SRDB18		28.20	30 Apr	Sales Day Book SDB50	129.40

Dr		Sales returns account (GL4100)				Cr
20-5			£ p	20-5		£ p
30 Apr	Sales Returns Day Book SRDB18		141.00			

Note: sales account not shown – see answer to Activity 4.5

RECEIVABLES LEDGER

Dr		Pershore Retailers (RL145)				Cr
20-5			£ p	20-5		£ p
5 Apr	Sales	SDB50	78.00	8 Apr	Sales returns SRDB18	24.00

Dr		E Grainger (RL055)				Cr
20-5			£ p	20-5		£ p
7 Apr	Sales	SDB50	33.60	12 Apr	Sales Day Book SRDB18	33.60

Dr			D Lloyd (RL095)			Cr
20-5			£ p	20-5		£ p
14 Apr	Sales	SDB50	79.20	16 Apr	Sales Returns SRDB18	39.60

Dr			Malvern Stores (RL110)			Cr
20-5			£ p	20-5		£ p
2 Apr	Sales	SDB50	66.00	28 Apr	Sales returns SRDB18	24.00
23 Apr	Sales	SDB50	56.40			

Dr			A Cox (RL032)			Cr
20-5			£ p	20-5		£ p
19 Apr	Sales	SDB50	39.60	30 Apr	Sales Returns SRDB18	48.00
29 Apr	Sales	SDB50	98.40			

4.7 **(a)** **General ledger**

Account name	Amount £	Debit	Credit
Sales	10,600		✓
Value Added Tax	2,120		✓
Receivables ledger control	12,720	✓	

Receivables ledger

Account name	Amount £	Debit	Credit
Bowne Ltd	960	✓	
Jamieson & Co	4,944	✓	
Pottertons	3,888	✓	
Wells plc	2,928	✓	

(b) **General ledger**

Account name	Amount £	Debit	Credit
Sales returns	1,520	✓	
Value Added Tax	304	✓	
Receivables ledger control	1,824		✓

Receivables ledger

Account name	Amount £	Debit	Credit
Lloyd & Co	576		✓
Wyvern Stores	1,248		✓

(c) **General ledger**

Account name	Amount £	Debit	Credit
Discounts allowed	50	✓	
Value Added Tax	10	✓	
Receivables ledger control	60		✓

Receivables ledger

Account name	Amount £	Debit	Credit
Sanchos Ltd	24		✓
Belton Stores	36		✓

4.8

Customer name	Receivables ledger account code
Dymock Trading Co	DYM003
Hedgehog Fashions	HED001
Jones & Co	JON002

Note: Dymock Trading Co is numbered '003' because an '002' account number has been allocated already for 'D'; similarly for Jones & Co where '001' has been allocated already for 'J'.

4.9 **(a)** and **(b)**

Sales day book

Date 20-9	Customer name	Invoice number	Total £	VAT £	Net £	Sales type 1 £	Sales type 2 £
30 June	Yanez & Co	1621	1,440	240	1,200		1,200
30 June	Napier Stores	1622	1,920	320	1,600	1,600	
30 June	Beale Ltd	1623	768	128	640		640
	Totals		4,128	688	3,440	1,600	1,840

4.10 **(a)**

Daybook	
Sales day book	✓
Sales returns day book	
Purchases day book	
Discounts allowed day book	

Date 20-4	Name	Invoice number	Total £	VAT £	Net £
15 Jul	Sparks & Co	24761	240.00	40.00	200.00

(b)

Purchases: toner cartridges	
Sales: copier paper	
Sales: toner cartridges	✓
Sales returns: toner cartridges	

(c)

as a debit entry	
as a credit entry	✓

4.11

20-2	Details	Amount £	20-2	Details	Amount £
1 June	Balance b/f	3,627	10 June	Bank	1,483
4 June		2,184	21 June	Sales Returns	210
			30 June	Balance c/d	4,118
		5,811		Total	5,811
1 July	Balance b/d	4,118			

CHAPTER 5: PROCESS RECEIPTS FROM CUSTOMERS

5.1 (d) Invoice, receivables ledger account, customer statement

5.2 (b) The prompt payment discount percentage is shown

5.3 (a) The remittance advice does not take account of the credit note issued on 10 November and so includes an overpayment of £49.00. Cool Socks should advise the customer, Trends, of this discrepancy and suggest that an adjustment could be made when the next month's payment is due, the credit remaining on the account for the time being.

(b) The remittance advice does not include payment of an invoice for £625.85 issued on 17 November and so the discrepancy is an underpayment. As the amount is large, Cool Socks should contact Vogue Ltd and ask for payment. If the invoice is disputed, the problem should be looked into and resolved as soon as possible.

(c) RTC Fashions has underpaid its account because it has deducted 5% prompt payment discount when it was not offered (it is not included in the terms on the Chico Importers invoice). Additionally it has adjusted and underpaid the VAT by £5.60. Chico Importers should either ask RTC Fashions for payment of the shortfall of £33.60 immediately or advise the company of the problem and suggest that an adjustment could be made when the next month's payment is due, the debit remaining on RTC Fashions' account for the time being. The decision depends on the relationship that exists between the supplier and customer.

5.4 (a)

20-4	Details	£	Discrepancies
3 April	Invoice 7624	1,410	No discrepancy
10 April	Credit note 105	-340	Incorrect date
19 April	Invoice 7711	1,875	Incorrect amount
25 April	Credit note 115	-65	Incorrectly recorded
28 April	Invoice 7769	2,350	Incorrect invoice number

(b) (b) £40 overpaid

(c) *£ 4,539.36

* £3,860 – £77.20 PPD = £3,782.80 + £756.56 VAT = £4,539.36

(d)

Date 20-4	Detail	£	Outstanding amount £
1 April	Opening balance	3,150	980
15 April	Invoice 7695	1,875	550
28 April	Credit note 121	−325	0

CHAPTER 6: FINANCIAL DOCUMENTS FOR PURCHASES

6.1 **(a)** purchase order

  (b) delivery note

  (c) goods received note

  (d) invoice

  (e) credit note

6.2 A delivery note is sent by the seller with the goods; a goods received note is an internal document used by the purchaser to record and action any discrepancies found when the goods arrive.

6.3 (a) The delivery note and the invoice

6.4 Credit note

6.5 The errors are:

  (a) the goods were delivered to the wrong address

  (b) an incorrect customer discount has been applied (10% instead of 15%)

  (c) the wrong goods were sent (product code 4574 instead of 4573)

  The total should have been £95 less 15% discount = £80.75 plus VAT of £16.15 = £96.90.

  The email should point out these errors and state that the disks are being returned for credit.

6.6 **(a)** Errors on credit note:

  – Wrong reference – should be 17643

  – Product code incorrect – should be 919BK

  – Should be gel pens, not rollerball pens

  – credit should be for 2 boxes, not 3

  The email should point out the errors on the credit note and ask for a revised document to be issued.

  (b)

supplier code	general ledger code
HE001	5010

6.7

Purpose	Document
Document stating the cost of goods or services to be provided	Quotation
Document stating the amount owing and the terms of payment	Invoice
Document listing and accompanying the goods	Delivery note
Document reducing the amount owing	Credit note

6.8

Discrepancy	
Buyer details	✓
	✓
Quantity of goods	✓
Date of credit note	
Net amount	
VAT amount	
Total amount	✓

CHAPTER 7: ACCOUNTING FOR PURCHASES, RETURNS AND DISCOUNTS

7.1 (c) Purchases returns day book

7.2 (d) Credit note issued; purchases returns day book; purchases returns account; VAT account; payables ledger control account; supplier's account

7.3 (b) Debit payables ledger control; credit discounts received; credit VAT

7.4 (a)
- The financial documents for credit purchases transactions are purchases invoices, received from suppliers, that have been checked and authorised.

- The details and amounts of the invoices are entered into the purchases day book. In the money columns of purchases day book are recorded:
  - total column, the final total of each invoice
  - VAT column, the VAT amount shown on each invoice
  - net column, the net ('goods or services total') amount of each invoice

- After purchases day book has been written up for the week or month, it is totalled and the information from it is transferred into the double-entry system.

- The bookkeeping entries are:
  - the total of the total column is credited to payables ledger control account in general ledger
  - the total of the VAT column is debited to VAT account in general ledger
  - the total of the net column is debited to purchases account in general ledger
  - the amounts from the total column for each separate transaction are credited to the subsidiary accounts of the suppliers in payables ledger

(b) • The financial documents for purchases returns transactions are credit notes, received from suppliers, that have been checked and authorised.

• The details and amounts of the credit notes are entered into purchases returns day book. In the money columns of the purchases returns day book are recorded:

– total column, the final total of each credit note

– VAT column, the VAT amount shown on each credit note

– net column, the net ('goods total') amount of each credit note

• After purchases returns day book has been written up for the week or month, it is totalled and the information from it is transferred into the double-entry system.

• The bookkeeping entries are:

– the total of the total column is debited to payables ledger control account in general ledger

– the total of the VAT column is credited to VAT account in general ledger

– the total of the net column is credited to purchases returns account in general ledger

– the amounts from the total column for each separate transaction are debited to the subsidiary accounts of the suppliers in payables ledger

7.5 (a)

Purchases Day Book						PDB36
Date 20-5	Supplier name	Invoice number	Account code	Total £	VAT £	Net £
2 Apr	Severn Supplies	6789	PL721	300.00	50.00	250.00
5 Apr	I Johnstone	A241	PL604	252.00	42.00	210.00
9 Apr	L Murphy	2456	PL659	222.00	37.00	185.00
15 Apr	Mercia Manufacturing	X457	PL627	216.00	36.00	180.00
19 Apr	AMC Enterprises	AMC456	PL520	414.00	69.00	345.00
26 Apr	S Green	2846	PL574	474.00	79.00	395.00
30 Apr	Totals for month			1,878.00	313.00	1,565.00
				GL2350	GL2200	GL5100

(b)

GENERAL LEDGER

Dr	Value added tax account (GL2200)		Cr	
20-5		£ p	20-5	£ p
30 Apr	Purchases Day Book PDB36	313.00		

Dr	Payables ledger control account (GL2350)		Cr	
20-5		£ p	20-5	£ p
			30 Apr Purchases Day Book PDB36	1,878.00

Dr	Purchases account (GL5100)		Cr	
20-5		£ p	20-5	£ p
30 Apr	Purchases Day Book PDB36	1,565.00		

PAYABLES LEDGER

Dr	Severn Supplies (PL721)		Cr	
20-5		£ p	20-5	£ p
			2 Apr Purchases PDB36	300.00

Dr	I Johnstone (PL604)		Cr	
20-5		£ p	20-5	£ p
			30 Apr Purchases PDB36	252.00

Dr	L Murphy (PL659)		Cr	
20-5		£ p	20-5	£ p
			9 Apr Purchases PDB36	222.00

Dr	Mercia Manufacturing (PL627)		Cr	
20-5		£ p	20-5	£ p
			15 Apr Purchases PDB36	216.00

Dr	AMC Enterprises (PL520)		Cr	
20-5		£ p	20-5	£ p
			19 Apr Purchases PDB36	414.00

Dr	S Green (PL574)		Cr	
20-5		£ p	20-5	£ p
			26 Apr Purchases PDB36	474.00

7.6 **(a)**

Purchases Returns Day Book						PRDB11
Date	Supplier name	Credit note number	Account code	Total £	VAT £	Net £
20-5						
7 Apr	Severn Supplies	225	PL721	60.00	10.00	50.00
14 Apr	L Murphy	X456	PL 659	96.00	16.00	80.00
21 Apr	AMC Enterprises	3921	PL 520	150.00	25.00	125.00
29 Apr	S Green	SG247	PL 574	81.60	13.60	68.00
30 Apr	Totals for month			387.60	64.60	323.00
				GL2350	GL2200	GL5110

(b)

GENERAL LEDGER

Dr		Value added tax account (GL2200)			Cr
20-5		£ p	20-5		£ p
30 Apr	Purchases Day Book PDB36	313.00	30 Apr	Purchases Returns Day Book PRDB11	64.60

Dr		Payables ledger control account (GL2350)			Cr
20-5		£ p	20-5		£ p
30 Apr	Purchases Returns Day Book PRDB11	387.60	30 Apr	Purchases Day Book PDB36	1,878.00

Dr		Purchases returns account (GL5110)			Cr
20-5		£ p	20-5		£ p
			30 Apr	Purchases Returns Day Book PRDB11	323.00

Note: purchases account not shown – see answer to Activity 7.5

PAYABLES LEDGER

Dr		Severn Supplies (PL721)				Cr
20-5		£ p	20-5			£ p
7 Apr	Purchases Returns PRDB11	60.00	2 Apr	Purchases	PDB36	300.00

Dr		L Murphy (PL659)				Cr
20-5		£ p	20-5			£ p
14 Apr	Purchases Returns PRDB11	96.00	9 Apr	Purchases	PDB36	222.00

Dr		AMC Enterprises (PL520)				Cr
20-5		£ p	20-5			£ p
21 Apr	Purchases Returns PRDB11	150.00	19 Apr	Purchases	PDB36	414.00

Dr		S Green (PL574)				Cr
20-5		£ p	20-5			£ p
29 Apr	Purchases Returns PRDB11	81.60	26 Apr	Purchases	PDB36	474.00

7.7 **(a)** **General ledger**

Account name	Amount £	Debit	Credit
Purchases	8,040	✓	
Value Added Tax	1,608	✓	
Payables ledger control	9,648		✓

Payables ledger

Account name	Amount £	Debit	Credit
Seng Ltd	1,152		✓
Peall & Co	2,832		✓
Knightons	4,176		✓
Galeazzi plc	1,488		✓

(b) **General ledger**

Account name	Amount £	Debit	Credit
Purchases returns	1,440		✓
Value Added Tax	288		✓
Payables ledger control	1,728	✓	

Payables ledger

Account name	Amount £	Debit	Credit
Martin & Co	1,056	✓	
Wentworth Stores	672	✓	

(c) **General ledger**

Account name	Amount £	Debit	Credit
Discounts received	60		✓
Value Added Tax	12		✓
Payables ledger control	72	✓	

Payables ledger

Account name	Amount £	Debit	Credit
Kumar Ltd	12	✓	
Prior & Co	60	✓	

7.8

Supplier	Payables ledger account code
Bridon Ltd	BRI003
Foster & Co	FOS001
Hirst & Co	HIR002

Note: Bridon Ltd is numbered '003' because an '002' account number has been allocated already for 'B'; similarly, for Hirst & Co where '001' has been allocated already for 'H'.

7.9 (a) and (b)

Purchases day book

Date 20-4	Supplier name	Invoice number	Total £	VAT £	Net £	Purchases type 1 £	Purchases type 2 £
30 June	Canoy Ltd	C350	1,608	268	1,340	1,340	
30 June	McVeigh & Co	5148	2,340	390	1,950		1,950
30 June	Robinsons	R/862	2,952	492	2,460	2,460	
	Totals		6,900	1,150	5,750	3,800	1,950

7.10 (a)

Daybook	
Sales day book	
Purchases returns day book	
Purchases day book	✓
Discounts received day book	

Date 20-6	Name	Invoice number	Total £	VAT £	Net £
5 Apr	Razaq Ltd	2470	650.82	108.47	542.35
12 Apr	Coffee Supplies	96331	433.74	72.29	361.45
22 Apr	Francis Fashions	FF/274	993.48	165.58	827.90
24 Apr	Etter Trading	691	209.54	34.92	174.62
28 Apr	Coffee Supplies	96348	400.32	66.72	333.60
	TOTALS		2,687.90	447.98	2,239.92

(b)

as a debit entry to receivables ledger control account	
as a debit entry to payables ledger control account	
as a credit entry to receivables ledger control account	
as a credit entry to payables ledger control account	✓

(c)

as a debit entry	✓
as a credit entry	

7.11 (a)

Account name	Amount £	Debit	Credit
Purchases Returns	610		✓
VAT	122		✓
Payables ledger control	732	✓	

(b)

Account name	Amount £	Debit	Credit
Bisain Ltd	54	✓	

7.12

20-1	Details	Amount £	20-1	Details	Amount £
12 May	Bank	1,054	1 May	Balance b/f	2,109
18 May	Purchases Returns	218	24 May	Purchases	1,727
31 May	Balance c/d	2,564			
		3,836		Total	3,836
			1 June	Balance b/d	2,564

CHAPTER 8: PROCESS PAYMENTS TO SUPPLIERS

8.1   (c)   The supplier statement and the supplier's payables ledger account in the books of the buyer

8.2   (a)   Supplier invoice

8.3   (b)   Deduct £250 from the amount owing to the supplier as shown on the statement

8.4   (c)   To accompany a cheque when paying a supplier

8.5   Invoice £150 on 8 March ref 76333 has been entered twice on the statement of account but only once in the payables ledger. It is likely to be a duplication and should be queried with Luxon Traders. The likely outcome is a payment of £100 (invoice for £150 less credit note for £50).

8.6   Credit note £72.90 on 22 April appears in the payables ledger account but not on the supplier statement. Having checked that the credit note has been correctly posted to the payables ledger account, you should query it with A Krauss Limited, as the company may have posted it to the wrong account, or not posted it at all. The likely outcome is a payment of £269.85 (invoices for £233.25 and £109.50 less credit note for £72.90).

8.7

BACS REMITTANCE ADVICE

FROM:

Hetherington Limited
Unit 23 Wessex Estate
Langborne Road
Seatown SE8 5VZ

TO
Aldersgate Supplies
10 Aldersgate Street, London
EC1A 7GH

date: 3 October 20-5

date	your reference	our reference	payment amount £
08 09 20-5	Invoice 10945	PO85262	120.75
14 09 20-5	Invoice 10963	PO85271	380.25
20 09 20-5	Credit note 109	PO85248	(46.00)
		TOTAL	455.00

THIS AMOUNT HAS BEEN PAID BY FASTER PAYMENTS TRANSFER DIRECTLY INTO YOUR BANK ACCOUNT AT HRBC BANK ACCOUNT NO 79001875 SORT CODE 41 22 01

8.8

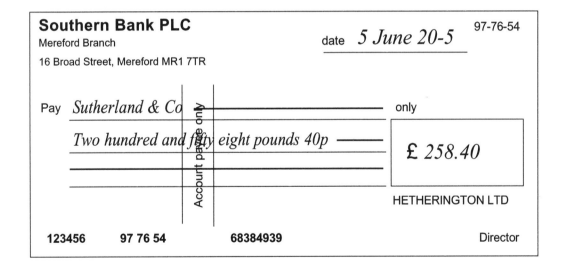

REMITTANCE ADVICE

FROM:

Hetherington Limited

Unit 23 Wessex Estate

TO

Langborne Road

Sutherland & Co

Seatown SE8 5VZ

67 Great March Street

Eastwick, EA3 9JN

date: 5 June 20-5

date	your reference	our reference	payment amount £
23 May 20-5	Invoice 7856	472984	345.90
29 May 20-5	Credit note 4562	472975	(87.50)
		CHEQUE TOTAL	258.40

Southern Bank PLC

Mereford Branch

16 Broad Street, Mereford MR1 7TR

97-76-54

date *5 June 20-5*

Pay *Sutherland & Co* only

Two hundred and fifty eight pounds 40p

£ 258.40

Account payee only

HETHERINGTON LTD

123456   97 76 54   68384939   Director

8.9 **(a)**

Ribeiro & Co				
Hillier Road, Rimmington, RM2 5TP				
STATEMENT OF ACCOUNT: Rannie Ltd				
Date 20-9	**Document number**	**Details**	**Amount £**	**✓**
2 May	CN 34	Goods returned	−236	
12 May	4176	Goods	1,215	
15 May	4198	Goods	878	✓
18 May	4218	Goods	2,608	
25 May	4265	Goods	964	
28 May	CN 45	Goods returned	−147	✓
31 May	4310	Goods	1,876	✓

(b)

Rannie Ltd		
BACS Remittance Advice		
To: Ribeiro & Co		
Date 20-9	**Your reference**	**Amount £**
2 May	CN 34	−236
12 May	4176	1,215
18 May	4218	2,608
25 May	4265	964
	TOTAL	4,551

8.10

20-7	**Details**	**£**	**Discrepancies**
3 June	Invoice 5621	2,310	Incorrect amount
7 June	Credit note 105	−225	Not on statement
15 June	Invoice 5722	1,804	No discrepancy
18 June	Credit note 109	−151	Incorrect credit note number
20 June	Invoice 5794	976	Incorrect date

CHAPTER 9: CASH BOOK

9.1 (d) The book of prime entry for bank receipts and payments

9.2

GENERAL LEDGER

Dr			**Capital account**			Cr
20-7			£	20-7			£
				30 Apr	Cash	CB70	2,000
				30 Apr	Bank	CB70	8,000

Dr			**Bank loan account**			Cr
20-7			£	20-7			£
				30 Apr	Bank	CB70	5,000

Dr			**Rent paid account**			Cr
20-7			£	20-7		£
30 Apr	Bank	CB70	1,000			

Dr			**Wages account**			Cr
20-7			£	20-7		£
30 Apr	Cash	CB70	800			

Dr			**Drawings account**			Cr
20-7			£	20-7		£
30 Apr	Bank	CB70	500			

Dr			**Vehicles account**			Cr
20-7			£	20-7		£
30 Apr	Bank	CB70	10,000			

9.3 **(a)** True

(b) False – the balance b/d of £918 on 1 May shows that, according to the cash book, there is a bank overdraft.

(c)

GENERAL LEDGER

Dr		Sales account			Cr
20-5		£	20-5		£
			30 Apr	Cash CB32	40

Dr		Commission received account			Cr
20-5		£	20-5		£
			30 Apr	Bank CB32	48

Dr		Receivables ledger control account			Cr
20-5		£	20-5		£
			30 Apr	Bank CB32	2,400

Dr		Bank loan account			Cr
20-5		£	20-5		£
			30 Apr	Bank CB32	2,000

Dr		Payables ledger control account			Cr
20-5		£	20-5		£
30 Apr	Bank CB32	3,200			

Dr		Purchases account			Cr
20-5		£	20-5		£
30 Apr	Bank CB32	96			

Dr		Office equipment account			Cr
20-5		£	20-5		£
30 Apr	Bank CB32	2,600			

Dr		Wages account			Cr
20-5		£	20-5		£
30 Apr	Bank CB32	1,550			

Dr		General expenses account				Cr
20-5			£	20-5		£
30 Apr	Cash	CB32	80			

(d)

RECEIVABLES LEDGER

Dr		**Lindum Limited**					Cr
20-5			£	20-5			£
				30 Apr	Bank	CB32	2,400

PAYABLES LEDGER

Dr		**Mereford Mills**				Cr
20-5			£	20-5		£
30 Apr	Bank	CB32	3,200			

9.4 (c) Bank transfer from a trade receivable for £1,350

9.5 (a) Cheque to a trade payable for £870

9.6 (a), (b) and (d) are true; (c) is false

9.7 **(a)** and **(b)**

Dr (Receipts)								
Date	**Details**	**Account code**	**Cash**	**Bank**	**VAT**	**Cash sales**	**Trade receivables**	**Other income**
20-7			£	£	£	£	£	£
12 May	Balances b/d		205	825				
12 May	Sales	GL		600	100	500		
13 May	Sales	GL	180		30	150		
13 May	T Jarvis	RL		155			155	
14 May	Sales	GL		720	120	600		
15 May	Cash	C		250				
15 May	Sales	GL	288		48	240		
16 May	Wyvern Council	RL		560			560	
			673	3,110	298	1,490	715	–
17 May	Balances b/d		387	1,816				

Cr (Payments)

Date	Details	Account code	Cash £	Bank £	VAT £	Cash purchases £	Trade payables £	Other responses £
20-7								
12 May	Rent	GL		255				255
13 May	Terry Carpets	PL		363			363	
14 May	Trade Supplies	PL		145			145	
14 May	Purchases	GL	36		6	30		
15 May	Bank	C	250					
15 May	Longlife Carpets	PL		291			291	
16 May	Purchases	GL		240	40	200		
16 May	Balances c/d		387	1,816				
			673	3,110	48	230	799	255

(c)

RECEIVABLES LEDGER

Dr		T Jarvis		Cr
20-7		£	20-7	£
			13 May Bank	155

Dr		Wyvern Council		Cr
20-7		£	20-7	£
			16 May Bank	560

PAYABLES LEDGER

Dr		Terry Carpets		Cr
20-7		£	20-7	£
13 May Bank		363		

Dr		Trade Supplies		Cr
20-7		£	20-7	£
14 May Bank		145		

Dr		Longlife Carpets		Cr
20-7		£	20-7	£
15 May Bank		291		

9.8 **(a)** **Cash book – credit side**

Details	Cash £	Bank £	VAT £	Trade payables £	Cash purchases £	Vehicle expenses £
Balance b/f						
Knowles & Co	30		5		25	
S Goulding	96		16		80	
Liyan Ltd		920		920		
Nelson Street Garage		132	22			110
Sandhu & Co		645		645		
Totals	126	1,697	43	1,565	105	110

(b) **Cash book – debit side**

Details	Cash £	Bank £	Trade receivables £	Other income £
Balance b/f	254	1,598		
Watkin Ltd		429	429	
P Pandya		1,522	1,522	
Matt Martin	235			235
Totals	489	3,549	1,951	235

(c) £363

(d) £1,852

(e) Debit

9.9 **(a)**

Cash book	
Cash book – receipts	✓
Cash book – payments	

Description for details column	
Total	
VAT	
Trade receivables	
Sales	✓

Date 20-9	Details	Total £	VAT £	Net £
10 May	Sales	4,589.04	764.84	3,824.20

(b)

Information required	Document
Details of payments made to credit suppliers	Internet banking payments schedule
Details of regular payments made through the bank account	Standing order and direct debit schedule

9.10

Cash book	
Cash book – receipts	
Cash book – payments	✓

Date 20-8	Details	Total £	VAT £	Net £	Frequency	Recurrences
1 Jun	OfficeFast Ltd	138	23	115	Monthly	12

CHAPTER 10: PETTY CASH BOOK

10.1 (c) Is the book of prime entry for low-value cash payments

10.2 (a) Is a financial document against which payments are made out of petty cash

10.3 (d) The petty cashier starts each week or month with a fixed amount of money

10.4 Debit

10.5 General ledger

Account name	Amount £	Debit	Credit
Petty cash book/Petty cash account	75.00	✓	
Bank	75.00		✓

10.6

	Expense (excluding VAT)	VAT	Total
	£	£	£
(a)	8.00	1.60	9.60
(b)	4.00	0.80	4.80
(c)	2.00	0.40	2.40
(d)	2.05	0.41	2.46
(e)	4.67	0.93	5.60
(f)	2.90	0.58	3.48
(g)	7.30	1.46	8.76
(h)	0.80	0.16	0.96
(i)	0.83	0.16	0.99
(j)	7.86	1.57	9.43

10.7 (a)

GENERAL LEDGER

Dr			Value added tax account				Cr
20-9			£	20-9			£
31 Mar	Petty cash book	PCB20	4.56				

Dr			Travel account				Cr
20-9			£	20-9			£
31 Mar	Petty cash book	PCB20	29.26				

Dr			Postages account				Cr
20-9			£	20-9			£
31 Mar	Petty cash book	PCB20	16.65	12 Mar	Petty cash book PCB20		8.50

Dr			Stationery account				Cr
20-9			£	20-9			£
31 Mar	Petty cash book	PCB20	9.60				

Dr			Payables ledger control account				Cr
20-9			£	20-9			£
31 Mar	Petty cash book	PCB20	13.50				

Dr			Petty cash account				Cr
20-9			£	20-9			£
1 Mar	Balance b/d		100.00	31 Mar	Petty cash book PCB20		73.57
31 Mar	Petty cash book PCB20		8.50	31 Mar	Balance c/d		100.00
31 Mar	Bank	CB	65.07				
			173.57				173.57
1 Apr	Balance b/d		100.00				

Dr			Cash book				Cr
20-9			Bank	20-9			Bank
				31 Mar	Petty cash	PCB20	65.07

(b)

PAYABLES LEDGER

Dr		P Andrews				Cr
20-9				£	20-9	£
18 Mar	Petty cash book	PCB20		13.50		

10.8

					Petty Cash Book						PCB42
Date 20-3	Details	Amount	Date 20-3	Details	Amount £	VAT £	Travel £	Postages £	Stationery £	Misc £	
1 Aug	Balance b/d	150.00									
			4 Aug	Taxi fare	9.60	1.60	8.00				
			6 Aug	Post office	5.50			5.50			
			9 Aug	Marker pens	3.84	0.64			3.20		
			11 Aug	Rail fare	10.50		10.50				
			12 Aug	Window cleaner	14.40	2.40				12.00	
			16 Aug	Envelopes	4.80	0.80			4.00		
			18 Aug	Donation	10.00					10.00	
			19 Aug	Rail fare	10.60		10.60				
			20 Aug	Post office	8.30			8.30			
			23 Aug	Printing tape	2.40	0.40			2.00		
			25 Aug	Post office	1.50			1.50			
			27 Aug	Taxi fare	14.40	2.40	12.00				
					95.84	8.24	41.10	15.30	9.20	22.00	
31 Aug	Bank	95.84									
			31 Aug	Balance c/d	150.00						
		245.84			245.84						
1 Sep	Balance b/d	150.00									

10.9 (a)

Total of petty cash payments for June:		£56.72
Cash remaining should be:		£93.28
Actual cash remaining is:		
	as at 30 June	
	number held	value £
£10 notes	3	30.00
£5 notes	8	40.00
£1 coins	15	15.00
50p coins	11	5.50
20p coins	6	1.20
10p coins	11	1.10
5p coins	5	0.25
2p coins	6	0.12
1p coins	11	0.11
TOTAL		93.28
Amount of discrepancy (if any)		£ nil

(b) If there is a discrepancy – whether a shortfall or a surplus – it should be investigated promptly and, if it cannot be resolved, should be referred to the accounts supervisor.

10.10 (a)

VAT £	Net £
4.47	22.35

(b) £100.71

(c)

Details	Amount £	Debit	Credit
Bank	264.16	✓	

CHAPTER 11: THE TRIAL BALANCE

11.1

Account name	Balance £	Debit	Credit
Value Added Tax	6,585		✓

11.2 (c) A list of balances of all general ledger accounts, separated into columns for debit balances and credit balances, which shows the total of each column.

11.3

Account name	Debit	Credit
Cash	✓	
Sales		✓
Purchases returns		✓
Receivables ledger control	✓	
Machinery	✓	
Discounts received		✓
Rent paid	✓	
Bank loan		✓

11.4

Trial balance of Brian Montagu as at 28 February 20-1		
Account name	Debit £	Credit £
Cash	250	
Sales		28,000
Bank (cash at bank)	1,350	
Vehicles	12,300	
Capital		7,150
Purchases	17,200	
Payables ledger control		2,400
Receivables ledger control	3,600	
Sales returns	450	
Discounts received		150
Wages	2,550	
TOTALS	37,700	37,700

11.5

Trial balance of Sara Greenwell as at 31 March 20-1		
Account name	**Debit £**	**Credit £**
Bank (overdraft)		650
Purchases	43,400	
Petty cash	80	
Sales		68,200
Purchases returns		150
Receivables ledger control	15,300	
Office equipment	3,650	
Drawings	5,840	
Vehicles	19,500	
General expenses	13,760	
Payables ledger control		6,220
Value Added Tax (owing to HMRC)		720
Discounts allowed	330	
Capital		25,920
TOTALS	101,860	101,860

Index

for your notes